ENGLISH ETHICAL SOCIALISM

ENGLISH ETHICAL SOCIALISM

SOCIALISM

Thomas More to R. H. Tawney

NORMAN DENNIS
AND
A. H. HALSEY

CLARENDON PRESS · OXFORD
1988

Oxford University Press, Walton Street, Oxford OX2 6DP
Oxford New York Toronto
Delhi Bombay Calcutta Madras Karachi
Petaling Jaya Singapore Hong Kong Tokyo
Nairobi Dar es Salaam Cape Town
Melbourne Auckland
and associated companies in
Berlin Ibadan

Oxford is a trade mark of Oxford University Press

Published in the United States
by Oxford University Press, New York

British Library Cataloguing in Publication Data
Dennis, Norman
English ethical socialism: from Thomas
More to R. H. Tawney.
1. Socialism. English theories, to 1960
I. Title II. Halsey, A. H. (Albert Henry),
1923–
335'.1
ISBN 0–19–827284–7

Library of Congress Cataloging in Publication Data
Dennis, Norman.
English ethical socialism: from Thomas More to R. H. Tawney/
Norman Dennis and A. H. Halsey.
p. cm.
Includes index.
1. Socialism—England—History. I. Halsey, A. H. II. Title.
HX250.E53D46 1988 335'.1'09—dc 19 88–10035
ISBN 0–19–827284–7

Typeset by Cambrian Typesetters
High Street, Frimley, Surrey
Printed in Great Britain
at Oxford University Printing House, Oxford
by David Stanford
Printer to the University

FOR OUR FAMILIES

Audrey Dennis *Margaret Halsey*
Julia Dennis *Ruth Halsey*
John Dennis *Robert Halsey*
 Lisa Halsey
 David Halsey
 Mark Halsey

PREFACE

This study has come to completion over half a lifetime of conversation. We see ourselves as heirs of a British radical tradition of ethical socialism. Our intention is to set out what we take to be the sources and nature of our political inheritance. We are by profession sociologists and therefore mindful that what we take to be true, and what we believe to be good, are born of experience in our particular generation, class, and country. Accordingly we begin with a sketch of our background so that the reader can interpret our account of public as well as personal issues.

We were undergraduates immediately after the Second World War during R. H. Tawney's last years at the London School of Economics. Our political and social outlook was heavily stamped by that experience. We were members of a group of students of sociology at 'the School' who became the first generation of professional sociologists in Britain.[1] These sociologists were born in the slump years between the wars. They came from the periphery of English society, not from the central circle of the well-born and well-connected. By no means all of their parents were working class, but none of them, Gentile or Jew, sprang from the metropolitan professional or administrative families or from the business class. Some were of wholly uncomplicated proletarian origin—in our own case sons of a tram driver in Sunderland and a railway porter in Kentish Town. Others had their childhood in families on the margin of the working class, their fathers in petty trade or clerical work. Almost all looked back on a home dominated by political radicalism and awareness of 'the Labour movement'. All, as Wyndham Lewis would have put it, were 'branded on the tongue'. Short of strenuously sustained efforts of elocution their class and region would henceforth claim them.

Most of them had 'won the scholarship'.[2] There were no public-school boys among them. They went to their grammar schools and absorbed the curious provincial patriotism which that experience

---

[1] For a fuller account, see A. H. Halsey, 'Provincials and Professionals: The British Post-War Sociologists', *Arch. Europ. Sociol.* 23 (1982), 150–75.

[2] A competitive examination for state-school children before 1944, giving a minority free places at grammar schools.

afforded in the 1930s and 1940s—a national and nationalistic history and literature which with science and mathematics were taught, often with high skill and devotion, in a refined version of the local dialect. 'My country right or left'[3] was as much a principal component of the hidden agenda of the provincial grammar school as it was of Orwell's Eton. And, combined with education in the kitchen from fathers or grandfathers who had served in the First World War, it was effective. J. A. Banks was a conscientious objector, but the rest completed their pre-university schooling in the armed services. More than one came across the word 'sociology' reading H. G. Wells in a Nissen hut. Most argued themselves into democratic socialism and enthusiastic support for Attlee's government on His Majesty's ships, on airfields, and in army camps. They acquired the resolve which Orwell had formulated for them during the war:

They will have to take their destiny into their own hands. England can only fulfil its special mission if the ordinary English in the street can somehow get their hands on power. We have been told very frequently during this war that this time, when the danger is over, there should be no lost opportunities, no recurrence of the past. No more stagnation punctuated by wars, no more Rolls-Royces gliding past dole queues, no return to the England of the Distressed Areas, the endlessly stewing teapot, the empty pram, and the Giant Panda. We cannot be sure that this promise will be kept. Only we ourselves can make certain that it will come true, and if we do not, no further chance may be given us. The past thirty years have been a long series of cheques drawn upon the accumulated goodwill of the English people. That reserve may not be inexhaustible. By the end of another decade it will be finally clear whether England is to survive as a great nation or not. And if the answer is to be 'yes', it is the common people who must make it so.[4]

Few of them had any notion while at school of going on to a university; for some that aspiration was a product of war service and the FET grant.[5] They chose to come to LSE. They carried a picture of their country as a status hierarchy, still strongly

---

[3] George Orwell's essay of that title is reprinted in his *Collected Essays, Journalism and Letters*, ed. S. Orwell and I. Angus (Harmondsworth, 1970), i. 587–92.   [4] Ibid. iii. 55.
[5] A British scheme, similar to the American 'G. I. Bill', which gave studentships to servicemen who had—or who were willing to say they had—university intentions frustrated by the war.

entrenched, but now threatened by the social democratic revolution which the war had promised, which a Labour government was undertaking, and for which Laski's LSE was an intellectual instrument. They came to study at a place which, though physically in London, they knew was outside, and was shunned by the cognoscenti of what Edward Shils later depicted as the 'Oxford–London–Cambridge axis'[6] of politics, power, and letters. Yet the LSE was an intellectual and political Mecca to them. The tradition of first-year undergraduate lectures given by the most eminent professors was fully and conscientiously practised. So they listened to Robbins, Popper, Tawney, Laski, and Ginsberg, and absorbed the excitement of the social sciences.

Our aspirations then and since were academic. We did not see the university as a point of entry into a political career. None of the group was active in the politics of the student union or LSE Labour Club—organizations fairly or unfairly dismissed as the property of political careerists, among them John Stonehouse.[7] They all read Max Weber's two essays on science and politics as vocations and chose the former for themselves while in no way abandoning their political enthusiasms.

Classical sociology may perhaps be best thought of as the liberal reply to Marxism. If so it was a central feature of their provincialism that the LSE sociologists were unschooled in, and conditioned to be resistant to, both the marxist thesis and the liberal sociological antithesis. John Westergaard was the exception. He was an avowed Marxist. Nevertheless, what was most vital for him was also salient for the group as a whole—hostility to social inequality, combined with a professional commitment to empirical research.[8]

[6] E. Shils, 'British Intellectuals in the Mid-Twentieth Century', in his *The Intellectuals and the Powers* (London, 1972), 135–53.

[7] An LSE Labour Club activist of the day, who later became a Labour MP, was involved in a spectacular scandal, and was finally jailed.

[8] Tom Bottomore was also a Marxist, but it is significant that after 1968 he came to be seen as tainted with the reformist empiricism of the group discussed here. Thus Martin Shaw disparages his 'neutral commentary' style and his use of sources 'rather tilted in the direction of early 20th century reformism'. Shaw is shocked to find that Bottomore is also capable of statements such as 'Marxism has brought into existence political oppression and cultural impoverishment'—which, Shaw complains, 'might have come straight out of *The Open Society and its Enemies*'. Bottomore obviously feels, Shaw concludes, 'that Marxism would be better off without its socialist political commitment'. (M. Shaw, *Sociology*, 10 (1976), 519.)

Some of the others have spent their subsequent sociological careers in at least partially successful search for a viable synthesis of Marxism and classical sociology. A Marxist such as Perry Anderson would dismiss such a claim as preposterous. Insisting on the view that Britain never produced its own sociology, his judgement in 1968 was unequivocally hostile:

To this day, despite the recent belated growth of sociology as a formal discipline in England, the record of listless mediocrity and wizened provincialism is unrelieved. The subject is still largely a poor cousin of 'social work' and 'social administration', the dispirited descendants of Victorian charity.[9]

The point about such a sneering dismissal is not so much the view of social theory that lies behind it as its rage against any sociology which is not subordinate to revolutionary politics as defined by Marxists. The fact is that by 1968, after a quinquennium in which the number of social scientists in British universities had tripled, the character of sociology had shifted decisively towards a chaos of conflicting ideologies, Marxism among them. Anderson's prejudice prevented him from appreciating the radicalism of the early post-war British sociologists. Their radicalism was indeed provincial, but none the less passionate for that, and none the less powerful in its impact on the consciousness of the ruling academic and political élite. The war-service students had had a childhood in their Labour families, to which had been added the war experience of siege socialism, the sense of a just cause against Fascism, and the promise of a planned and open society without the unfreedom of a communist state. With these social experiences they felt no need of Marx to support a radical fervour.

As an interpretation of their experience as working-class children and patriotic soldiers, Marxism was read and heard more as the shifting propaganda of the Russian foreign ministry than as an analysis of the social structure of their own country. The polarization thesis they knew to be at least as much rhetoric as reality, quite useful to score an occasional debating point against Them (the Conservative rulers and their representatives), but rhetoric for which they had viable and powerful alternatives, whether derived from the Magnificat or Tawney or William Morris

[9] P. Anderson, 'Components of the National Culture', *New Left Review*, 50 (1968), 8.

or Orwell. Marxism was for middle-class pre-war intellectuals. Russia was for the Webbs. Such events as the Hitler–Stalin Pact of 1939, the communist take-over of Czechoslovakia in 1948, the Twentieth Congress, and the Hungarian Revolution of 1956 only confirmed the stubbornly held conviction that Marxist-Communism had nothing to do with the socialism to which they were committed—a democratic socialism without secret police and suppression of free speech.

They did not hate or reject their country. For all its persistent inequality, the snobbery which branded the tongue of every British child, the stupidity and incompetence of the slump Tories, and the stuffy closedness of the culture, they knew Britain as a decent society. They were confident that the democratic institutions invented by the Victorian and Edwardian working class, the trade unions, the co-operative societies and the Labour party, were the foundations of a free and socialist Britain, of the New Jerusalem. If their party and their Attlee government lagged behind, their idealistic impatience called for renewed radical persuasion. It did not require a total therapy of revolution and the massacre of their own countrymen. Resolve, pressure, argument, and firm insistence on democratic action would be repeatedly necessary over a long haul. But democracy and decency need never be abandoned. In short, the LSE post-war sociologists were committed to a socialism which had no need for Marxism and no time for Communism precisely because this was a socialism deeply rooted in English working-class provincialism.

The intellectual experience of the sociology they learned from Ginsberg, Glass, Popper, and Marshall added a further factor which led them to a confrontation with marxist theory. The confrontation was not at first direct. Ginsberg's synthesis of rational ethics and the evolution of social institutions harmonized with the Labour programme of radical reform. Clearly, national-ization of industry was institutional evolution in the service of justice to workers, and the increase in free grammar-school places promised parallel justice to workers' children. Glass's direct application of the method of political arithmetic to the systematic exposure of inequality strongly reinforced the bridge leading from social theory to political action. Yet more important was the impact of Karl Popper's justification of 'piecemeal social engineering'. While they may have chafed under its implications of extreme caution, Popper's post-war sociology students were comforted and encouraged by a theory which simultaneously offered reassurance that reformist rather than revolutionary change was likely to be most effective and (what they ardently wanted to believe) that the logic of discovery permitted an important role to the social scientist in the process of social reform. Sociology could be seen as an intellectual trade union of those trying to solve problems by the hypothetico-deductive method. There was a logically justified place in it for ideals, theory, method, and substance—for morality, research, understanding, and politics.

The group left the LSE still looking for a solution to the problems of the relationship between quantification and understanding in sociology, and of the integration of sociological thought with political action. Carrying the marks of their intellectually and culturally ingrained provincialism, they continued to study the works of the Germans Weber and Marx, the Frenchmen Comte and Durkheim, and the Italian Pareto. Some defined sociology as cumulative and explanatory in its aspirations, with due (but not slavish) respect for natural science models and attempts at quantification and comparison. Others assimilated the subject to the liberal arts, as intellectual history and interpretative under-standing—a different but a related and also credible definition.

The search had taken many of them to the United States, physically as well as intellectually, where from Harvard, Columbia, and Chicago there radiated an orthodoxy of sociological theory expounded by Parsons, Merton, Shils, and Riesman, with a litany on quantitative method supplied by Lazarsfeld. But after the 1960s the simple world of an organized orthodoxy distintegrated. Berkeley rose and fell. Factions fought for dominance. The 'critical sociologists' of the Frankfurt School fiercely attacked the idea that conventional sociology could make any contribution to humane social reform. Piecemeal social engineering was anathema to all brands of neo-marxist radicalism. Positivism, with its tedious counting of heads, became a term of abuse, relieving students of the obligation to read any book so labelled, or to learn the methods which had been regarded by the LSE group as indispensable to professional competence. Epistemological nihilism and moral relativism stripped respectability from everyone who was not a totally committed and permanent opponent of contemporary society, the welfare state provisions of which were characterized as sops to soften the wrath of the otherwise revolutionary proletarian, or as a more sophisticated way of maximizing the capitalist's exploitation of the worker.

To resist the blandishments of governmental bureaucracy on the one hand and to survive the assaults of the newer radicalisms on the other were the preoccupations of the 1970s for a beleaguered minority in the sprawling profession they had done so much to create. Some retreated into inactivity or administrative busy-work. Others went on with their research and teaching, persisting in their belief in the political value of attempting to study social facts objectively. As one of us has put the positivist view:

When confronted with things every effort must be made to remove the influence of one's own fears of what the facts may show, and the influence of one's own desires about what the facts ought to show if the world were benign and just. Science is a set of procedures which over a range of activities and practitioners has been shown to have been effective in diminishing subjectivity. It is impossible to diminish subjectivity to zero anywhere. It is extremely difficult to get it below a very high level in the study of social affairs. Some researchers pretend to follow the protocols of science but do not. There are difficult topics and dishonest men. To say that a social science is value free is never, therefore, to describe what has been achieved. It only indicates the direction of endeavour.[10]

The polarizing tendencies originating in the late 1960s and early 1970s—in the one direction towards the use of the campus as a base for direct political action, in the other towards its use as

[10] N. Dennis, 'Sociology, Education and Equality', *Oxford Rev. of Edn.* 6 (1980), 114. This point of view has nothing to do with the anti-Kantian 'positivism' which claims that only those aspects of reality available to be studied by the nineteenth century 'methods of the natural science' are worthy of human consideration (or which even claims that nothing else 'exists'). Nor has it anything to do with the 'positivism' that claims that the basic laws of society have already been discovered—that social science has already had its Newton or Darwin. Nor has it anything to do with the associated claim, that further empirical research is redundant, because what is significant and true, now and into the future, can be predicted from established theory. Given that these extreme *positivistic* claims, especially the last two, are commonly made by self-styled Marxists, it was surprising but explicable that some Marxists should have been at the forefront of the *attacks* on 'positivism' in the 1960s and 1970s. It was explicable because by positivism they meant empirical research the conclusions of which were non-marxian. Such research continued to question, for example, the theory that the social structure of advanced industrialist countries was simplifying itself into an ever-richer, smaller class of owners and an ever-larger, more poverty-stricken class of proletarians, and that the proletariat of those countries was, barring false consciousness, straining on the leash of communist revolution.

protection for non-communicating worlds of private knowledge in which excellence is merely a function of fashion and amnesia a virtue—continue to be inimical to the pursuit of sociology as an academic discipline. But the underlying issue, the extent to which value commitment can be allied to objective methods of study, remained to torment the post-war British sociologists as it did their predecessors, and as it will their successors.

Such is the personal and professional background that we bring to a book about a moral and political tradition which we believe to be the best available guide to a good life for our children—ethical socialism.

CONTENTS

I

THE TRADITION OF ETHICAL SOCIALISM

Ethical socialism is a radical tradition which makes heroic claims on people and on the society that nurtures them. It offers both a code of conduct for individuals and a guide to social reform aimed at creating optimal conditions for the highest possible moral attainment of every person. It assumes a theory of human nature—what is possible in a human personality—and a theory of society—what is possible in a human social structure. Its credibility therefore is doubly tested: not only as an intellectually adequate and morally compelling prescription of private individual virtue, not only a benign blueprint for the social conditions of virtue, but as both. It has to face each test. Yet the first is primary. The good society can encourage but cannot ensure the creation of exemplary citizens. Circumstances can only make personal moral choices harder or easier: they cannot absolve the individual from making them.

The tradition reiterates consistent principles of responsibility and altruism—for the individual from conscience, for society through democracy. Conscience in the European context derives from the Judaic-Christian moral inheritance. European democracy has evolved as universal opinion mobilized by subscribers to this traditional conscience who apply it to politics. Ethical socialists adopt the underlying theory of human nature that people live by ends as well as means. They posit free will and a self-consciousness which enable a man or woman to aspire beyond immediate desires or appetites towards the rational realization of a best possible self. Their underlying theory of society is of complex relationships constraining but also sustaining the exercise of choices which enable the world to be moved to fellowship, a *koinonia* of equal respect for every morally free person within it. In such a society every person is free to the highest degree consistent with the equal freedom of all others. *Koinonia*, the fellowship of sharing, allows new vistas of freedom to expand day by day rather than being closed by social irresponsibility or exploitation. All members of such a society flourish in freedom because they are held together by mutual regard.

THE GREAT NAMES

'But wait', the reasonable critic will say, 'can this be realistic morals and practical politics for the twenty-first century?' The challenge is fair. We shall try to answer it by examining the ethical-socialist tradition, its successes and failures, and finally its relevance to contemporary Britain. We shall do so in the main by reviewing the personal values and social analyses of six outstanding English writers who have lived and expounded the culture and politics that we advocate.

This biographical method has its dangers. We could have chosen six or sixty others. And traditions properly narrated describe a culture: the totality of a collective possession is greater than the sum of the lives of its distinguished devotees. Nevertheless our decision is not arbitrary. For all its hazards the discussion of individuals enables us to illustrate concretely the abstractions of long-debated principles. If it be objected that we have thereby confused an element of popular culture with a saga of heroes we can at least reply with John Plamenatz that 'the authority of great names is less oppressive than is fashion . . . if we neither neglect great names nor defer to them, but seek, to the best of our ability, to take their measure, we are then better placed to take our own'.[1]

We see R. H. Tawney as the great modern master of ethical socialism: he offered the most complete expression of the tradition we seek to understand. In him the tradition reaches its highest point of personal accomplishment and its most comprehensive range of argument. Much of what he had to say had been developed by L. T. Hobhouse, the first Professor of Sociology in Britain, under whom Tawney undertook his early researches at the London School of Economics. Although their message was similar and reached an increasingly receptive public until about the time of Tawney's death in 1962, as the master rose to fame his precursor passed into oblivion. Yet it remains true that Hobhouse provided the philo-sophical and empirical underpinning for many of the assertions the

[1] J. Plamenatz, *Man and Society* (London, 1963), vol. i, p. xii.

truth of which Tawney felt able to take for granted and thus to propagate with clarity and confidence. In the twentieth century the London School of Economics was the principal channel through which ethical socialism was conveyed by Tawney's contemporaries and successors, notably T. H. Marshall, and the sociologists influenced shortly after the Second World War by Marshall's theory of citizenship.

Ethical socialism, however, was the exclusive product of neither academics nor the twentieth century. In order to demonstrate that the attitudes and ideas of ethical socialism are deeply rooted in English culture we deal with two famous figures from very different centuries and backgrounds: Thomas More, the sixteenth-century statesman responding to an England on the threshold of capitalist agriculture, and William Cobbett, the plough-boy turned pamphleteer, responding to an England in the throes of the Industrial Revolution.

Thomas More has his place if only because his Utopians are ethical socialists to a man and woman. Cobbett is included as the tireless proponent of two essential ideals of the tradition—freeborn individuals and the common weal. Cobbett consistently taught confidence to working people that they would, by painstaking civic resolve, construct and keep a high civilization of free, equal, and fraternal compatriots. Both men embodied the ethical-socialist code in their personal lives.

Then as a reminder that the tradition continued to flourish mightily outside the universities in the twentieth century we have included George Orwell, the energetic interpreter of yet another phase in the passage of Britain through advanced industrialism and world war.

These writers are, to repeat, not the whole tradition. Many other individual socialists such as Robert Owen, William Morris, G. D. H. Cole, or R. M. Titmuss could be claimed at least in part for the ethical-socialist camp. But our main objective is not to offer a complete biography of any individual: it is to make clear the elements and the unity of the tradition as it crystallizes in the works of Tawney.

Whether directed at academicians or activists, our method is sociological. We try in each case, and at greater length for Tawney, to analyse the political engagement of an individual in the way that Max Weber recommended for the understanding of all social action. We ask what ends were sought as possible and desirable, what the actor took to be true about the circumstances in which he lived, what means he proposed as effective to move his country from its past and present to or towards the preferred future, and what state of affairs ensued when his efforts had been exhausted. In that way and in these terms we can offer an understanding of what, how, and how far ethical socialism has informed the lives and transformed the environment of some remarkable champions of a social ideal.

Their experience has been widely scattered over the history of agrarian and industrial Britain. So their preoccupations have varied with circumstances. What they have in common is a steady gaze in search of common wealth. In modern political language they have all sought an optimal combination of liberty, equality, and fraternity.

THE TRADITION DEFINED

Socialism, like Marxism or liberalism, is an inevitably imprecise concept because it refers to an ideology of many dimensions all of which vary in significance under different historical conditions. As cultures and social structures change and words change their meanings, political taxonomies are defied. The history of socialism is marked with simplistic identification of the concept with, for example, collectivism or statism or common ownership of property. In reality divisions within socialism have been as bitter and crucial as conflict between socialism and its competing ideologies.

Ethical socialism abhors idleness and is suspicious of intellectuals. It gives socialism a marked bias towards individual autonomy, and an anti-historicist slant.[2] It distrusts the bureaucratic state. It is aware of the enemies and false friends and freedom on the Left as well as the Right, and is implacably opposed to totalitarianism from either of these directions. It gives egalitarianism a pronounced emphasis on the importance of respect and dignity rather than material equality. It gives fraternity a no less distinctive sense of history, love of country, dislike of violence, and above all faith in

---

[2] This is anti-historicism in the sense given the term in K. R. Popper, *The Poverty of Historicism* (1944–5) (London, 1957), where Popper summarizes his 'refutation of historicism' on pp. v, vi.

the good sense of ordinary people. Accordingly it favours parliamentary government while seeking also to extend the democratic principle to participatory citizenship in all spheres of public and especially industrial life.

There is no formal doctrinal constitution of ethical socialism. But six common factors make up the totality of the tradition, their combination varying to produce the uniqueness of each individual representative. First, second, and third are positive commitments to fraternity, liberty, and equality. Fourth is the anti-historicism referred to above—the rejection of the 'historicist' view that a society's future is ineluctable and will be the result of social laws working themselves out with an iron necessity towards an inevitable goal. Fifth, nevertheless, is a sense of the enormous contribution that a society's past makes to its present morality and institutions, and that its present choices and failures to choose will be profound in their consequences. Sixth is a shared belief in the power of moral character to perfect a person and ennoble a nation. This belief in the efficacy of moral commitment informs the distinctive attitude of socialists to the meaning of liberty, equality, and fraternity.

Fraternity is the ethical socialist's *sine qua non*, 'without which nothing'. Max Weber, in 'Class, Status and Party',[3] deals with three modes of social organization which have been both vigorous and widespread. One of these modes is the allocation of rights and duties to individuals on the basis of ineradicable features of their person or history—for example, their sex or their skin colour or their class origin or the religion of the community within which they were brought up. This is allocation by 'status', characteristic of 'estate' societies in which sacred claims and obligations are solidified in tradition and buttressed by ritual. In pre-literate and other small-scale societies kinship is frequently a principal status factor, with a stress on unselfishness, loyalty, and other 'community' values. Some status factors produce caste societies (e.g. the apartheid society of South Africa) possibly with community-like solidarity within each caste, but with an absence of solidarity between castes.

The second is allocation on the basis of bargaining. In this mode of social organization, regarded as a pure type, fraternal relation-

---

[3] M. Weber, *From Max Weber: Essays in Sociology*, ed. H. H. Gerth and C. W. Mills (London, 1948).

ships are reduced to a minimum. The allocation of tasks in a society and the distribution of goods and services (ranging from tangible objects of consumption to emotional fulfilment) are the result of a process of rational uncoerced exchange of equivalents between self-regarding competitors, who may or may not be equally well equipped for success. All are out to maximize their own advantages, but each must secure the best bargain he can. Any relationship of exchange endures for only so long as it suits all the parties to it. On a large scale this is most familiar where money is the principal measure of value in a market system. While recognizing both the existence and importance of free altruistic choices (and frequently being themselves philanthrophists) the theorists of *laissez-faire* capitalism, from the classical economists of the latter half of the eighteenth to the monetarists of the latter half of the twentieth century, deal with the principles of this egoistic mode in its nearly undiluted form.

The third is allocation by authority. In this system some people are accorded the right by the rest of the population both to specify what the rights and duties of individuals shall be and to ensure, by force if necessary, that individuals carry out their duties and are protected in their rights. In such a relatively stable country as the United Kingdom many of the activities of the state over most of the national territory are of this type.

These are not, of course, the only analytically pure modes of social organization. Among the many, two other very different modes are conceptually familiar and empirically important. At one extreme is allocation by brute force—'he shall take who has the power, he shall keep who can'—pillage, armed robbery, rape, and so forth. At the other extreme is selfless giving, expressed more or less effectively by such words as love, altruism, service, self-sacrifice, philanthropy, community—and fraternity.

It was a feature of the period following the death of R. H. Tawney that the Left and Right in England devised new mixtures of these pure forms of social organization. The Labour party had formerly emphasized the ideal of fraternity (with nationalization, a National Health Service, state education, and council estates being justified as more benign environments for the realization of the ethic of service). It turned increasingly towards the advocacy of relationships of authority in some areas of life, and to the advocacy of market-type relationships in others. On the one hand the authority of the state was to be enhanced as an external controlling factor in the economy. On the other (more innovative for the Labour party and much more disturbing to the Tawney-type socialists whose model of the good society was family life) procreation and child-rearing, which had been set within a freely chosen and daily renewed life-long altruistic relationship of marital and parental love, were to be governed by the egoistic bargains of individuals. Though their arguments were never part of an official national programme, Labour party representatives were prominent among those who publicly maintained that family services and functions should be liberated from the outmoded Hebrew and Christian ethics of heterosexuality, pre-marital chastity, intra-marital fidelity, and the joint responsibility of the biological parents for their children at least during the years of childhood.

The Conservative party, historically the carrier of the ancient ballast of paternalism, inherited a welfare state which since 1945 (and earlier) had steadily, and over some periods rapidly, expanded its command over real resources. In the 1980s, while cutting certain welfare services, practically it was able to do no more overall than restrict the rate of further growth to the same pace as the growth in the national income. But ideologically, without denying or deploring the possibility and existence of altruistic choices, its leaders became the vigorous advocates of market relationships in the production, allocation, and management of consumer goods, housing, education, health services, and much else. To the great fraternal organizations of the working class, which themselves in some cases had drifted in the direction of group egoism, authoritarianism, and violence, it applied the same panacea of private calculation. It looked at the same time, however, to the authority of the central state, at the expense of lesser authorities within the community, to set the framework for egoistic choice. While it reduced authority, it concentrated the authority that remained, and in the area of civil rights it resorted to the heavy hand of governmental control.

The mainstay of the Labour party in the years of its growth and victory, the respectable working class, with its ethical-socialist commitment to 'fraternity across the board', was thrown into a state of dismay, confusion, and political homelessness.

Whatever their circumstances, all ethical socialists have had a hatred of individual unfreedom at the centre of their social thought and political action. A passion for autonomy is a necessary if not sufficient condition for membership of the ethical-socialist tradition. But there have been other socialists more concerned with equality than with liberation from tyranny. The task of the ethical socialist is to reconcile any contradiction between these two values by enveloping them within the values of a fraternal society.

Traditional discussion of the origins of inequality turned on a crude distinction between nature and society. Plato confidently argued from natural to political inequality. Hobbes expressed a contrary view in 1641:

Nature hath made man so equall, in the faculties of body, and mind; as that though there bee found one man sometimes manifestly stronger in body, or of quicker mind than another; yet when all is reckoned together, the difference between man, and man, is not so considerable, as that one man can thereupon claim to himselfe any benefit, to which another may not pretend, as well as he.[4]

Hobbes's formulation still defines the debate. Egalitarian claims, especially with respect to race and gender, are more strident now than they were in the seventeenth century, and we would now say that Hobbes was making empirical propositions from both genetics and sociology, the one referring to natural differences and the other (about claiming and pretending) referring to the social psychology of man's perceptions of social rights. But the central assertion is about the values which ought to be reflected in the actual relations of men and women in society.

In this sense the debate, turning as it does on ethical priorities between equality, liberty, and fraternity, may never be finally resolvable. There have been, to be sure, notable recent contributions to greater conceptual clarity as to the meaning of terms. John Rawls[5] adopts the device of the 'original position'—an 'if so' story of the rational choices that might be expected from an individual contemplating different societies with known different equalities or inequalities of positions but an unknown placement for the contemplator—to illuminate the problems of value choice. Brian Barry[6] takes the discussion further to demonstrate how a small adjustment to Rawls's social and psychological assumptions opens the possibility of a crucial shift of preference towards egalitarian

---

[4] T. Hobbes, *Leviathan* (1651) (London, 1914), 63.
[5] J. Rawls, *A Theory of Justice* (Cambridge, Mass., 1971).
[6] B. Barry, *The Liberal Theory of Justice* (Oxford, 1973).

rather than liberal forms of society. But no amount of conceptual clarification, sophisticated or erudite, solves the problems of evaluation. In discussing the ethical socialists we shall be looking for a convergent evaluation of what is possible and desirable in modern society.

Meanwhile we can note the provenance of different priorities. One mundane but momentous perspective recurs down the ages—recognition of mortality. Thus Horace (65–8 BC) wrote: 'Pale Death kicks his way equally into the cottages of the poor and the castles of kings.'[7] And James Shirley (1596–1666) reminds us that:

> Death lays his icy hand on kings.
> Sceptre and crown
> Must tumble down.
> And in the dust be equal made
> With the poor crooked scythe and spade.[8]

This attitude was integral to Christian social teaching which dominated the evaluation of social relationships at least until the eighteenth century. It was not that natural inequalities between individuals were denied so much as deemed irrelevant in discussing the rights and wrongs of dictatorship or democracy, freedom or slavery. Christians were not only 'equal before the Cross' but, as the Church Fathers insisted, would, if they eschewed sin, live like brothers without inequalities of property and power. The fall of Adam had created earthly inequality. Political inequality might be necessary to protect order and restrain evil. But it did not arise, as Plato had imagined, from natural inequality. It arose from original sin. Political inequality in Christian tradition must be endured but by no means implied a necessary respect or admiration for the rich and the powerful. On the contrary, position in the next world was typically held to be threatened by privilege in this. 'He hath put down the mighty from their seat and hath exalted the humble and meek', says the Magnificat. The prescription for Christians on earth was to seek the fellowship of sharing.

The break with Christian attitudes of submission to inequality dates from the eighteenth century, with the decline of religious belief and the beginnings of a secular optimism. Ethical socialism spans the ancient and modern conceptions of social harmony. We

---

[7] *Odes*, I. iv. 13.   [8] *The Contention of Ajax and Ulysses* (1654).

shall see below that the ethical socialists (including Orwell who formally disavowed Christian belief) are each in their different way people crucially influenced by both the Christian ethic and belief in at least the possibility of social progress. They are all pilgrims to a New Jerusalem.

Egalitarianism as a movement is commonly associated with Rousseau. But Rousseau, though believing that the evils of unfreedom and inequality were socially created, was a remorseless pessimist. He held that freedom was impossible except in a community of equals, but held out scant hope of social transformation towards equality. In this sense he too was a child of Christianity. If the early socialists (Fourier, Proudhon, Saint-Simon, Robert Owen, William Thompson) were his intellectual children, they were also crucially different in entertaining the hope of progress. Modern egalitarianism derives from this form of sociological optimism and though encouraged by, it was by no means identical with, either the Hegelian idealist or marxist materialist theories of the inevitability of social transformation. Hegel's elaborate analysis of the relation between masters and slaves, and Marx's development of it into a prediction of a victorious working class, both hold out the possibility of a community of equals.

However, ethical socialism does not presuppose either the idealist or the marxist theory of history. It proceeds on assumptions of openness or voluntarism as opposed to necessitarianism. We would postulate as a fourth condition of membership in the ethical-socialist tradition this refusal to espouse historicism. We emphasize this fourth condition, which is met most closely and explicitly by R. H. Tawney and T. H. Marshall, because of its moral implications. Free men and women, to be free, must make their own history in however difficult circumstances. And socialism is not inevitable nor irreversible if attained.

T. H. Marshall's analysis of the development of citizenship,[9] for example, brings out the important truth that the forces which influence the distribution of life chances are neither mechanical nor inexorable. Class displaced feudal status with formal equality of market relations as well as ushering in new inequalities of social condition. Citizenship promotes unequal rewards, for example, state scholarships to selective university admission as well as equal

[9] Notably in his Alfred Marshall Memorial Lectures, delivered in 1949. (T. H. Marshall, *Citizenship and Social Class* (Cambridge, 1950).)

rights, for example, universal political franchise. More generally, it may be noted that no social goal—equality, efficiency, liberty, order, or fraternity—may be regarded as absolute. Public policies are perforce compromises aiming at optimal balance between desired ends.

A continuing objection to egalitarianism is the alleged obstacle of genetic differences between races and classes of which Jensen has been an outstanding proponent.[10] As to classes, and against Jensen's marshalling of the evidence from studies of twins reared apart, there is the opposed conclusion of Schiff[11] from his studies of cross-class adopted children in France. As to race, it has to be said that we do not yet have the techniques or the data to measure definitively the genetic and environmental influences on race–IQ differences. Nor does the answer really matter, for there are more important issues of equality and justice in present-day society which do not have to wait upon further advance in the social sciences. Value choice is always the nub of the issue.

Certainly the writers we discuss did not wait for scientific resolution of issues in social biology. They advocated and acted with confidence for two reasons which may be postulated as the fifth and sixth characteristics of the ethical-socialist outlook: a sense of history and a stress on morality. All our authors interpret their age as one of transition. Even Thomas More, though medievally Christian in his belief that the only really important transition was for the individual to the next world, and for the collective in the second coming, had an acute sense of historical deterioration in his England and of historical continuities and discontinuities with the Hellenic age which were being rediscovered by his fellow humanists.

Of the criteria postulated, the sixth is paramount. It is a theory of personality and society which places moral motivation as the mainspring of individual conduct and social organization. Socialism can only be built on moral character and history is a never-ending struggle to develop the altruism of individuals, to mould social institutions in its image and to pass on its tradition to each new generation. This essential theory of human nature is interpreted contextually according to the social experience of each devotee. But

[10] A. Jensen, *Genetics and Education* (London, 1972).
[11] M. Schiff and R. Lewontin, *The Irrelevance of IQ Genetic Studies* (London, 1986).

its vision of an improvable if not perfectable person is always there. Moral commitment can surmount any material obstacle. More discovered this truth among the Carthusian monks of the Charterhouse, Cobbett on his *Rural Rides*, Orwell in anarchist Barcelona, Hobhouse observing trade-unionists at Toynbee Hall, T. H. Marshall watching imprisoned sailors in a German prison camp, Tawney with working men in tutorial classes at Rochdale.

These then are the common features of a succession of ethical socialists whom we may now consider in turn. Our purpose is to show the continuing vitality of the ideas of these writers in an England once more in the throes of transition. For it is a society of rapid technological and social change, rich in essential or ennobling things that can be bought and sold for money. But it is a society also which is well supplied by markets in what is trivial or degrading— and a society which is neglectful of many values which escape pecuniary calculation. Even on the economic side inequality has persisted. A majority are securely attached to a materially prosperous country while minorities are trapped in deprivation. The relevance of the ethical-socialist idea is therefore perhaps even greater than it ever was, for much of what the past masters were able to take for granted as having been already achieved or as giving grounds for hope in their time has to be argued for and accomplished anew in ours. The quest is and always must be for a moral community in which freedom is gained for every member through the sharing of what they have, in equal mutual respect for the freedom of all.

2

A PRACTICAL UTOPIA
Thomas More (1478–1535)

The tradition of ethical socialism we inherit is old, very old. A culture of respect for law and love of freedom has lately been once again traced back to the thirteenth century, distinguishing England from the peasant societies of medieval Europe and Asia.[1] In other chapters we deal with both Cobbett's and Tawney's, as well as Marx's, interest in the early development of the free-born but communitarian Englishman, and these of course pre-date Macfarlane's treatment. Marx regarded More's work as a response to the distinct worsening of the position of the common Englishman:

In England, serfdom had practically disappeared in the last part of the fourteenth century. The immense majority of the population consisted then, and to a still larger extent in the fifteenth century, of free peasant proprietors ... A comparison of the writings of Chancellor Fortesque [*Laudes legum Angilae*] and Thomas More reveals the gulf between the fifteenth and the sixteenth century.[2]

Heroes and heroines doubtless practised the combination of brave independence and sober orderliness permitted and encouraged by this culture in a distinctively prosperous, mobile, and uncaste-like society. They are mostly lost to us now as persons. But we do have a record, voluminous and detailed, of an exceptionally distinguished early son of the tradition, Thomas More. His life and times are both remote and yet also crucial to the interpretation of the ethical-socialist tradition in our own time: remote because he deliberately accepted martyrdom on behalf of his version of the tradition against the authority of the secular power; crucial because his is a statement about the meaning of life itself, though set in the busy day-to-day activities of a public and political career at the high point of power which was the Lord Chancellorship of England.

[1] A. Macfarlane, *The Origins of English Individualism: The Family, Property and Social Transition* (Oxford, 1978).
[2] K. Marx, *Capital* (1867–94) (Moscow, 1958), 717, 719.

More was a martyr, a hero, and a saint.[3] But he was also a privileged courtier, a man of vanity and mocking self-display, and an angry, vengeful persecutor of heretics. Modern scholarship[4] has rescued him and us from one of those 'creations of sterile and impossible virtue who so tantalized and corrupted the desperately romantic Middle Ages'.[5] For us now he is a human if mysterious figure, a man of frailty and imperfection as well as what Erasmus first called him—a man for all seasons.

More was born in London in 1478 and went to the scaffold in the same place on a July morning in 1535. In the years between he had difficulties in choosing lay against priestly life, marriage against celibacy, and professional honour against monetary gain. But the final test was to uphold the Christian tradition against the will of the national throne. It was not that he gave precedence to sceptre over crown, and far less that he respected the papal rather than the kingly incumbent—he was no less enthusiastically an English patriot than a European humanist. It was that for him ultimately moral authority resided in Christ's Church, separated from the inescapable corruption of state power. The collective conscience of all Christendom, most perfectly expressed in the lives of the saints in every age and handed down from generation to generation through the faithful practice of the Sacraments in 'one holy and apostolic church'—*that* was the fount of earthly authority. Loyal obedience to that tradition was the idea for which he died.

PERSONAL ENDS

More's personal as well as his social ideals are essentially Christian, medieval, and monastic. In his time the idea of both persons and peoples had to be shaped within the taken-for-granted assumption that the world is unalterably as it is. It cannot be perfected before the second coming of Christ and is incapable of transformation by unaided human agency. The accessible milieu of least imperfection is the monastery and the life and character of the individual is to be found at its best in the diligent pursuit of the discipline imposed by

[3] He was canonized by Pope Pius XI in 1935.
[4] See especially the most recent biography by R. Marius, *Thomas More* (London, 1984) for a detailed and dispassionate assessment. For the most convincing eulogy of More, see R. W. Chambers, *Thomas More* (London, 1935). For a more hostile interpretation see G. R. Elton, 'The Real Thomas More' in *Reformation Principle and Practice*, ed. P. N. Brooks (London, 1980).   [5] Marius, *More*, 520.

a religious order because most pleasing to God. We cannot know why the world is as it is because the mind of the Deity is inscrutable. Nevertheless it is inconceivable to postulate a human being without an immortal soul or to suppose that the fate of an individual is not determined by a providence which includes rewards and punishments beyond the present life. All these assumptions lie behind both More's practice in England and his theory in *Utopia* of the good life for an individual in his ideal community.

More's personal ideal was thus set by the disciplined life of the monks at the Charterhouse in London with whom he lived daily for about four years, sharing their rituals, admiring their austere piety, and believing that theirs was the most assured path to heaven. He spent more time with monks than George Orwell was to spend with his source of moral inspiration, working men. Yet More decided in the end for the secular life. It must have been a decision wrung from deep ambivalence. For his ancient model, Saint Augustine, had taught that all sensuality was evil and his friend Erasmus was adamant that he would never enter the service of any monarch. If More married to make himself 'a faithful husband rather than an unfaithful priest' he later regretted his weakness, recognizing ruefully that it may be easier for a bachelor than a married man to control lust. For the rest of his days he lived under a self-imposed discipline of personal denial and prodigious labour (his abhorrence of idleness was compulsive). And if he also entered public life through Parliament in the year of his marriage, he finally gave his life in defence of the priority of Church over State.

More is personally remote from us now, both as a saint distinguished from ordinary mortals, and as a man who continually seemed to enact the private virtues of the good husband, father, and friend as if on a public stage and larger than life even in his own household. Perhaps still more important, he is a distant figure because deeply rooted in medieval Christian views of human nature and the relation between personal character and social structure. He had in full measure the medieval belief in original sin, the Christian conviction of the vanity and the ephemeral unimportance of worldly desires, the invaluable worth of each individual immortal soul, and the utter dependence of every person on the grace of an almighty God. Modern sceptics may well suspect the personal description as a hallowed idealization from repeated hagiography. They may detect supervening elements of the social actor masking a more complex, less perfect person. What they can less readily doubt is that the definition of moral character which ethical socialism inherits is here revealed as a tradition of awesome simplicity and power. A moral kingdom not of this world could firmly guide the conduct of an individual throughout an earthly life.

In this perspective we can glimpse the vast distance between More and the majority of our own contemporaries by recalling a scene from the last year of his life. More was awaiting execution in the Tower of London. His daughter came to visit him. From the window of his death cell they saw the procession of Dr Reynolds and three Carthusian monks towards Tyburn and the horrifying agony of death by hanging and disembowelling which was a common enough fate in those days for those who defied the secular power. More turned to his daughter:

Lo, dost thou not see, Meg, that these blessed fathers be now as cheerfully going to their deaths as bridegrooms to their marriage? Wherefore, thereby mayest thou see, mine own good daughter, what a great difference there is between such as have in effect spent all their days in a strait and penitential and painful life religiously, and such as have in the world, like worldly wretches (as thy poor father hath done), consumed all their time in pleasure and ease licentiously. For God, considering their long-continued life in most sore and grievous penance, will no longer suffer them to remain here in this vale of misery, but speedily hence taketh them to the fruition of his everlasting Deity.

Within the year, More followed his brothers with no less dignity and with that cheerful self-disregard which informed his whole life and character as one who had worn the hair shirt throughout a lay life. Weak from long imprisonment, at the foot of a rickety scaffold, he took leave of his friend, Thomas Pope, with a characteristic joke: 'I pray you see me safe up, and for my coming down, let me shift for myself.'

Such an attitude towards self, life, and death is so remote from suburban twentieth-century cosiness and metropolitan sophistication as to raise immediately the question of whether our author or his *Utopia* can be relevant to the contemporary world. We shall argue that they are. *Utopia* was indeed published nearly five centuries ago in Louvain and in Latin. Britain now has nearly twenty times the population of England then. It is industrial, technological, capitalist, protestant, and secular whereas More was born into an England of probably less than three million people and a society which was agrarian, pre-scientific, catholic, and religious. His kings were illiberal autocrats. Our Queen is the constitutional and ritual product of some centuries of evolved political liberalism.

Nor can contemporary relevance rest on the banal continuities of human nature—that men are men and the species for ever social. The arguments for attention both to the man and the book are neither the dramatization of historical contrast nor the distillation of the universals of man in society. They are, we think, that More stood at the beginning and we stand at the end of a capitalist era and that just as then, with his brilliant contemporaries, Erasmus, Michaelangelo, Machiavelli, Luther, he struggled to relate a tradition to radicalism in a world felt to be in exciting but dangerous transformation, so too must we. By his private life and his public writing More exemplified in his time what we hold to be the most valuable civic inheritance in ours—ethical socialism. We write under this title—knowing that some might deem it a contradiction in terms—without which English political life and thought is incomprehensible and of which Thomas More is a founding father.

Of course, we could praise this compatriot in quite other ways. For example, it would be plausible to claim More as an academic entertainer. Books were commonly written to be read aloud in those days, and *Utopia* is aptly cast in the form of dialogue between the author and the sea-faring Raphael Hythloday, returned to Holland from travels with Amerigo Vespucci. The result is a marvellously dramatic script and we could use Ralph Robinson's 1551 translation of More's Latin into English to demonstrate the quaint vigour and range of vocabulary of the vernacular which Erasmus disdained. And so we would be reminded of More as a tributary source of the sparkling flood of Elizabethan English prose. In his own English writing, More anticipated the blend of simplicity and majesty of the anglican liturgy, as when he prayed:

Good Lord, give me the grace to spend my life, that when the day of my death shall come, though I feel pain in my body, I may feel comfort in my soul; and with faithful hope of Thy mercy, in due love towards Thee, and charity towards the world, I may through Thy grace part hence into Thy glory.

Alternatively More could be extolled as the inventor of a literary genre. He bestowed Utopia as a new word on the English language.

Nor was this merely an imitative resuscitation of the Hellenic pictures of earthly paradise of ideal states which had appeared with Plato and disappeared with Lucian. With his book, More established the direct topical juxtaposition of the ideal against the real imperfections of current morals and manners. Utopias and dystopias—well over one hundred—have been added in subsequent centuries. They include that of another Lord Chancellor of England, Francis Bacon's *New Atlantis*, and Campanella's *City of the Sun* in the seventeenth century, Jonathan Swift's *Gulliver's Travels* in the eighteenth, William Morris's *News From Nowhere*, and Samuel Butler's *Erewhon* in the nineteenth, and H. G. Wells's *Time Machine* and George Orwell's *Nineteen Eighty-Four* in the twentieth century—all addressed to solving the moral and material problems of their own societies under conditions made conceivable by the scientific developments of their day.

What, assuredly, we would not want to do is to dehumanize More. He has been the victim of this treatment by interpreters of diverse motive. The hagiography of pious Catholics tends to turn the man into a myth, especially since he was beatified by Pope Leo XIII in 1886. In the secular sphere, Robert Bolt's play was intended to eulogize More as a man of independent opinion, puritanical self-discipline, cheerful virtue, and unfailing personal courage unto death. But the popularization of an image by television and cinema, and the sale of thousands of prints of Holbein's portrait of More in pop art shops, have the same tendency. They all too easily generate contradictory untruth—the destruction of idols at the behest of the same impulse towards fashionable dramatization. The defence of myth-making is thin. For example, Sir Vivian Fuchs once complained against Roland Huntford's debunking of Scott of the Antarctic by appealing to the argument that a country needs heroes. But *A Man For All Seasons* is all too likely to become a creature for all critics. So Woodrow Wilson and T. E. Lawrence were made popular heroes in the First World War only to be savaged later by psychoanalytic biographies, the one by Freud himself, the other by Richard Aldington.

Equally we want to avoid a more subtle denigration to which More has been vulnerable. It comes by neglect or by adverse judgement from those protestant and secular progressives who have dominated Anglo-Saxon philosophy and history in modern times. Thus, in a reference to *Utopia*, we are told by one biographer in

1926, G. R. Potter, that 'the verdict of history may be that he had seen the light and had deliberately closed his eyes to it . . .' 'To his religion', Potter adds, 'he sacrificed many of the convictions of his early years, and subjugated what the modern world regards as his better self to the claims of papal supremacy within England.' Bertrand Russell is the modern philosophical progressive *par excellence*. He affords More four of the thousand pages of his *History of Western Philosophy*. The passage, however, is a summary of *Utopia* and a sketch of its author in Russell's worst mood of mandarin disdain.

Rather more seriously disappointing is the fact that the standard modern survey of political and social theory—John Plamenatz's *Man and Society*—makes only passing reference to More in a discussion of Durkheim and socialist thought in the nineteenth century. This is puzzling for several reasons. Plamenatz was a meticulous scholar who makes much of Machiavelli, to whose *Prince* More's *Utopia* is exactly the contemporaneous reply we might have expected if these two sixteenth-century authors had been aware of each other's books. He also refers to Erasmus and Vives (who warmly admired More's contribution to the New Humanism) and then goes on to an authoritative and lucid discussion of the way in which the notion of liberty of conscience developed out of medieval disputes into a central concept of modern political theory in Europe.

'Liberty of conscience', Plamenatz rightly argues, 'was born, not of indifference, not of scepticism, not of mere open-mindedness, but of faith.' He then contrasts two propositions. First, 'Faith is supremely important, and therefore all men must have the one true faith.' And second, 'Faith is supremely important, and therefore every man must be allowed to live by the faith which seems true to him.' Having set these two quite different arguments against each other, Plamenatz shows how the first gradually gave way to the second in a Christendom which had long been accustomed to think of itself as a single community of the faithful and was now in schism. Thomas More, we would say, was the first martyr to that terrible dilemma, and his *Utopia* was offered as a solution by a radical who also understood what was both precious and precarious in the traditions of European Christianity.

Thomas More has, of course, been claimed for the competing radicalism of our time, Marxism. For Karl Kautsky he was one of two great figures looming 'on the threshold of socialism' (the other being Thomas Munzer).[6] He was 'the father of utopian socialism' and 'utopian less on account of the impracticability of [his] aims than on account of the inadequacy of the means at [his] disposal for their achievement'. Kautsky, even as a revisionist Marxist, had to affirm that More's life was a tragedy not in terms of the moral dilemma that we have suggested but 'the whole tragedy of a genius who defines the problems of his age before the material conditions exist for their solution'.[7] However for those not imprisoned by the strait-jacket of the marxist theory of ineluctable history, More and his *Utopia* can be appreciated both in the context of the protestant convulsion in Europe and in the timeless conception of socialism as a set of personal and political principles that people are challenged to apply to themselves, their institutions, and their government in any age.

MEANS

More did not directly present a programme for reform. Instead he included in *Utopia* some direct criticism of European society in Book I which relates an invented conversation between himself and Raphael Hythloday in Antwerp in 1515. Book II is a descriptive monologue by Hythloday of the institutions of a new-world commonwealth. The sailor reflects More's social priorities in which above all the conscience of the community is set above individual judgement, the spiritual above the physical life, the next world above this, reason above passion, simplicity above sophistication, and industriousness above idleness or frivolity.

Seen as a balance between what the modern world of political discussion is inclined to treat as the value triangle of liberty, equality, and fraternity, More gives unhesitating preference to fraternity. He denies both privacy and property to the individual and places him under the remorseless surveillance of the community. Equality is thereby substantially achieved but at high cost to liberty. The social order, apart from its religious base of Christianity without revelation, bears uncomfortable resemblance to the self-idealization of a modern Eastern European communist society.

[6] K. Kautsky, *Thomas More and his Utopia* (London, 1927).
[7] Ibid. 249.

What manner of society, then, was to be found among the remote Utopians of the southern hemisphere? To answer that utopian institutions put the principles of peace, equality, and justice into practice is true but vacuously unhelpful since it describes the social dreams of most men and women whether of the sixteenth century or our own. In fact, More described in practical terms how the Utopians realized these ideals, and thus presented to his English and European contemporaries a vivid alternative social system, all the more telling in that Utopians worked it out solely on the basis of the four cardinal virtues of antiquity—wisdom, fortitude, temperance, and justice—that is, without the divine revelation of the Christian virtues of faith, hope, and charity.

Sixteenth-century Europe was impoverished and oppressed by warfare at the whim of kings and princes seeking their own aggrandizement. The Utopians despised martial glory. They assumed that men should behave internationally with the same moral scruples as do kinsfolk and neighbours. They avoided war by every possible device of generous foreign aid, diplomacy, and, if necessary, intrigue to foment discord among their enemies. They would go to war only if these measures failed and only then to defend their country, to restore justice to an ally, or to deliver a people from tyranny. They took up the sword, in short, only to defend internationally the justice and freedom they gave to their own citizens. And even then they preferred, when possible, to use mercenaries and bribery so as to minimize the bloodshed of innocents. But if invaded they fought bravely, training all, men and women alike, in the military skills.

Life in early sixteenth-century England was precarious in every sense. The expectation of life at birth was about thirty-five years— less than half of what it is now. Infants could be regarded only very tentatively as potential adults. Not only mortality, but also morbidity were ever present in a world of ill-understood endemic disease, high risks of fire, and uncertain food supply. London was a squalid, insanitary mess of crowded hovels. More described it himself in a letter written about 1504 to his older friend John Colet, Dean of St Paul's Cathedral. The city, according to More, is a place of wickedness. 'No matter where you go, you find feigned love and the honeyed poison of flatterers, and there are always hatred, quarrels and the din of the market. Wherever you turn your eyes, what else will you see but confectioners, fishmongers, butchers, cooks, poulterers, fishermen, fowlers, who supply the materials for gluttony and the world's lord, the devil? Houses block out light and hide us from the heavens.' By contrast, in the country, 'wherever you cast your eyes, the smiling face of the earth greets you, the sweet fresh air invigorates you, the very sight of the heavens charms you. There you see nothing but the generous gifts of nature and the traces of our primeval innocence.'[8]

More's London, though a small town by modern standards of some 45,000 people, reminds us of the urban priority areas described in the 1985 report by the Archbishop of Canterbury's Commission, *Faith in the City*.[9] Such welfare organization of poor relief and hospitals as had existed was being plundered by royal greed. Utopia stood in total contrast and its capital Amaurot was a glorious vision of London reformed. More writes here in the exuberant spirit of a renaissance social engineer. A piped water supply, wide streets in front, and delightful gardens behind three-storey houses with flat roofs and glass windows all commonly owned. Four great hospitals served the town, clean and devotedly staffed. There was a guaranteed provision, to the young, the old, the healthy, and the sick, of adequate food, clothing, shelter, and nursing.

Nor was Utopia a mere fancy of escape from poverty and toil. By contrast with his England, More put all his Utopians to work save those selected for scholarship on rigorously meritocratic tests and retests. His pacific country allowed no idle hands, whereas, as More saw it, in England many women, all the nobles with their parasites and attendants, those engaged in luxury trades, the clergy, and the 'sturdy beggars' were kept by the labour of their fellow citizens. In Utopia, because economic growth was not sought, because idleness was not tolerated, because everyone learned the agricultural skills and took his or her turn for labour in the countryside, and because private consumption was discouraged, fashion banished, and private wealth forbidden, it was wholly practicable for the Utopians to work but six or eight hours a day and to maintain communal institutions of gorgeous splendour. Contempt for gold was instilled by its use only for chamber pots, prisoners' chains, and children's toys.

Politically, Utopia was a representative democracy in which the

[8] Marius, *More*, 3.   [9] (London, 1985).

elected prince could be deposed for tyranny, office-holders dismissed for corruption, and the powerful punished more severely than the weak for crime. The laws were few and simple, there was no capital punishment, and convicts redeemed themselves by arduous labour.

More's contemporaries were too close to medieval Christendom to be at all surprised by the utopian assumptions of the existence of God and the immortality of the soul. They would not have been surprised that in Utopia disbelief in either of these propositions was sanctioned by withdrawal of citizenship or that deliberate and persistent propaganda against these beliefs might incur exile or enslavement. But through sixteenth-century eyes, *Utopia* appears vastly more radical than traditional. What would have been radically dazzling to them was the vision of religious toleration, hygienic urban life, a short working day, the abolition of private riches, and the ending of tyranny and war.

Twentieth-century Britons might well share some of this wonder. They, too, find equality and international peace elusive. But *Utopia* for them must appear more traditional than radical. At the end of the capitalist era they are no strangers either to the difficulties of full employment in a fair division of labour or of private affluence amidst public squalor. More's community houses for eating, education, and conviviality—his essentially monastic socialism—are easily dismissed as a traditional relic, as irrelevant as an Oxford college. Privatization is our legacy from the capitalist centuries between. More's assumption of directed labour and standardized plain clothing offend too against the modern spirit of individualism, demanding a return to ancient un-freedom. No less archaic is the assumption that increasing wealth or, as we would now say, economic growth, is not to be sought. Liberal individualism sets no limit to the proliferation of wants or to the hope of their satisfaction.

Indeed, it is scarcely an exaggeration to say that conceptions of life and death have been reversed between the beginning and the end of the capitalist era. For More life was a short, precarious interlude to be endured, and death a beginning. For us life is a long protection to be enjoyed, and death is an ending. We accordingly make virtually infinite demands on this life in this society.

What More is saying to us is that growth does have its limits and that as we reach them we are forced back to the problem of how we can agree on the distribution of limited worldly goods. He is saying that what matters is not efficiency to maximize production, but care and justice in the sharing of what we have. He invites us to contemplate the moral imperatives with which we would govern our lives and which would give us a disciplined protection against futile pursuits of Maeterlinck's blue bird.[10]

The Utopians lived commodiously and left ample time for the cultivation of their mental and spiritual life. They suspected private property as the corruptor of morals, they disregarded its function as the motive for further wealth production. And they were able to do so because social control for them was not, as with us, a shifting bargain over the share out of today's production and tomorrow's promise of greater abundance. Instead they took it for granted that it was the obligation of the individual to store up treasures in heaven through unselfish duty on earth. Harsh material conditions in life and the promise of religion beyond death made More's passage to Utopia possible in the sixteenth century.

But impossible now, the pagan will say, knowing that even Karl Marx set the seal of disapproval on such utopian socialism.[11] But is it? Thomas More deliberately denied Christian revelation to his Utopians. They created their society solely in the light of reason. He did this *vis-à-vis* his contemporaries to show them that virtuous pagans could create a better commonwealth than they had made shift to do as bad Christians. He wanted to encourage them not merely to emulate but to excel the limits of what was possible to utopian reason. For us his message is not wholly different. It is a call to find our unchanging radical aspirations in our fast-moving tradition. He appeals to us to understand the limits of reason as an apparatus for the satisfaction of unlimited earthly ambition, to rediscover the value of community as against individualism, and in the end to recognize that the only enduring community is that of the Saints.

[10] *The Blue Bird* (London, 1909).
[11] Marx's own vision of communist society is, of course, highly utopian. He condemns as utopian the visions of others; but he especially condemns as 'utopian socialists' those who fail to recognize the validity of his explanation of how communist society will be brought about.

AND YET

And yet the example of Thomas More, myth or reality, must finally belong to the inspirational rather than the relevantly practical inheritance of modern ethical socialism. Political transformations need but cannot be solely dependent on heroes. He incomparably more than Henry VIII deserved the title of Defender of the Faith, but that faith is much less available to be defended in a post-Christian world. Adapting Maréchal Bosquet's comment on the charge of the Light Brigade in the Crimean War, the contemporary critic might well say, 'C'est magnifique, mais ce n'est pas la politique'. As inspiration to the individual socialist and as model to the socialist society More's life and his *Utopia* respectively still point heroically in the direction of the good life in the good society.

Nevertheless both ends and means remain in question under vastly transformed circumstances. For all his noble example we still have sordid poverty alongside arrogant riches, corrupt rulers and apathetic subjects, warfare in precedence over welfare. Neither liberty nor equality nor fraternity were conspicuously advanced in sixteenth-century England as a result of More's efforts. He did persecute heretics, and the Reformation and Counter-Reformation were to continue in bitterness and slaughter. *Utopia* after all was not a political programme but rather a possible alternative history produced out of a remarkable renaissance imagination.

What is left to us is, in the best sense, a dream. We are bequeathed a vision of personal courage and loyalty to the ideal of a spiritually united community. As Anthony Kenny has so well put it:

More is that rare figure, an Establishment martyr: a man to whom the world and all its promises were open, who had riches and power to hand, which he could have kept if he had been willing to bend to the wind and who went to his death without bitterness and with a jest. The Utopians would have been proud of him: when a good man dies 'No part of his life is so oft or so gladly talked of, as his merry death'.[12]

---

[12] A. Kenny, *Thomas More* (Oxford, 1983), 104.

3

THE FREE-BORN ENGLISHMAN AND THE COMMON WEAL
William Cobbett (1763–1835)

COBBETT'S LIFE AND DEATH

Two centuries after Thomas More the tradition of ethical socialism had to come to terms with the transition from agrarianism to the early forms of classical industrialism. At this point the magnificent figure of William Cobbett rode across southern England as the extraordinary champion of ordinary people. He comes down to us now in popular legend as the convinced carrier of belief in freedom and independence as the English birthright. His was a long life of unceasing effort on behalf of common men in the common weal, displaying inexhaustible wit and righteous anger against all enemies of liberty and sturdy self-reliance. Had he been born in chains he would somehow have become free through sheer force of moral and physical strength. In him we see a precursor of Tawney, advocating in his time the tradition of individual freedom within the context of communal order. His morals and politics were grounded in Christianity. He encouraged the English working class to believe that common wealth and freedom of persons was not only their legitimate aspiration, but already their rightful inherit-ance. He thus claimed the ethical-socialist tradition for all his compatriots.

His forebears were labouring men. He learnt, not from school, but from the culture of his childhood in a farming community and from his father's thrifty and industrious ambition. He lived in a society of independent individuals in his native Farnham where there was full private ownership, a 'chain of connection' between richer and poorer, and considerable geographical and social mobility. Such an upbringing gave him a natural sympathy with the theories being developed in his day on the basic presumption of rationality and freedom. Thus, even in the insurrectionary years of 1811, 1817, and 1830, Cobbett's radicalism never turned him towards the approval of class struggle, still less of armed class conflict. His devotion was to the independence of the small producer and the heroic potential of the plain man.

His moral outlook was rooted in thorough familiarity with that of the English eighteenth-century parish. 'Our religion was the Church of England', he wrote, 'to which I have ever remained attached; the more so, perhaps', he adds, 'as it bears the name of my country.'[1] The *Book of Common Prayer* required the curate of each parish to instruct children in a catechism summarizing the morality the national Church sought to inculcate. Cobbett's morality was that of a Church of England Christian of his day. All his life, too, he followed the book's stylistic rule: to say things in such a language 'as is easy and plain for the understanding both of . . . Readers and Hearers'. The authors of the Preface taught him another important lesson, that institutions are only as good as the people who operate them. 'There was never any thing by the wit of man so well devised, or so sure established, which in the continuance of time has not been corrupted.'[2]

Cobbett had the knack of turning all good fortune and misfortune into educative experience. When he was fourteen, and had run away to work at the Royal Gardens at Kew, he picked up a copy of Swift's *A Tale of a Tub*; it produced in him 'a sort of birth of intellect'. In 1781 he was in Wapping and heard John Wesley preach. In 1782 he helped at a school near Portsmouth run by a relative. Later, he worked for a time for the author of *A Complete and Universal English Dictionary*, who allowed Cobbett to use his books. In May 1783 he again ran away from home, and found a job as an attorney's clerk in London.

From the solicitor's office he joined the army. Because of his experience as a clerk, he was made copyist to the garrison's commander. He did not spend his time in 'the dissipations common to such a way of life', but in reading and study. He subscribed to a circulating library, and read novels, plays, history, and poetry with avidity. He learned Lowth's *Grammar* by heart.[3] He educated himself in the inhospitable circumstances of the barrack room. What excuse, he demanded to know, could there be for any youth,

[1] G. D. H. Cole, *The Life of William Cobbett* (1924) (London, 1927), 16.
[2] Preface, *The Book of Common Prayer* (1662) (Oxford, n.d.).
[3] G. Spater, *William Cobbett: The Poor Man's Friend* (Cambridge, 1982), i. 17.

however poor, for not accomplishing the same?[4] Military life was turned to autodidactic purposes. Posted to Canada, he studied geometry and read Vauban on fortifications. He taught himself French, and became so proficient that he was able to earn a living in the 1790s as a translator of French and as a teacher of English to French émigrés.[5] He eventually wrote a successful French grammar.[6] He discovered his flair for conveying information effectively to others. His *Little Book of Arithmetic* was 'for the teaching of young corporals and serjeants'. (Two beautiful pages are reproduced in Spater's biography.)[7] When the new discipline relating to military exercises were issued, it was Cobbett who taught them to his officers.

His military experiences led him to despise his superiors,[8] but to admire the courage, intelligence, and decency of the English common soldier.[9] He quit the army in order to institute proceedings against those officers whose guilt of peculation he felt he could prove.[10] Before the court martial took place, however, he suspected a plot against him and, now married, he fled to France. From France he went to the United States, where he observed at close quarters the gap between the ideals of democracy and the abuses from which it could suffer at the hands of unscrupulous men. From the United States he also watched events during the years in which Louis was guillotined, the Girondists were defeated by the armed force of the Commune under the control of Jacobins, and the Committee of Public Safety exercised its dictatorship. The Cult of the Goddess of Reason and anti-Christianity were officially propagated. It was the period of the Reign of Terror during which, as Lamartine said, the revolution seemed to consume her own

[4] W. Cobbett, *Advice to Young Men, and (incidently) to Young Women* (1829–30) (Oxford, 1980), 47. The classic account in fiction of self-education under adverse circumstances—by an 'ever-increasing army of martyrs'—is C. Kingsley, *Alton Locke: Tailor and Poet* (1850) (London, n.d. [1892]), 30.
[5] Cole, *Life of William Cobbett*, 53–4.
[6] W. Cobbett, *A French Grammar* (London, 1824).
[7] Spater, *Cobbett*, 23.   [8] Ibid. i. 21.
[9] *Pol. Reg.*, 6 Dec. 1817, in W. Cobbett and W. Cobbett (the Younger), *Cobbett's Annual Register*, called also *Cobbett's Political Register*, *Cobbett's Weekly Political Pamphlet*, etc. (London, 1802–35). There is a selection from the *Pol. Reg.* and other writings by Cobbett in G. D. H. and M. Cole (eds.), *The Opinions of William Cobbett* (London, 1944).
[10] Anon. (Cobbett, supposed author), *The Soldiers' Friend* (London, 1792); R. Powell, *Proceeding of a General Court Martial* (London, 1809).

children. He therefore knew the myths and realities of violent revolution. American support for the French and American abuse of England led to a powerful reaction from Cobbett, and he perfected his art of defending the institutions of his homeland against 'sans-culottes tomfoolery' in both its French and American versions.[11]

By the time Cobbett returned to England, in 1800, the enemies of liberty were different. 'Now that Napoleon is Emperor, the danger to English liberty posed by the false liberty of the Jacobins is removed', he wrote.[12] But in an England of inflation and heavy taxation, he believed that freedom was now being lost to an increasingly oppressive and centralized state controlled by the leader of the party in power; that the old aristocracy and the gentry were being replaced in the countryside by self-seeking war contractors and newly-rich dealers in the National Debt; and that the horizons of the rural labourers were being narrowed by high taxes, high prices, and sluggish wages.

He supported Burdett in the Middlesex by-election of 1804, and was henceforth exposed fully to (as well as powerfully influencing) radical perceptions and values. In 1806 he began his collaboration with the 'brave and serene' Major John Cartwright,[13] who taught him faith in the efficacy of a certain type of agitation—the petition, the address, and the open and free discussion of the county meeting, rather than that of the conspiratorial underground of the London tavern clubs; and faith, too, in the force of ancient constitutional precedent.[14]

Economic crises punctuated the war and the post-war period. Particularly important for moulding Cobbett's outlook were those associated with popular unrest. There were bad harvests and war embargoes on trade 1809–12. For the hand-workers there were the effects of newly introduced steam machinery. Food riots erupted in several parts of the country. One outbreak of the machine-breaking movement, Luddism, ended in the murder of an employer.[15] The agitation for parliamentary reform involved the death in 1819 of eleven peaceful demonstrators at St Peter's Field, Manchester—the Peterloo Massacre.[16]

[11] Spater, *Cobbett*, i. 46.   [12] *Pol. Reg.*, 1 Nov. 1804.
[13] E. P. Thompson, *The Making of the English Working Class* (London, 1965), 638.
[14] Ibid. 647–8.   [15] Ibid. 340–1.   [16] Ibid. 686–7.

Cobbett's view of the world, and the moral code by which he judged it, reflected a particular interpretation of the history of English society. Whether or not the result of successful ruling-class propaganda, the linked ideas of 'the free-born Englishman' and 'the common weal' were deep-rooted and persistent in the culture of the common people. England was popularly the blessed isle of truth and concord, the impregnable stronghold of liberty,[17] which had enjoyed over a century free from civil war.

Certainly these were Cobbett's most basic assumptions. Even when government repression drove him to a second exile in America he remained faithful to this view of his native land:

I wished nothing for my country but its liberties and its laws. England has been very happy and *free*; her greatness and renown have been surpassed by those of no nation in the world; her wise, just and merciful laws form the basis of that freedom which we here enjoy, she has been fertile beyond all rivalship in men of learning and men devoted to the cause of freedom and humanity.[18]

In its obituary Tait's *Edinburgh Magazine* called him 'the Last Saxon'.[19] 'Throughout the bulk of the campaigning years of Cobbett . . . the dominant language of radicals was a form of constitutional rhetoric, which used precedent to justify images of an organic community and elaborated a mythical history of Saxon or medieval England to reclaim rights which historically belonged to the English people.'[20] He carried into the nineteenth century, as Tawney carried into the twentieth, a memory of the *Rectitudines Singularum Personarum*, the Anglo-Saxon *Rights and Duties of All Persons*.[21]

It was Marx's opinion that Cobbett was the greatest pamphleteer England had ever produced, and that as a master of English he had not been surpassed.[22] To Hazlitt he was one of England's best

[17] W. Wordsworth, 'The Excursion' (1814), *The Poetical Works of William Wordsworth*, ed. T. Hutchinson (London, 1908), viii, ll. 145–7, p. 876.

[18] W. Cobbett, *Journal of a Year's Residence in the United States of America* (1819) (Gloucester, 1983), 303–4.

[19] *Tait's Edinburgh Magazine*, Aug.–Sept. 1835. Hood expressed the same idea in his biography of Cobbett. (E. P. Hood, *The Last of the Saxons* (London, 1854).)

[20] G. S. Jones, *Languages of Class: Studies in English Working Class History 1832–1982* (Cambridge, 1983), 125.

[21] A. E. Bland, P. A. Brown, and R. H. Tawney, *English Economic History: Selected Documents* (London, 1914), 5–9.

[22] K. Marx and F. Engels, *Collected Works* (London, 1979), xii. 189.

writers, combining the qualities of Swift, Defoe, and Mandeville.[23]
To Henry Morley, the plain speech of Cobbett was as resolute as
the plain speech of Luther.[24] Cobbett strove for such plainness. He
believed that mastery of grammar was the key to clarity of
expression and comprehension. *A Grammar of the English
Language* was written by him to provide the tools of liberation and
personal development to everyone, but most especially to the
poor—to soldiers, sailors, apprentices, and plough-boys.[25] He was
able to draw on vast resources of the classics of English literature,
as well as those of other countries. The basis of his literacy was the
Bible, a never-failing store of authoritative doctrine, vivid imagery,
and pungent vocabulary.

Mary Mitford has pictured the expansive Cobbett at the height
of his powers. A tall, stout man, fair and sunburnt, with a bright
smile, and an air compounded of soldier and farmer. 'He was, I
think, the most athletic and vigorous person I have ever known.'[26]
When he died on 18 June 1835, old age had ruined his body. He
was probably, since the early 1820s, disturbed in mind, paranoid
after decades of persecution. But Ebenezer Elliot's elegy catches him
as he wanted to be remembered, riding out in the rain and the wind
with one of his young sons by his side, and now to be buried with
his ancestors at Farnham. 'Yes! Let the wild-flower wed his grave',
Elliot wrote,

> That bees may murmur near,
> When o'er his last home bend the brave,
> And say—'A man lies here'.[27]

SELF RESPECT

Cobbett deals extensively with the strictly self-regarding aspects of
the ideal character. The indispensable foundation of self-development is freedom from hunger, cold, and other physical hardships

[23] W. Hazlitt (the Elder), *The Spirit of the Age*, 2nd edn. (London, 1825), 333.

[24] Cobbett, *Advice* (London, 1887), John Morley's Introduction, 7.

[25] W. Cobbett, *A Grammar of the English Language* (1823) (Oxford, 1984).
Cobbett's views on the importance of grammar for the disadvantaged stands in stark
contrast to those of some educational progressives in the 1980s. See National Union
of Teachers, Response to HM Inspectorate of Schools, *English from Five to Sixteen*,
The Times, 12 Jan. 1985.

[26] M. R. Mitford, *Recollections of a Literary Life* (1852), 2nd edn. (London,
1859), 199 ff.

[27] 'Elegy of the Death of Cobbett', quoted in *Life of William Cobbett*, p. vii.

which render a person incapable of raising himself by his own efforts. If a person has not the means to obtain physically necessary food, clothing, and shelter, no matter how hard he strives to obtain them, all other good things are mere words.[28] The body should be capable of supplying the simple joys of rude health.[29] Intellectually, people should be curious about the world and be equipped with knowledge useful to them. But merely to read books is not the way to self-improvement. Directionless reading can be a mask for the vice of idleness, and reading is foolishness without remembering.[30]

Cobbett dismissed much fashionable literature as a false factual account of the world.[31] The influence of artists and authors could be a morally destructive impediment to the formation of an admirable personality. The purpose of his own monthly pamphlets was explicitly to inculate industry and sobriety.[32] His final piece of advice to young men and women is, 'be industrious, be sober'.[33] In much great art, he maintained, there is direct incitement to habits destructive of personal morality and therefore of personal happiness.[34]

But he opposed censorship. The people of England could and should judge and comment for themselves. The purpose of freedom of expression was not to confound and confuse vice and virtue or truth and falsehood, but to survey vice in order that virtue may be more firmly constituted, and to scan error for the confirmation of truth. Liberty of expression did not mean only freedom to produce malignant works. It meant just as strongly the liberty, and the duty, forthrightly to condemn them. He was neither a libertarian nor a moral relativist. He embraced all the arguments of Milton's *Areopagitica*.[35] The forms of virtue were multifarious, human beings were frail, and circumstances altered cases: tolerance was therefore itself a great virtue. But the forms of vice were also multifarious. He did not believe for a moment that he should be

[28] W. Cobbett, *Two-penny Trash: or Politics for the Poor* (London, 1831–2), 5 Jan. 1831.
[29] W. Cobbett, *Rural Rides* (1821–32) (London, 1912), i. 294.
[30] Cobbett, *Advice* (1980), 305–6; Sir. P. Sidney, 'An Apology for Poetry' (1595), *English Critical Essays 16th and 17th Centuries*, ed. E. D. Jones (London, 1922), 31.
[31] Cobbett, *Advice*, 296. (Cobbett directs his wrath here at Shakespeare's Henry V as Prince Hal and as monarch.)
[32] *Pol. Reg.*, 5 June 1830.   [33] Cobbett, *Advice*, 335.
[34] Ibid. 295. (Here Cobbett belabours Fielding's *Tom Jones*.)
[35] J. Milton, 'Areopagitica' (1644), *The Portable Milton*, ed. D. Bush (Harmondsworth, 1976).

neutral on the subject of decency and decadence—any more than Orwell did when he wrote of a twentieth-century artist's way of life that if it were possible for a book to give off a physical stink from its pages, Salvador Dali's memoirs would.[36]

Cobbett's emphasis was on the selfhood of *all* human beings. Happiness is found in the successful development of all one's own powers, and in the successful exercise of one's own will, for man was born to express himself in activity and exertion.[37] Happiness is the great object and it is to be found only in personal liberty. Life in the woodlands, where by his own efforts the labourer can gather fuel and snare animals for food, was to be preferred to arable or pastoral districts where there is only bare pay.[38] He wrote *Cottage Economy* to help working people to lead a more independent existence in all circumstances.[39]

Respect for the person of independent character, as well as contempt for selfish and corrupt public officials, led him to favour a large element of private control of property. He extended this principle of property to justify trade-unionism of a Friendly Society type. Every man's labour was his property.[40] But private property in personal labour-power was ineffectual to its purpose unless people could freely establish strike funds. Only thus could workers survive long enough to secure a fair price for their labour.[41] This stress on personal independence led Cobbett to fierce hostility towards people willing to depend on charity. 'What! are you to come crawling, like sneaking Curs, to lick up alms . . . round the rims of a soup kettle!' Dependency should be rejected with scorn and indignation,[42] for it necessarily involved interference on the one side and the weakening of character on the other.[43]

One aspect of the will to independence is freedom from submission to one's own greed or socially defined standards of well-being beyond those necessary for a fully creative life. This is one of Cobbett's most important links with ethical socialism. To live upon little is the great security against slavery. He condemned

[36] G. Orwell, *Collected Essays* (London, 1961), 229.

[37] W. Cobbett, *Sermons* (London, 1822), 121.

[38] See, e.g., Cobbett, *Rural Rides*, i. 294, where he contrasts the round, red faces of the labourers in agriculturally poor districts like the Weald of Kent with the pale, starved look of the labourers on the 'beautiful and productive'—and therefore fully developed—downlands of N. Hants.

[39] W. Cobbett, *Cottage Economy* (1821–2) (Oxford, 1979).

[40] Jones, *Languages of Class*, 108–9.   [41] *Pol. Reg.*, 30 Aug. 1823.

[42] Ibid. 30 Nov. 1816.   [43] Ibid. 16 July 1808.

those who hankered after food and drink beyond the absolute demands of nature. Certainly, poverty was the enemy of liberty, independence, and happiness, and no one should accept it for himself or permit it to be the fate of anyone else. But poverty meant for him an insufficiency of the food, clothing, and housing actually necessary to health and decency, not that 'imaginary poverty of which some persons complain'.[44]

But riches, too, create dependence. Men and women are debased by frivolous enjoyments, they are rendered powerless by their imaginary wants.[45] He despised from the bottom of his soul, he said, 'what is called *wealth*'. The great thing was to be able to *work*. In so far as possessions promoted happiness, the wise man would accumulate those which survived external vicissitudes, i.e. those of his own character, and the skills and experiences at his own disposal.

However strongly committed a person is to freedom from subservience, however well-equipped freely to work for a common enterprise, and however prudent in expectations, nevertheless disappointment and suffering can be the actual outcome. Thus fate makes fortitude the friend of liberty. When in 1817 he lost nearly everything for the third time in his life, his resolve was undaunted:

I knew an Englishman in the Royal Province of New Brunswick who had a very valuable house . . . He was out of town when the fire broke out, and he happened to come home just after it had exhausted itself. He came very leisurely up to the spot, stood about five minutes looking steadily at the rubbish, and, then, stripping off his coat, 'Here goes', he said, 'to earn another!' . . . This noble-spirited man I had the honour to call my friend; and if this page ever meets his eye, he will have the satisfaction to see, that though it was not possible to follow, I at least remembered his example.[46]

[44] Cobbett, *Cottage Economy*, 3.   [45] Cobbett, *Advice* (1980), 59–60.
[46] W. Cobbett, *The Autobiography of William Cobbett* (London, 1947), 83. This 'autobiography' was compiled by William Reitzel. This story well illustrates that for Cobbett 'independence' did not signify 'self-centredness'. It meant being free of domination by given circumstances. A person may at one extreme be killed by a bolt from the blue, where he has had no control whatsoever over an event of decisive consequence. At the other he may on his own whim clasp or unclasp his own hand, quite unconstrained externally by either social or physical forces. He wanted as many actions as possible to come out of the 'Cobbettness' of the Cobbett he was at the moment of choice and *in that sense* out of his 'free will', and he wanted *mutatis mutandis* the same for all others *whose 'free will' led them to act with wisdom and magnanimity*.

Admiration for fortitude was the origin of his enthusiasm for sports and customs demanding bravery from the combatants and inculcating respect for endurance in the general population. By 'bravery' he did not mean the readiness to kill or to hurt, 'but the capacity to venture, and to bear the consequences'.[47]

Independence of character should reveal itself in political life, in the insistence that decisions affecting the common good should be made democratically. Where people do not share in the making of laws, whether because they are excluded or exclude themselves, the inevitable consequence, says Cobbett, has been and will be taxes pressing down the industrious, and state coercion to compel them to pay. There will be liberty and luxury for those who make the laws and receive the taxes, while the lives of those who bear the burdens will be cramped mentally by ignorance, and physically by material want.[48]

PUBLIC SPIRIT

Cobbett did not contribute consciously to anything he thought of as socialism. But he supplied strong strands to the culture of the English working class which Tawney was to use in weaving the full cloth. He was not a moral philosopher like Hobhouse. Nor was he a scientist; he adduced no proofs to support his assumptions about the levels and distribution of abilities in the population, or about the conditions which make social institutions viable. In his own eyes and those of his working-class audiences he dealt with nothing but the common sense of the community on what was true and good.

We do not find in his works, therefore, any theory of ethics which requires that happiness should be sought through altruism. He simply took for granted that on the whole people stood a better chance of having a happy life if they were not selfish. He did not separate the independent character from the co-operative character. In his ideal, independence and altruism were bound together in the same person. Those who were 'proverbially the most *independent* part of the people' were in general 'more *public spirited* than other men'.[49] He proclaimed duties as well as rights, but duties which

---

[47] *Pol. Reg.*, 10 Aug. 1805.
[48] Cobbett, *Advice* (1980), 328.
[49] Ibid. 307. Emphasis added.

free people fulfilled as living impulses, not for monetary reward or because they were under constraint.[50] He did however allow one selfish motive to loom large: the desire to be thought well of by one's fellows. 'To be remembered with esteem, I prize beyond all the riches and all the honours of this world.'[51]

Cobbettian common sense attributed to the altruistic character the values of conjugal fidelity, filial duty, honesty towards employers, and devotion to the country.[52] In his advocacy of these virtues he was not merely repeating passively the catechism of his boyhood; from 1830, in his *Two-penny Trash*, his declared purpose was to teach them continuously to his working-class readers.[53]

The foundation of a fraternal character was, for Cobbett, tenderness towards all sentient things that needed protection—towards victims, not victimizers.[54] The admirable person, however, did not simply recoil from inflicting hurt; tenderness was to be associated with courage in preventing hurt being inflicted.[55] Cobbett lived according to these standards.[56] His ideal of character assumed a society in which people had to discover the means of living together harmoniously and protecting themselves from aggression. A person matching Cobbett's ideal, therefore, was one who enjoyed the rights and performed the duties of citizenship. Readiness to act as a citizen was no less important than the readiness to perform the duties and accept the benefits of spousehood or parenthood.[57] It was the citizen's right and duty to share in law-making. Where participation in law-making had been lost, or had been taken away by force or fraud, the citizen's first obligation was to do all in his power to restore it, and to discharge it was then his sacred duty.[58] ('Sacred' is a word he frequently uses in this connection.)

Cobbett was a passionate patriot. Defending himself against the

[50] *Pol. Reg.*, 7 June 1806 (he tells the electors of Honiton that he will serve them as MP without reward); *Pol. Reg.*, 20 Oct. 1827 (he makes the same promise to the electors of Preston).
[51] Ibid. 7 June 1806.   [52] Ibid. 5 June 1830.   [53] Ibid.
[54] Cobbett, *Advice* (1980), 322.
[55] Cobbett, *Grammar of the English Language*, 144.
[56] On his conduct in defending the common soldiers against their officers see Cobbett, *The Soldier's Friend*; on his conduct during a yellow fever epidemic see Spater, *Cobbett*, i. 5; on his early opposition to flogging, see *Pol. Reg.*, 6 Feb. 1802; on his later, more celebrated opposition to flogging, for which he was sent to Newgate goal in 1810, see Spater, *Cobbett*, ii. 325.
[57] Cobbett, *Advice* (1980), 314.   [58] Ibid. 329.

charge of seditious libel levelled against him in 1831, his last words to the jury were reminiscent of Sir Thomas More's—he would with his last breath pray to God to bless his country.[59] 'God has given us a country of which to be proud, and that freedom, greatness, and renown, which was handed down to us by our wise and brave forefathers, bid us perish to the last man, rather than suffer the land of their graves to become a land of slavery, impotence, and dishonour.'[60]

The person of independent character acted altruistically not only by displaying to others the benefits of his own conduct, but also by combating vice. There was such a thing as a 'crime of all-controlling necessities'.[61] But there was also clearly a 'crime of the perpetrator'. In the latter case, to 'forget or not to punish so far as we are able, and legally can punish, is a neglect of sacred duty'.[62] Cobbett did not challenge traditional judgements on 'sins crying out to heaven for vengeance' such as wilful murder, sodomy, the oppression of the poor, and defrauding labourers of their wages. He himself produced his *Sermons* to denounce hypocrisy, cruelty, drunkenness, bribery, oppression, unjust judges, sloth, murder, gambling, public robbery, tithes, and the Malthusian attempt to limit marriage among the poor. He had no fellow-feeling for ordinary criminals. He paid twenty guineas a week for 104 weeks for his own room at Newgate to keep himself 'out of the company of felons'.[63]

For immoral conduct, punishment was the most necessary thing imaginable. It was, indeed, a vice not to oppose vice. 'Not to prevent robbery or murder, having the power to do so, is to rob and murder; not to endeavour to prevent injustice is to be unjust.'[64] This was obviously so in combating the widespread miseries of poverty resulting from public policy.[65] But in the case of even drinking or

---

[59] *Pol. Reg.*, 10 Sept. 1831; W. Cobbett, *A Full and Accurate Report of the Trial of William Cobbett* (New York, 1831).

[60] Cobbett, *Advice* (1980), 333–4.

[61] W. Cobbett, *Poor Man's Friend* (London, 1826), 50.

[62] *Pol. Reg.*, 4 Apr. 1835.

[63] W. Cobbett, *Legacy to Labourers* (London, 1834), 32. For contrast see, for example, I. Taylor, P. Walter, and J. Young, *The New Criminology* (London, 1973), 282. 'For us, as for Marx and for other new criminologists, *deviance* is normal—in the sense that men are now consciously involved (in prisons that are contemporary society and in real prisons) in asserting human diversity.' The 'New Criminology' was fashionable in the 1970s and early 1980s.

[64] Cobbett, *Sermons*, 24.   [65] *Pol. Reg.*, 20 Oct. 1827.

gambling we were criminal, Cobbett wrote, not only if we gave them our countenance, but if we neglected any means in our power to expose them to hatred and contempt.[66]

THE INSTITUTIONS OF A FRATERNAL SOCIETY

In the state of nature everything is the common possession of all the people. Cobbett insists on everyone's original equal claim to what nature supplies, a claim which could never be lost or superseded. Everyone has a right to benefit from what is common to all men and women—the bounty of nature. Private property, therefore, can never be complete or absolute.[67] Civil society can never be justified except in terms of its benefits to all. 'These truths are written on the heart of man.'[68] What applies to property in land applies to all institutions: the limit of their operation is defined by the right of everyone to participate in the common good.[69]

In many if not all respects everyone was by right an *equal* beneficiary. All were equally entitled to draw human dignity from their membership of society.[70] He believed that in death as in life all were equally entitled to be treated with respect.[71] All men and women had the right to live in their homeland, and to share in the common good embodied in the natural resources and modes of co-operation found in the country of their birth. No one's right is superior to another's in these matters. Cobbett objected to proposals that the poor should be encouraged to emigrate, for this violated the right to live in the land of their birth 'in exchange for labour duly and honestly performed'.[72]

He maintained that all human beings are equal in their right to a minimum standard of living in all circumstances. This meant the supply of sufficient food, shelter, and fuel for survival. Englishmen

[66] Cobbett, *Sermons*, 49; this is the Cobbett commemorated in G. K. Chesterton, 'The Old Song', *The Collected Poems of G.K. Chesterton*, 3rd edn. (London, 1933), 71.   [67] *Pol. Reg.*, 8 May 1819.

[68] W. Cobbett, *Advice to Young Men, and (incidently) to Young Women* (1829–30) (London, 1887), 270. Emphasis added.   [69] *Pol. Reg.*, 17 Feb. 1821.

[70] His sense of the dignity of the human being was so strongly developed that it set him athwart the path of medical progress in more than one way. He objected, e.g. to Jenner's technique of injecting cow-pox, and to male midwives, both as offensive to the dignity of the person. (Cobbett, *Advice* (1887), 213–14.)

[71] He objected to the Dead Bodies Bill, which would have allowed the corpse of a pauper to be turned over to medical students for research. (Ibid. 191–6.)

[72] *Pol. Reg.*, 2 Nov. 1816.

had had the right to be maintained from the products of nature and social co-operation, to prevent death by starvation or from cold, 'since England had been called England'. Many were poor, not through any fault of their own, but because of feebleness of frame, ailments of the body, or distress of mind arising from congenital defect or Act of God. Any such person was correctly to be brought under the special protection of the government, for no human industry, care, or foresight could have prevented such misfortune.[73] Even for those who were poor because they were manifestly intractable, starvation and nakedness was too severe a punishment. Only wilful murder would justify a penalty so harsh. When civil society superseded the state of nature, access to the means of obtaining wealth became institutionally determined. Then everyone by virtue of being a human being had a claim to subsistence, if necessary derived only from the efforts of other people. Cobbett assumed here that the numbers of the improvident and idle would be small, and the subsistence standard manageable.

In his ideal society there would be equality of opportunity for individuals to develop their abilities. The wealthy and powerful in the imperfect society of his time owed their good fortune to birth, not to their own efforts. He thought the way must always be left open to those who proved themselves effective not only in training but also in practice. He demanded the abolition of 'the odious innovation of naval academies' and the reopening of the door of promotion to 'skill and valour'.[74] Allocation by achievement must replace allocation by ascription. The vigour of this demand sprang from his sense that all men were potential William Cobbetts, and that William Cobbett was a match for any man on earth.

But he did not envisage the emergence of a society of equally admirable and equally competent men and women. He demanded absolute equality of certain basic rights and of opportunity, but he did not expect equality of outcomes. His ideals of personality and social organization (which laid so much emphasis on self-reliance and uncoerced co-operation) produces, paradoxically, an *ideal* of an *imperfect* Utopia. He believed that in his ideal society many more people would make the 'correct' moral choices and thus take the path to self-development and fraternity; but some people would not take advantage of their opportunities and some would succumb

---

[73] Spater, *Cobbett*, ii. 333; Cobbett, *Sermons*, 75.
[74] *Pol. Reg.*, 10 Sept. 1831.

to the temptations of idleness, dissipation, and selfishness. Cobbett would not have it otherwise. For that would mean the destruction of autonomy and voluntary altruism on the one hand, and of collective commitment to liberty on the other. Indeed, the fear of descending into a state of personal degradation, falling prey to avoidable diseases, or becoming the subject of public disapprobation is salutary. It is the great source of provident carefulness, attentive observation, reasoning on causes and effects, skills in the performance of labour and in the arts and sciences, public spirit, military courage, and the search for renown.[75]

He strove, in short, for a society in which people had different jobs, and different standards of living above the subsistence minimum and below the level of injurious wealth. But these differences were to be based upon personal achievement, and relationships were to be governed by altruistic practices of decency and good fellowship.

In politics as in the economy he looked for a compressed hierarchy, and deplored a polarized society of few governors and many governed. His ideal state was democratic and constitutional. He believed in parliamentary institutions. For their own benefit people had to submit themselves to general rules. But every person had the right to have an equal say in making them.[76] Among males, only minors, men stained with indelible crimes, and insane persons were properly to be excluded from a voice in choosing their governors by secret ballot.[77]

He believed in representative, not delegatory democracy: where there are large numbers, the means must be found of choosing the few to speak and act on behalf of the many. He believed in constitutional, not populist democracy: representatives ought to approach their decisions through the orderly presentation of fact and argument, not as mouthpieces of rowdy mobs. But fact and argument themselves will rarely eliminate disagreement: 'there will hardly ever be perfect unanimity amongst men assembled for any purpose whatsoever.' Business had to be transacted, and a convenient arrangement was to adopt the rough-and-ready rule that the decision of the majority should be the decision of the whole.[78]

[75] Cobbett, *Sermons*, 74.   [76] Cobbett, *Advice* (1887), 271.
[77] *Pol. Reg.*, 2 Nov. 1816. His remarks about women are read today with great offence. He recognized that abuses could arise due to 'scamps of all sorts', including poor scamps.   [78] Cobbett, *Advice* (1887), 271–2.

In the end, however, this system could only work if there was individual commitment to the spirit of democratic give and take.

The rich oppressed the poor through their control of the coercive power of the law. But Cobbett looked to a democratic Parliament to sweep away the old bad practices of the oligarchic state. The democratic state ought also to control oppressive private interests. The freedom of some must be limited to enlarge the freedom of many. In the 1820s he became increasingly conscious of the plight of the industrial workers. In his article 'To the Cotton Lords' he attacked the 'signeurs of the Twist, sovereigns of the Spinning Jenny, great yeomen of the Yarn' as tyrants. It was a proper use of the state to penalize and suppress such abuses.[79] The state had historically been a major source of tyranny. The democratic state could be the patron and protector of liberty.

Cobbett had little faith, on the other hand, in the capacity of the state to produce and distribute goods and services. With his experience of the sinecurist, the incompetent official, and the corrupt politician, he concluded that measures of improvement undertaken by the state must be only in those areas of life in which it is truly effective and benign.[80]

In a good society, Cobbett argued, parents should play a major part in the education of their own children—and he believed it was possible in far more cases than was generally acknowledged.[81] As parent he controlled the early environment of his own children. 'They heard no talk from fools or drinkers; saw me with no idle, gabbling, empty companions; saw no vain and affected coxcombs, and no tawdry and extravagant women . . . and other nonsense that fit boys to be lobby-loungers, and girls to be the ruin of industrious and frugal young men.'[82] As in education so in other spheres of life: voluntary co-operation was a form of social organization superior to bureaucracy or professional expertise.[83]

The role for the Church in his ideal society was to encourage good conduct. There was a tendency in human nature to corruption and perversion which had to be combated. 'The Word of God has

---

[79] *Pol. Reg.*, 10 July 1824.

[80] He was scornful of Spence's scheme for what would now be called Keynesian measures of public works; they would do no more good than giving the unemployed money for 'throwing stones against the wind'. (*Pol. Reg.*, 28 Nov. 1807.)

[81] Cobbett, *Advice* (1887), 236–7. (Cobbett provides a wonderful account here of how he educated his own children—who, irrespective of their sex, all went on to distinguished careers.)   [82] Ibid. 242.   [83] Ibid. 200.

been given for a *rule of conduct*; and religion consists in obeying the rule.'[84] Cobbett's moralizing, reflecting Christian doctrine, remained powerfully attractive to ethical socialists until well into the twentieth century, and especially to those who clung to its working-class, chapel-and-temperance version.

ARCADIA LOST

Cobbett's perception of England was of a once happy society now racked with problems. From one end of England to the other, he writes, the labourer looks back upon his starving children, 'while, from the door, he surveys all around him the land teeming with the means of luxury to his opulent and overgrown master'.[85] Women labourers are 'as ragged as colts and pale as ashes'.[86] The men 'shirk and shiver about in canvas frocks and rotten cottons'.[87] The dwellings of the labourers are little better than pigsties. Wretched hovels are stuck upon little bits of ground on the road side, he notes of some farm labourers' dwellings just outside Cricklade, as if they had been swept off the fields by a hurricane. 'Fine fields and pastures all round; and yet the cultivators of the fields so miserable!'[88] Formerly prosperous areas are impoverished and depopulated. Along the Upper Avon in Hampshire, the churches would now not only hold all the inhabitants, but all their household goods, tools, and implements as well. In some villages the church *porches* would be large enough to serve all the existing population.[89]

Marx put forward the oversimplified view that Cobbett was a revolutionary who looked not to the creation of a new age, but the rehabilitation of the old.[90] It is true that he wanted back the best of the past. He wanted the supposed prosperity and humane social relationships of the past preserved in the new world. But he wanted it with modern technology selected and fully used to the extent that human beings generally benefited from it.

In some cases, poverty was a person's own fault.[91] But in general the cause of poverty was pre-eminently *not* the conduct or character of the poor, least of all of the agricultural labourer.[92] The

[84] Cobbett, *Sermons*, 26. (James 2: 19.) [85] *Pol. Reg.*, 15 Mar. 1806.
[86] Cobbett, *Rural Rides*, i. 16. [87] Cobbett, *Advice* (1887), 193.
[88] Cobbett, *Rural Rides*, i. 17–18. [89] Ibid. ii. 47–9.
[90] Marx and Engels, *Collected Works*, xii. 189. On the lament for arcadia lost among industrial workers, in this case women working in Bolton, see Thompson, *Making of the English Working Class*, 417. [91] Cobbett, *Sermons*, 122.
[92] Cobbett, *Autobiography*, 285.

poor were in poverty, *in spite of* all the ingenuity, industry, and frugality they practised.[93] Technological advance was not the cause of poverty. In agriculture Cobbett was an enthusiastic innovator, supporting the use of better techniques and machinery, and condemning the attempt to prevent their introduction.[94] Nor was it the greed of the employers in agriculture or manufacturing that caused poverty.[95] It was the sum taken from those who labour, to give to those who did not, which was the cause of all misery.[96] The main basis of exploitation was the system of state borrowing and taxation, compounded by periodic inflation and deflation.[97] It is rare indeed to find Cobbett mentioning any useful purpose for taxation. At the head of the system of exploitation were the great families of the nobility who controlled the House of Commons. They had become nothing more than what he called 'a prodigious band of spungers' living off the labour of the industrious members of the community. Taxes supported sinecurists who never did work and never intended to. Poor rates, by contrast, were available to the labourer who had worked to create the available wealth. He was out of work one day, but could work, and then would be set to work, the next.[98]

Cobbett's view of London recalls More's: 'the Wen'—the most detestable manifestation of the system of state exploitation through compulsory taxation to finance idle consumers. Fully a third of all the good food in the whole country was drawn up to the metropolis, yet of its million and a half inhabitants, more than a million had no business there.[99] The state itself consumed directly enormous quantities of building materials and labour in constructing government offices and all the buildings needed to make the system secure—barracks, prisons, hospitals, and madhouses.[100]

The centuries-long movement towards the enclosure of the open fields and commons, condemned by More, accelerated in Cobbett's lifetime, and had almost run its course by the time of his death. He was not a principled opponent of enclosure, but he recognized that

[93] *Two-penny Trash*, July 1830.   [94] *Pol. Reg.*, 30 Nov. 1816.
[95] See, e.g. *Pol. Reg.*, 30 Nov. 1816, 14 Apr. 1823, 7 Dec. 1833.
[96] *Pol. Reg.*, 2 Nov. 1816, 30 Nov. 1816; Cobbett, *Rural Rides*, ii. 42–6, where he calculated the surplus value extracted from the labourers of Milton.
[97] This was Cobbett's constant theme. See, e.g., *Pol. Reg.*, 30 Nov. 1816.
[98] See, e.g., *Pol. Reg.*, 2 Nov. 1816; and Cobbett, *Rural Rides*, i. 300; see also Marx and Engels, *Collected Works*, xii. 45, where the identical view is expressed.
[99] *Pol. Reg.*, 5 Feb. 1825.   [100] Ibid. 12 July 1823.

the poor man often lost, not only materially, but also in terms of personal demoralization. He used the power of the Old Testament prophets to assist him in his denunication of the oppressive consequences—as R. H. Tawney was to use the language of the Bible a century later. 'These are the words of the prophet AMOS, let the GRASPALLS, young and old, bear in mind.'[101]

THE STRENGTHS OF ENGLAND

Cobbett observed prosperity as well as poverty. The fuel for his indignation was the sight of wretchedness in the midst of plenty. Lincolnshire produced and possessed 'more good things than man could have the conscience to ask of God'.[102] In Warwickshire, every object seemed to say: 'Here are resources! here is wealth! here are all the means of national power, and of individual plenty and happiness!' On the route to Liverpool, 'every object seemed to pronounce a eulogium on the industry, skill, and perseverance of the people. And why, then, were these people in a state of such misery and degradation?'[103] There was enough and to spare, if people received their full share, but no more than their fair share.[104]

He saw virtue as well as vice. The people of his native land were capable and kind to a degree not matched in other societies.[105] Cobbett's view was that the majority of the English were extraordinarily civilized. They had a strong sense of decent conduct and were ready and willing to help their fellows. English rural labourers, in particular, were in his opinion the most just, the most good-natured, and the most patient people in the world.[106] For hundreds of years the mass of the English had been 'the most orderly, the most independent, yet the most obedient; the best fed and the best clad, and, at the same time, the most industrious and adroit working people that ever lived upon the face of the earth'. They were industrious and honest, and by now unreflectively disposed to a 'laudable submission to the laws'.[107] They were the

[101] *Two-penny Trash*, 1 Oct. 1830. (Amos 8: 4, 10.)
[102] *Pol. Reg.*, 17 Apr. 1830.
[103] Cobbett, *Autobiography*, 175–6. For other descriptions of prosperity see, e.g., his visit to Upwaltham (*Rural Rides*, i. 179) and Sunderland (Ibid. ii. 294).
[104] *Pol. Reg.*, 2 Nov. 1816.
[105] See *Pol. Reg.*, 23 Mar 1816, 8 Jan. 1831; Cobbett, *Legacy to Labourers*, 39.
[106] *Two-penny Trash*, Nov. 1830.
[107] Cobbett, *Legacy to Labourers*, 8.

best parents, the best children, and the most faithful workmen that ever formed part of any civil community.

It was a feature of the civilized character of the English 'to sympathize with the oppressed, and to lend assistance to the weak in their struggles with the strong'.[108] E. P. Thompson argues that 'no one can suppose that the tradition of the "free-born Englishman" was merely notional who studies the responses to Peterloo'.[109] At the Spring Assizes of the Western Circuit, held in Dorchester in March 1834, six agricultural labourers were each sentenced to seven years' transportation for administering illegal oaths. 'To the eternal honour of England and, indeed of Scotland and Ireland too', Cobbett wrote, 'they have been roused from one end to the other by the sentence passed.'[110] Agitation did not immediately succeed in preventing the transportation of the Tolpuddle labourers, but in 1836 the remainder of their sentence was remitted. This injustice survives to this day in the annals of the English trade union movement as the great example of labour martyrdom. Yet in a century which has seen Nazi extermination camps, Stalinist labour camps, the 'ones who disappeared' in Argentina, and the apartheid system in South Africa, this memory confirms Cobbett's view that the tendency of England's regime of repression, in comparison with many other countries, was to be mild and law-bound. When Cobbett, aged and ill, was in despair over the action of the inadequately reformed Parliament in supporting the detestable new Poor Law, he clung to the belief in English decency. Even though the Poor Law would benefit the English landlords, the fault lay not with them, but with the few untypical ideologues who had invented the project—many of them Scottish, not English. Cobbett did not impute the oppressive principles of less eligibility and the abolition of outdoor relief to a majority of the landlords, 'or to any considerable portion of them'. Products of English culture they were, he wrote, 'too wise, as well as too just, to entertain any such wish'.[111]

Within all social classes there were, of course, to be found examples of weaknesses of character, of selfish and anti-social conduct, and indeed of persistent and active malice. But there was

[108] W. Cobbett, *An Answer to the Speech of the Attorney-General Against H. M. the Queen* (London, 1820).

[109] Thompson, *Making of the English Working Class*, 686–91.

[110] *Pol. Reg.*, 5 Apr. 1834.   [111] Ibid., 12 July 1834.

not only individual conduct, there were the culture and institutions of England. Here Cobbett was passionately favourable in his assessment. 'I know of no enemy of reform and the happiness of the country so great as the man who would persuade you that we possess *nothing good*, and that *all* must be torn to pieces.'

For what, then, did Hampden die in the field, and Sydney on the scaffold? and has it been discovered, at last, that England has *always* been an enslaved country from top to toe? The Americans, who are a very wise people, and who love liberty with all their hearts . . . took special care to speak with reverence of, and to preserve, Magna Charta, the Bill of Rights, the Habeas Corpus, and not only all the body of the Common Law of England, but most of the rules of our courts, and all our forms of jurisprudence.

He was therefore immovably attached to the great constitutional laws and principles of English society. There was no precedent and no regulation favourable to freedom which was not to be found 'in the laws of England or the example of our Ancestors'.[112]

Freedom enjoyed and maintained, especially by the relatively poor and powerless, depended both on cultural values that cherished liberty for all, and on the preservation of norms and institutions that ensured fair dealing between free people. For him, there had been such a system of liberty in 'the Constitution of England undefiled and uncorrupted'[113] until its present rulers sought to subvert it with their system of gagging and repression.[114]

Cobbett's experience in the courts was by no means unchequered. But he knew enough of the fair dealing built into the existing system of law to make him proud of English justice. This was notably the case with his second trial for seditious libel in 1831. Though able to claim no status other than that of a common citizen of England, he was able to subpoena as witnesses the Prime Minister, the Lord Chancellor, the Home Secretary, the Privy Seal, the Foreign Secretary, and the Secretary of War—and was acquitted.[115] At the other end of the scale, he was equally proud of the capacity of his fellow countrymen to evolve humane institutions at the level of their own 'old and amiable' parochial governments.[116]

---

[112] Ibid., 2 Nov. 1816.   [113] Ibid., 15 Apr. 1809.

[114] W. Cobbett, *History of the Last Hundred Days of English Freedom* (1817) (Westport, Conn., 1971).   [115] Spater, *Cobbett*, ii. 477–9.

[116] Cobbett, *Legacy to Labourers*, 8; W. Cobbett, *A History of the Protestant 'Reformation'* (1824–6) (Dublin, 1868).

Just as strong as his anger at England's distress, therefore, was his pride in his countrymen across all classes, and in the historical institutions of England. He wanted the best of old England preserved or restored, with England as great in the world, and her industrious, laborious, kind, and virtuous people as happy in the future as they were when he was born.[117]

PARLIAMENTARY OR VIOLENT CHANGE?

A reformed Parliament would be the totally effective instrument for the removal of injustice and the introduction of social reform. In 1816 Cobbett wrote, 'A *reformed Parliament*—we must have *that first*, or we shall have nothing good.'[118] The lack of a Parliament annually chosen by all the people was the 'root of all our suffering', and reform would cure them all at once.[119] Eleven years later his faith in Parliament had not waned.[120] At the height of the agitation for the Reform Bill, Parliament is still the key to desirable changes in society and character. A reformed Parliament was the organ of a unified nation, and a unified nation, not one class as the enemy of another, ought to secure that reform. 'Everywhere . . . I have endeavoured to show the necessity of such union.'[121]

In his time he was condemned by some as the apologist for working-class violence and praised by others as a powerful voice against it. He is seen by Trevelyan as the man who did more to prevent conflagration in this country than all the repressive measures ever passed.[122] Raymond Williams on the contrary makes him the supporter of any efficient means of redress, including riots and arson.[123] E. P. Thompson judges him adept at pitching his rhetoric just the right side of treason.[124] We may therefore ask whether Cobbett's contribution to the British radical tradition was favourable to violence or not.

He was certainly not a principled opponent of either private violence, or rebellion, or war between states. Especially early in his

---

[117] Cobbett, *Autobiography*, 287.   [118] *Pol. Reg.*, 2 Nov. 1816.
[119] Ibid., 30 Nov. 1816.   [120] Ibid., 20 Oct. 1827.
[121] Spater, *Cobbett*, ii. 410. Cobbett was welcoming the establishment of Attwood's Birmingham Political Union.
[122] G. M. Trevelyan, *Lord Grey of the Reform Bill* (London, 1920), 217.
[123] R. Williams, *Cobbett* (Oxford, 1983), 32.
[124] Thompson, *Making of the English Working Class*, 626.

career, he was a staunch defender of England's right to use force.[125]
On the side of private violence, he believed in fair physical contests
between people who were equally risking personal injury as a
method of settling personal quarrels.[126] As between the state and
its subjects he enunciated a doctrine of a *constitutional* right to
rebellion, appealing to the authority of Blackstone.

Whether or not in a particular instance the point had been
reached when the exercise of the right to rebel was valid could only
be decided by public opinion at the time. In these terms he defended
the conduct of the participants in a failed armed insurrection in
1817. They were wrong in thinking that oppression had reached
the pitch at which they were entitled to exercise the right; but they
were correct in claiming that *at some point* the right did come into
operation.[127] In much the same terms he honoured Thistlewood,
one of the leaders of the Cato Street Conspiracy of 1821,
comparing him to Sir Thomas More.[128] Cobbett also took the view
that there was an ultimate right of the hungry to use violence to
prevent starvation in the midst of plenty.[129]

He put forward a third, weaker condonation of violence. He
merely registered that in all the circumstances it was *understandable*
that it had occurred. 'How great are the allowances that we ought
to make for the poor creatures who, in this once happy but now
miserable country, are doomed to lead a life of constant labour and
half-starvation.'[130] In certain cases violence is simply an inevitable
result when there is a body of idlers, living chiefly on the taxes
levied on and impoverishing the industrious part of the community.[131]

The final major episode of civil disorder during Cobbett's
lifetime centred around one of the principal legislative measures of
the reformed Parliament—the new Poor Law. Except for medical
attendance, all relief whatever to able-bodied persons, other than in

---

[125] Spater, *Cobbett*, i. 120; ibid. ii. 319–21. Cobbett publicly and dangerously
opposed the popular Peace of Amiens; he supported the right of *HMS Leopard* to
use force to search the *USS Chesapeake* on the high seas; and he was at one point in
favour of an alliance with the United States to wage war against despotism.

[126] See, e.g., Cobbett, *Autobiography*, 174. (Here he tells a story about the
punishment of an unfair fighter at Barnett Fair.)

[127] *Pol. Reg.*, 23 May, 1818.

[128] Thompson, *Making of the English Working Class*, 704; he was more ready to
approve foreign revolutionary violence, see Spater, *Cobbett*, 493.

[129] Cobbett, *Advice* (1887), 274–5.

[130] Cobbett, *Rural Rides*, i. 295.   [131] *Pol. Reg.*, 7 Dec. 1833.

well-regulated workhouses, was to be declared unlawful. In the workhouse they would be—and would be seen to be—worse off than the worst-off of the independent labourers of the lowest class. In his very last article for the *Political Register* Cobbett dealt with the Poor Law and the violent resentment of the working class against it. In new scenes 'of turmoil and boiling blood', he wrote, half a dozen counties were in a state of commotion, and the jails were opening their doors to receive the rebels.[132]

The danger of dishonesty (including self-delusion) in pursuing the line that one is merely describing anger and in no way condoning it, is very great. At its worst it can be either all invention and incitement, or all wishful thinking. Undoubtedly Cobbett on occasion succumbed to temptation in both these respects.[133] It is therefore easy to appreciate why he can be seen as the advocate of destructiveness and violence for the achievement of political or economic ends, or as one of the 'nod and a wink' men who egg others on with their pious ambiguities. Nevertheless he offered little if any intellectual respectability to the civil disturbances to which he actually had to address his journalism. Each case has to be put into the context of his wider treatment of the subject.[134] Within that context it is clear that Trevelyan is right to place him within the working-class tradition of peaceable change and the rejection of unlawful violence.

Our interpretation is borne out by his treatment of the Captain Swing riots of 1830. The rioters burnt ricks and smashed machinery. Rural labourers were demanding better administration of the poor laws for the unemployed and better wages for the employed. Both these objectives were accomplished on a wide scale. Cobbett wrote that 'out of evil comes good', but was careful to add, 'we are not, indeed, upon that mere maxim, "to do evil that good may come of it" '.[135] At his subsequent trial, in July 1831, he unequivocally spoke against destruction of property and attacks on people. He was able to call the Lord Chancellor himself as his first

---

[132] Ibid., 13 June 1835. See also e.g. ibid., 12 July 1834.
[133] See, e.g., ibid., 1 Nov. 1834.
[134] For Cobbett on the Spa Fields riots, 1816, see Thompson, *Making of the English Working Class*, 636; *Pol. Reg.*, 25 Oct. 1817; and ibid., 30 Nov. 1816. For Cobbett on the Luddite disturbances of 1816 see ibid., 30 Nov. 1816. For the Pentridge Rising, 1817, see G. D. H. Cole and R. Postgate, *The Common People 1746–1946*, 4th edn. (London, 1949), 223; and for Cobbett's response to it see *Pol. Reg.*, 23 May 1818.   [135] *Pol. Reg.*, 11 Dec. 1831.

witness, for he had sought and obtained Cobbett's permission to republish his 1816 'Letter to the Luddites', calculating that it would have a pacifying effect on the rioters.[136]

In his defence of the rural labourers in 1830 and 1831 he did not argue that the British state, because it represented only partial interests within the community, lacked legitimacy. He made it quite plain that, had the labourers been guilty of serious crime or rebellion, the state would have been justified in treating them harshly. In fact the rioters had not attacked people seriously at all. 'Had they been *bloody*; had they been *cruel*; then it would have been another matter; had they burnt people in their beds, which they might easily have done; had they beaten people wantonly, which has also been in their power; had they done these things, there would have been some plea for severity; but they have been guilty of none of these things.'[137] At his trial, in referring to the death sentence against one of the Captain Swing arsonists, Cobbett says that he 'was left, and justly left, for execution, because there was no excuse for him'.[138]

Our interpretation is also confirmed by his lifetime devotion to the principle of peaceful persuasion. The injustices of society were sustained by definitions of the situation which favoured the privileged classes. With few guns and no state education, popular acquiescence was built into the system, he told his readers, by means of 'the numerous humbugs with which you have been so long amused'.[139] The intelligentsia generally was in the pay of the government, producing myths to order.[140] The ruling ideas of the age were the ideas of the ruling class. Unlike Marx, however, Cobbett believed that the system could be changed by people whose perceptions had been altered—and altered by factual knowledge and reasoned argument. It was his intention to produce 'uniformity of sentiment as to public matters'.[141] This was not to be accomplished at a revolutionary stroke. 'Among the virtues of a good citizen are fortitude and patience. He is not to expect the baleful tree to come down at a single blow; he must patiently remove the earth that props and feeds it, and sever the accursed roots one by one.'[142]

[136] Cole, *Opinions*, 323–3.
[138] Cole, *Opinions*, 318.
[140] Cobbett, *Advice* (1887), 260.
[142] Cobbett, *Advice* (1887), 283.

[137] *Pol. Reg.*, 11 Dec. 1830.
[139] *Pol. Reg.*, 23 Mar. 1816.
[141] *Pol. Reg.*, 2 Nov. 1816.

He trusted the power of words to direct human conduct. How often, he once exclaimed, did Pope's line occur to him: 'Heaven first taught letters for some wretch's aid'.[143] The person who honestly and clearly presented the facts and their logical inferences, and set them against the principles of common-sense ethics, would prevail against force and against ignorance, against the liar and against the corrupter of morals. To suppose that truth and virtue would not conquer, he said, was directly contrary to all experience.[144] Freedom of expression was therefore of paramount importance. Let journalists and authors take their own course. If they speak the truth with sense and reason they will gain readers. If they do the opposite, the only effect will be to gain them hatred and contempt.

He was well aware that civil disorder had powerful consequences. But its beneficial outcomes were rare and, good or bad, the effects were always unpredictable and uncontrollable. In every case, therefore, the predominant desire ought to be to employ no means beyond those of reason and persuasion. One hour spent soberly looking into the rights of things, he believed, was more likely to make people of good sense act with benign effect than whole years spent in demagoguery and disorder.[145]

FAILURE AND FULFILMENT

What then was the outcome of the expenditure of Cobbett's prodigious energy? His failures were many. True, by the time he died in 1835 a certain measure of parliamentary reform had been secured. But it fell far short of his intentions. Another thirty and more years were to elapse before further progress was made in his desired direction. He had thought that the structural change for which he had striven would at least have brought into Parliament MPs 'able and willing to plead the cause of the working millions'.[146] In fact the first House of Commons elected under the new Act contained only a minority who were not representatives of the landed interest: and that minority, the middle-class representatives, played a disappointing role.[147]

[143] Ibid. 247. [144] *Pol. Reg.*, 5 June 1813.
[145] Cobbett, *Legacy to Labourers*, 69.
[146] Spater, *Cobbett*, ii. 509.
[147] E. L. Woodward, *The Age of Reform 1815–1870* (Oxford, 1939), 87; *Pol. Reg.*, 2 Feb. 1833; Spater, *Cobbett*, ii. 510. 217 were sons of peers or baronets; only 158 were middle class.

He and a handful of other radical MPs attempted to cut expenditure on government pensions and sinecures—a reform at the heart of Cobbett's life-long criticism of English society. He was voted down by huge majorities. The inequitable burden of taxation was equally objectionable to him. His efforts to secure reform were fruitless. Worse was to follow, namely, the introduction of 'that great and terrible innovation the POOR-LAW BILL'.[148]

He supported the growing agitation for increased protection of factory children. But he failed here also. In October 1830 Richard Oastler, a country-estate manager of high-Tory views, published his first letter on 'Yorkshire Slavery'. The style and sentiments are such that it could have been written by Cobbett himself.[149] The agitation that followed led to the setting up of the Committee on Factory Children's Labour, which reported in 1832.[150] Coming back from the House of Commons, which had voted on the resulting Factory Act at 1 a.m., Cobbett was in bed at 2.30 a.m., but up again at six to write a bitterly sarcastic report on the proceedings for the afternoon's *Political Register*.

We have this night discovered that the shipping, the land, and the Bank and its credit, are all nothing compared with the labour of three hundred thousand little girls in Lancashire! Aye ... if we only deduct two hours a day, away goes the wealth, away goes the capital, away go the resources, the power, and the glory of England![151]

(Tawney was to use the same style of argument.) From Cobbett's point of view, therefore, a truly democratic Parliament, the main instrument of change to a better society and a major feature of that better society, was still far off. The basic causes of poverty continued to operate and were indeed exacerbated by the new Poor Law.

In his private life, too, Cobbett's achievements fell short of his intentions. The passions of radical politics led to ruptures between friends, and in his old age to the break-up of the family life by which he set so much store.[152] When he entered the reformed

---

[148] Cobbett, *Legacy to Labourers*, 7.
[149] *Leeds Mercury*, 16 Oct. 1830, in Bland, Brown, and Tawney, *English Economic History*, 592–3.
[150] Committee on Factory Children's Labour, *Report* (1831–2), in Bland, Brown, and Tawney, *English Economic History*, 510–11.
[151] *Pol. Reg.*, 20 July 1833.
[152] Spater, *Cobbett*, ii. 362, 483, 487, 515–16, 518–19, 523.

William Cobbett (1763–1835)   53

Parliament as MP for Oldham, he was seventy years of age. The abstemious man with once magnificent physique had become fat. His heels 'were always swelling in a most odious manner' and he experienced 'dreadful short breathing'. Macaulay considered that late hours in the House enfeebled not only the body of the old man, but his mind also. His egotism and his suspicion had at last attained such a height, he wrote, that Cobbett was 'really as mad as Rousseau'.[153]

From one point of view, indeed, his life was a complete failure. By the time of his death the England of capitalist industrialism had fully and securely established itself. Fate had made him, through his vitally important part in the Reform agitation, one of the principal instruments of the political victory of the English bourgeoisie. 'Cobbett fought for the old England; he helped in fact to consolidate the new.'[154] Nevertheless, he had been a great force in putting England on the path that was to lead to adult suffrage, and to nearly everything else he looked for in a parliamentary democracy. In Plamenatz's view, Cobbett (with Hunt) did more than anybody else to frighten the ruling oligarchy into sharing their power with the middle class.[155]

He fought for a free press that depended upon the good sense of readers and the integrity of editors, not upon the judgements of officials or the coercive power of politicians. Much of the attempt by the state to control the press had been directed at Cobbett himself. The emergence of independent radical journalism was, therefore, 'in great degree his personal triumph'.[156]

His message was that worthwhile values were being lost, and he strove to preserve and restore them. He was not alone in propagating the myth of a lost community. Feargus O'Connor, the Chartist leader, spoke in exactly the same terms of the old English times, when everyone lived by the sweat of his brow, and enjoyed 'old English fare, old English holidays, and old English justice'.[157] To describe these views as a myth is not to say that they are wholly fanciful. Cobbett knew with the absolute certainty of his personal experience that things had been better for him as a plough-boy in

[153] Spater, *Cobbett*, ii. 522.   [154] Cole, *Life*, 434.
[155] J. Plamenatz, *Mill's Utilitarianism* (Oxford, 1949), 98.
[156] Thompson, *Making of the English Working Class*, 720. In 1957 Hampshire NUJ members placed a stone to commemorate Cobbett's part in freeing the press from control by the state.   [157] Ibid. 230.

Farnham in the 1770s, and for his grandfather and father before him, than they were for the miserable labourers by the roadside near Cricklade in the 1820s. He had a sense from lifelong observation that the Cricklades and worse were multiplying and that the Farnhams were under threat. He had an intuition that personal conduct and social arrangements had been deteriorating for thirty or forty years. Decent, humane relationships were being superseded by relationships more brutalized, more selfish, and more stupid and stupefying. In such circumstances, not unique to Cobbett's age, the faith that things can be better is sometimes more easily sustained by treasuring a firmly remembered past than by yearning for a vaguely imagined future.

He sought to build working-class confidence and self-esteem, and succeeded in doing so. In that sense the last great spokesman for the English agrarian was, unbeknown or only partly known to himself, the first great spokesman for the self-respect of the English industrial worker.

Cobbett was the last man to deny that people were capable of acting as a rabble, for he was at the receiving end of mob behaviour on many occasions.[158] Destruction of property and violence against the person continued to mark both economic disputes and demands for political reform, with the last years of his life showing a resurgence of such unrest on both fronts. There were the Reform Bill riots. There were industrial riots—during the miners' strike of 1831, for example, there was widespread disorder in Co. Durham and Northumberland.[159] But there had been a change towards a culture of peaceability which Cobbett promoted. The Spa Fields riots, and then the bloody fiasco of the Pentridge Rising, strengthened his case that the destruction of property and physical intimidation of opponents was not the way forward. Late in 1817 he wrote approvingly of a '*change* in the character of the people'. Meetings of up to 40,000 had gathered 'and they had *talked sense*, and had *quietly separated*'. At one meeting he had been talking to a shoemaker, and, in order to maintain his opinion, the shoemaker

---

[158] On his treatment by a peace mob in London in 1802 see Spater, *Cobbett*, i. 120; on his treatment by an election mob in Coventry see *Pol. Reg.*, 25 Mar. 1820. No Roman said with more feeling or justification *odi profanum vulgus*, I loathe the profane rabble, when it *was* a rabble.

[159] R. Fynes, *The Miners of Northumberland and Durham: A History of their Social and Political Progress* (1873) (Sunderland, 1923), 20–1.

'pulled *a volume of Blackstone out of his pocket*'. *This* was the threat to the established order that could be effective.[160]

The new type of peaceful and orderly demonstration which, with interruptions, gradually came to dominate the English radical scene in the nineteenth century first matured in Lancashire.[161] Cobbett's role in helping to bring this about was recognized by writers at the time.[162] It was certainly claimed by Cobbett himself.[163] He risked unpopularity to prove that '*riot must make matters worse*'.[164] Repudiation of violence and respect for the law until it could be constitutionally changed spread into trade-unionism. The general rules of the Tolpuddle branch of the Friendly Society of Agricultural Labourers, for example, stated that 'the object of the society can never be promoted by any act or acts of violence, but, on the contrary, all such proceedings must tend to injure the cause and destroy the society itself. This order therefore will not countenance any violation of the laws'.[165] From 1817 to Chartist times this was the central tradition,[166] and with the end of the Chartist 'physical force' agitation, it strongly reasserted itself for decades. In 1941 Orwell felt able to describe as an 'all important' trait of the English that they respected 'constitutionalism and legality', and believed in 'the law' as something which was perhaps cruel and stupid, but in England 'incorruptible'.[167]

In denying that English common people were a rabble, Cobbett both contested the accuracy of a generalization, and asserted the hope of further improvement. In 1819 he claimed to have been 'the great enlightener of the people of England'. The *Westminster Review* commented, 'It is impossible to avoid laughing at him, and at the same time feeling, in our hearts, that the impudent fellow has some ground for his boast.'[168] He was proud to think that he increased the numbers of those who could intelligently understand

---

[160] *Pol. Reg.*, 25 Oct. 1817.

[161] The great early example of the peaceable mass meeting was that which preceded the Peterloo Massacre—see, e.g. Thompson, *Making of the English Working Class*, 679; and J. L. and B. Hammond, *The Skilled Labourer, 1760–1832* (London, 1919), 10.

[162] G. Wallas, *The Life of Francis Place, 1771–1854* (London, 1898).

[163] *Pol. Reg.*, 11 Apr. 1818.   [164] Ibid.

[165] Bland, Brown, and Tawney, *English Economic History*, 641.

[166] Thompson, *Making of the English Working Class*, 670.

[167] G. Orwell, *The Orwell Reader* (New York, 1949), 255. Orwell's views on this matter are dealt with at greater length in ch. 5.

[168] *Westminster Review*, Jan. 1824, 7.

their situation, and who desired to alter it without entering the cul-de-sac of private violence and counter-violence, of prejudice and revenge. W. E. Adams writes of the 'earnest and reputable' people whom Cobbett 'multiplied'.[169] E. P. Thompson attributes to Cobbett the main role in the creation of this aspect of English working-class culture.[170]

Cobbett was not only a participant in and advocate of such a culture of moral and intellectual seriousness and sobriety in the literal sense of the term. Radicals like him sought to rid working people of the label of drunken and violent louts. 'I look upon drunkenness', Cobbett wrote, 'as the root of much more than half the mischief, misery, and crimes with which society is afflicted.'[171] The roots of the temperance movement lay in the Radical campaign for sobriety (particularly after the drunken rioting at Spa Fields in 1816 and 1817) to which he lent his powerful voice. This movement of moral earnestness (of which total abstinence was a part) was successful. It was one of the things that allowed working-class socialists to feel for a time that there was a distinctive working-class culture, and that it was superior in every way to the dissipated, frivolous, self-indulgent life led by the decadent bourgeoisie.

The usual primary distinction made in politics is some variation on the theme of 'Left' and 'Right'. Cobbett was unusual in making his primary distinction between what he called true reformers and sham reformers, that is, between those who pursued effective and those who pursued ineffective measures. Advance towards the nurturing of good people in an ideal society required the abolition of clear abuses and the reinstatement and strengthening of known virtues and the known conditions of social well-being, not a leap into utopian innovations.[172] He thus put at the centre of his thought the same distinction as Weber was later to identify as fundamental. At one pole are responsible politicians. They assess the environment within which they have to attain their objectives. They calculate as best they can all the foreseeable results, good and

[169] W. E. Adams, *Memoris of a Sociai Atom* (London, 1903), i. 164.
[170] Thompson, *Making of the English Working Class*, 746.
[171] *Pol. Reg.*, 13 Jan. 1821. Cobbett was never in favour of total abstinence. Indeed he frequently fulminates against the waste of the labourer's money on nutritionally useless tea, and recommends the consumption of beer, a wholesome and (especially when brewed according to his instructions at home) cheap drink.
[172] Spater, *Cobbett*, ii. 484–5.

bad, of their actions. At the other are the doctrinaire politicians, who will do what is 'right' whatever the situation, whatever the chances of success, and whatever the likely subsidiary consequences. Those who do not share Cobbett's and Weber's evaluations of the two opposed styles condemn the one as 'pragmatism' and extol the other as 'the politics of principle'. It is to the radical tradition of pragmatism that Cobbett made his contribution. He was that rarity who in Weber's belief made the ideal political actor. He combined commitment to a cause with common sense, and united within a single character both passion and perspective.[173] He served the tradition of ethical socialism not only through his writings, but also by showing throughout his life that a *passion* for responsible conduct is a human possibility.

Even if he had succeeded in nothing else, his ideal of the self-improving, sober, industrious, responsible, and altruistic working man was passed down so as to eventually form the Thomas Burts, the Peter Lees, the Jack Lawsons, and the ethical-socialist convictions of thousands of unknown people like them in the mining villages of Co. Durham, the textile towns of the Pennines, and all over Britain in the respectable working-class communities of the first half of the twentieth century. Above all he handed down a personal example of strenuous self-improvement and life-long effort on behalf of those who gave service to the community and were poor. He fought against those, rich or poor, whose way of life wasted or abused their own abilities, or made them parasites or predators on the lives of their fellow countrymen. That is what, in his *Legacy to Labourers*, he himself saw as his main contribution. He wanted to remind them, he wrote,

that they once had a friend, whom neither love of gain on the one hand, nor fear of loss on the other, could seduce him from his duty towards God, towards his country, and towards them; to remind them, that that friend was born in a cottage, and bred to the plough, and that his name was—William Cobbett.[174]

[173] M. Weber, 'Politics as a Vocation' (1918), in M. Weber, *From Max Weber: Essays in Sociology*, ed. H. H. Gerth and C. W. Mills (London, 1948).
[174] Cobbett, *Legacy to Labourers*, 41–2.

4

LIBERTY, EQUALITY, AND THE COMMON GOOD

Leonard Trelawney Hobhouse (1864–1929)

CHRISTIANS, GENTLEMEN, AND OTHERS

Hobhouse was born in 1864. His father, an anglican clergyman in a small Cornish village, was remorseless in requiring that duties be fulfilled and any neglect repaired. But for a generation scientific discoveries had been sapping naïve faith in the Bible. With the publication of *The Origin of Species* in 1859 the beliefs of ages simply crumbled away in the minds of the educated young. Like so many others from similar backgrounds, Hobhouse discarded what Carlyle called the old Hebrew clothes of his parents, but held to their example.[1] As a pupil at Marlborough he abandoned Christianity intellectually, though not ethically. He studied the work of the recently deceased George Eliot. Like him, she had been brought up in a strictly religious atmosphere against which she had rebelled, while dedicating herself to the cause of truth and goodness. Hobhouse focused his admiration on the radical cause, which was espoused in the language of unremitting, exalted morality. His hero was John Stuart Mill, whom he described as the greatest and best man of the nineteenth century. Cobden he described as a genius along with Shakespeare and Newton. It was through his uncle, Arthur (later Lord) Hobhouse, rather than his father, that he imbibed the culture of the English gentleman.[2] Like

---

[1] By 1860, and then for about 20 years, it was generally accepted among advanced thinkers that the only source of knowledge properly so called was the scientific method. Furthermore, many prominent figures were influenced also by Comte's whole positivist philosophy, which eventually developed into a religion of Humanity. (See A. Comte, *A General View of Positivism*, trans. J. H. Bridges (London, 1865).) Mill owed a direct debt to Comte. Ruskin felt obliged to define his position in relation to him. (R. Harrison, *Before the Socialists* (London, 1965), 251–2.) Annan's 1959 Hobhouse Memorial Lecture was on 'The Curious Strength of Positivism in English Political Thought'. (*Hobhouse Memorial Lectures 1951–60* (London, 1962).)

[2] B. Webb, *My Apprenticeship* (1926) (Harmondsworth, 1971), 188, 309. Beatrice Webb took the Hobhouses as typifying the 'country gentleman and public

the Trevelyans of Northumberland (whose most famous sons were Sir Charles Trevelyan, a member of the first Labour cabinet, and G. M. Trevelyan, the historian) such families inculcated within an ambience of cultivated refinement a strict sense of social obligation.

Hobhouse left Marlborough for Oxford in 1883. For radical, idealistic undergraduates Oxford was under the influence of T. H. Green (1836–82) and Arnold Toynbee (1852–83). Green also had been brought up in an evangelistic rural vicarage. He was the prophet of strenuous social duty. For him, both faith and reason found their highest expression in good citizenship.[3] It was under the influence of this doctrine that Hobhouse took up the cause of the local agricultural labourers.[4] The ideal of self-sacrificing service was even more dramatically represented by Toynbee. It was during Hobhouse's first term, in November 1883, that Canon Barnett made his influential plea to Oxford men to reside among the poor, as Toynbee desired, in order to weld the classes together in society.

In the 1880s socialism became an issue for educated people. Henry George had published *Poverty and Progress* in 1879. When he visited England in connection with the Irish land agitation his impact on public opinion was 'immediate and astonishing'. Land nationalization itself was a good old radical cause, not at all restricted to socialists. But Hobhouse was drawn towards the socialist camp. He came into contact with the Fabians. In the late 1880s he was friendly with Sidney Webb, and his cousin married one of Beatrice Potter's sisters. He was a close ally of Sidney Ball, one of the few socialist dons of those days.

Alfred Marshall taught at Oxford in 1883, and Hobhouse was a member of his Balliol discussion group. Through Marshall and Green, as well as his own already formed inclinations, Hobhouse

service family' and Arthur Hobhouse as typifying the English gentleman. Hobhouse's own delight in the culture of 'well-mannered gentlemen and elegant ladies' is evident in his essay written on the centenary of Jane Austen's death. (J. A. Hobson and M. Ginsberg, *L. T. Hobhouse* (London, 1931), 345–9.) His own life-work can be seen as an endeavour to universalize the ideal of gentlemanliness. Weber also believed that, unlike that of the Junker, the idea of the English gentleman was one which could be embraced by all sections of the population. (M. Weber, *From Max Weber*, ed. H. H. Gerth and C. W. Mills (London, 1948), 391.)

[3] T. H. Green, *Works* (London, 1888), vol. iii, p. xi.

[4] Hobson and Ginsberg, *Hobhouse*, 28–30. He was drawn into the circle of the eccentric Lady Carlisle, and was sent out on temperance propaganda in the villages around Castle Howard. (P. Clarke, *Liberals and Social Democrats* (Cambridge, 1978), 23.) Green had been prominent in the temperance movement.

was turned in a Christian-Socialist direction. The Christian Socialists believed that working people ought to prepare themselves for citizenship through Friendly Societies and co-operatives. The state was not external to the citizens who composed it, but one of the forms through which the citizen's personality was expanded. By means of the state, social harmony was contrived in the interests of everyone. These all became essential components in Hobhouse's political views.

Alfred Marshall was one of the tribe of sages and pastors of the period.[5] He was the foremost economist of his day, and it was from him (and later from J. A. Hobson) that Hobhouse derived his economic theory. He also looked to Marshall for facts about contemporary life. During Hobhouse's undergraduate years more and more sensational studies began to appear on the condition of England.[6] Soon, however, both the shrewd observations of Marshall and the vivid reports of the social explorers were supplemented by the work of Charles Booth. It was to his and to similar work that Hobhouse looked for his factual information, together with what he gleaned about the working class through his contacts with other researchers, especially Beatrice Potter.[7]

Among competing frames of reference to his own, Marxism did not feature at all largely. This was not because Marxism was regarded as an upstart doctrine, and its potency for the future overlooked. Hobhouse's view was, on the contrary, that this once interesting body of ideas had been already fully assessed and comprehensively refuted. Machine industry was spawning a multitude of special skills. Poverty had not increased more quickly than population and wealth. Modern industrial society had exhibited a growing heterogeneity of class and other interests. Capitalism's self-destruction in a more or less imminent revolution—possibly peaceful, probably violent—looked less, not more likely as the nineteenth century progressed. No well-informed person could

---

[5] A. Marshall, *Memorials of Alfred Marshall*, ed. A. C. Pigou (London, 1925), 8.
[6] See, e.g. G. R. Sims, *How the Poor Live* (London, 1883); W. P. Carnall [A. Mearns], *The Bitter Cry of Outcast London* (London, 1883).
[7] See, e.g. C. Booth, *Life and Labour of the People in London*, i. (London, 1892); B. S. Rowntree, *Poverty: A Study of Town Life* (1901), 2nd edn. (London, n.d); B. S. Rowntree and M. Kendall, *How the Labourer Lives* (London, 1913); A. L. Bowley, and A. R. Burnett-Hurst, *Livelihood and Poverty* [Introduction by R. H. Tawney] (London, 1915). Beatrice Potter's views on this matter were eventually made public in her *My Apprenticeship*.

possibly deny it. Exposed to the rigours of time, the whole structure had silently collapsed. For Hobhouse's world-view look not to Marx but to his exact contemporary, George Eliot; not to the proletariat but the choir invisible. He also sifted his observations in opposition to another type of socialism. The dangerous contender was, he believed, bureaucracy, imported from Bismarckian Germany, which he later came to associate with his old friends the Fabians.

On the Right, the main enemy was anti-state individualism. In the late Victorian period its influential champion was the auto-didact and polymath Herbert Spencer. In 1884, when socialism and anti-socialism were beginning to join battle in this country, Spencer produced his pungent *The Man versus the State*. He argued that the trend of progressive nations had been from regimes based upon compulsory co-operation to regimes in which individuals could after due notice join or leave social organizations as they desired. Historically Tories had stood for the former, status; Liberals for the latter, contract. Now Liberalism was transforming itself into a new Toryism by favouring the intrusion of the state once more into social life. This policy was at best futile. More often, Spencer argued, it was actually damaging to the interests of those whom it was designed to serve.[8] Popularly (though wrongly) associated with Spencer's name was another frame of reference, Social Darwinism, against which Hobhouse had to defend his own. Social Darwinism harnessed anti-state doctrines to biological theory, with its immense nineteenth-century prestige. Throughout his work, and most directly in *Morals in Evolution* and *Development and Purpose*,[9] Hobhouse attempted to show that evolution properly understood supported the ethical socialist's rather than the Social Darwinist's world-view. In society the fittest to survive was not the person who was exacting and merciless. It was the person who was generous and just, and who would rather, with Plato, suffer wrong than inflict it.[10]

[8] H. Spencer, *The Man versus the State* (1884) (Harmondsworth, 1969), 63, 70–1.

[9] L. T. Hobhouse, *Morals in Evolution: A Study in Comparative Ethics* (1906), 7th edn. (London, 1951); *Development and Purpose: An Essay Towards a Philosophy of Evolution* (1913), rev. edn. (London, 1927). For the relationship between Hobhouse's and Spencer's thought see G. Hawthorn, *Enlightenment and Despair* (Cambridge, 1977), ch. 5.

[10] L. T. Hobhouse, *The Labour Movement* (1893), 3rd edn. 1912 (Brighton, 1974), 151.

THE IDEAL OF THE FULLY DEVELOPED PERSON

Hobhouse's political philosophy was centred on his ambition to improve 'character'. In this he followed Green. Theirs was the Aristotelian ideal of the fullest possible development of each individual's powers, which depended on two beliefs: first, as they unfolded, the powers of each person in all their variety were mutually reinforcing; secondly, each person's full development was assisted by the full development of the powers of other people, in their immensely greater variety.

The fully-developed personality emerged and maintained itself under the guidance of practical reason, which operated within the individual's feelings and desires and harmonized discordant elements. Hobhouse was therefore hostile to anything that diminished this first trait of ideal character, rational self-control. He habitually contrasted the 'public house' labourer unfavourably with the working man of the trade union, co-operative, and Friendly Society type. His attitude to rational self-control also fixed his attitude to the standard of living to be aimed at. He argued, as did Cobbett, that everyone capable of the rationally self-controlled development of personality must have the basic material means to make that possible. But no more. Ruskin told a story of a passenger in a holed ship who wanted to save his gold. He strapped it in a pocket-belt round his waist and promptly sank to the bottom of the sea. Did he control his wealth, Ruskin asked, or did his wealth control him? Wealth was only useful, Hobhouse argued, if it was under the rational control of the possessor, and was used for the purposes of thought and creation. Beyond that it ceased to be wealth and became 'illth'. Private opulence corrupted life and destroyed the simplicity of men and women from cottage to castle.[11]

The second trait of the person of ideal character was that he was actively engaged in the task of working out harmoniously latent capacities in all their fullness. Hobhouse assisted with the work of Toynbee Hall, and a typical week's programme offered to the inhabitants of Whitechapel during the period of his involvement included lectures on Socrates, the Saxon Chronicle, and the

---

[11] J. Ruskin, *Unto This Last* (1862) (London, n.d. [1912]), 30, 93–4, 119; *Labour Movement*, 113.

Chemistry and Arts of Manufacture; a reading party on Spinoza; a meeting of the Shakespeare Club; a lantern-slide talk on Normandy; and classes in shorthand, carpentry, wood carving, clay modelling, Greek, Latin, and German.

The third trait of the ideal character was its unselfish promotion of the welfare of others. Selfishness could not achieve its aims. 'Vulturous greediness', as Carlyle said, 'cannot live.' Carlyle's language of 'naked egoism' and 'cash-payment alone' was not different from Marx and Engels's in the *Communist Manifesto*.[12] Ruskin denounced a society based upon the pursuit of self-interest as one which God always crushed out with calamity or revolution. For Hobhouse, as for others in this tradition, altruism was also a truer expression of human nature. The characters of men and women should be so composed that they work as earnestly and strenuously for others as for themselves, for they themselves are better for it. This was a matter of fact, demonstrated in medicine, the Churches, education, the Civil Service, and even in industry pure and simple. That hired, selfish, reluctant work was unnatural, inferior, and transitory was also Marx's view. The great social experiment of the co-operative movement, Marx said, showed that the true character and destiny of labour was to ply its toil with a 'willing hand, a ready mind, and a joyous heart'.[13]

Hobhouse's ideal character, fourthly, fulfilled these duties towards others out of a sense of inner commitment. A keen sense of justice and social responsibility ought, certainly, to find a congenial framework of rules within which individuals can work together in harmony. But the mere machinery of social interaction was worthless unless it was an expression of the spirit and feeling of those who operated it.[14] If they had renounced their private virtue, it was impossible for people to build a public good.

---

[12] T. Carlyle, *Past and Present* (1843) (London, 1899), 188; K. Marx and F. Engels, *Selected Works* (Moscow, 1951, 1958), i. 36.

[13] *Labour Movement*, 116; K. Marx, 'Inaugural Address to the WMIA' (1864), in Marx and Engels, *Selected Works*, i. 383.

[14] *Labour Movement*, 18. Some of the Fabians shared this emphasis on personal commitment. Sydney Olivier's Fabian Essay was on 'Socialism and Morals'. He told the Marxist Hyndman that a socialist system would suffer 'inevitable evils' if there were no revolution in morality. (M. Olivier, *Letters* (London, 1948), letter dated 22 Jan. 1884.) Ball's article, 'The Moral Aspects of Socialism', *Int. Journ. Ethics*, vi. (1896), was republished as a Fabian pamphlet. 'For Ball like Hobhouse, the root questions of socialism were ethical.' (Clarke, *Liberals and Social Democrats*, 45.)

THE IDEAL OF THE VARIEGATED BUT HARMONIOUS COMMUNITY

The traits of an individual's character and the attributes of his or her social relationships were, for Hobhouse, inseparable. It was therefore meaningless to consider the concept of the ideal character without simultaneously considering the ideal community. A community advanced towards Hobhouse's ideal as it increased in scale, efficiency, mutuality, and freedom. Human life was carried forward only if all these advanced together.[15] He was principally interested in mutuality and freedom—liberty, equality, and fraternity—and the relationship between them.

By mutuality Hobhouse means service to an end in the benefits of which all can share. Such an end is 'a common good'. The complex system of such ends is 'the common good'. Efforts applied to the production of common goods, and devotion to the common good, produce beneficial results for the individual. Devotion to selfish interests to the exclusion of the interests of others produces only detrimental results, though in the short term the appearance may be to the contrary. To be a member of the ideal community is to hold inviolate the principle that all claims by a person to common goods are conditional upon the recognition of the like claims of others. People who from their character do not habitually act, as it were instinctively, upon that principle are by that fact, *whatever their wealth or social rank and whether governors or governed*, members of what Marx called the 'dangerous classes'. They have made outlaws of themselves.[16] For these ideas of mutuality and the common good Hobhouse was greatly indebted to Green. The concrete form of devotion to the common good is 'citizenship'. All Hobhouse's work deals with these matters, but his most ambitious treatment on the empirical side is *Morals in Evolution* and on the ethical *The Rational Good*.[17]

By freedom, Hobhouse means scope for the emergence of

[15] L. T. Hobhouse, *Social Development: Its Nature and Conditions* (1924) (London, 1966), 79.

[16] T. H. Green, *Lectures on the Principles of Political Obligation* (London, 1921), sect. 121.

[17] M. Richter, *The Politics of Conscience: T. H. Green and his Age* (London, 1964), 344; L. T. Hobhouse, *The Rational Good: A Study of the Logic of Practice* (London, 1921). See also C. M. Griffin, 'L. T. Hobhouse and the Idea of Harmony', *Journ. Hist. Ideas*, 35 (1974).

character. Liberty is the indispensable condition of mental, spiritual, and physical growth, for to try to form character by coercion is to destroy it in the making. The ideal community is a set of relationships which secures the external and material conditions for a free and unimpeded development of personal life.[18]

Hobhouse's ideal of community also postulates equality: free scope for the development of the personality of each and every member. In what sense 'equal'? He does not imply identical genetic endowments. He envisages equality of neither resource allocation nor outcome. His community is one of equality in the sense that all have an equal right to the conditions for the fullest development of personality of which they are capable. Any inequality of treatment would have to be based solely upon the consideration that 'when we have well weighed the good and evil of all parties concerned we can find no alternative open to us which could do better for the good of all', in terms of the harmoniously full development of personal powers.[19]

The ideal community is democratic. But Hobhouse's argument for democracy is not that the individual has the moral right to use his political rights to pursue narrowly conceived private interests in the public domain. It is that all sane adults have the duty to contribute instructed judgements to the formation of the common good. Intelligent interest in all manner of public things is immediately effective in the growth of the powers of personality, and in the long run the individual's own best interests are served by participation in generally available benefits. He finds his own good in the common good.

The ideal community is pluralistic. In any conceivable society people need a host of organizations to link them into the complex of persons, social relationships, cultural products, and material artifacts that make up the community. Through them they are helped to appreciate intellectually and emotionally the ramifications of their own conduct upon others, and that of others upon them. They are thus led to a recognition of the way of life which does or does not result in maximum benefits for all.

[18] L. T. Hobhouse, *Social Evolution and Political Theory* (New York, 1911), 199–200.

[19] L. T. Hobhouse, *Liberalism* (London, n.d. [1911]) 131. This view, which is clearly expressed in the 1789 Declaration of the Rights of Man ('social inequality can only be founded on common utility'), has been revived and given extended treatment in J. Rawls, *A Theory of Justice* (Oxford, 1972).

The ideal of the fully-developed personality in the community of free and equal citizens contributing to the common good depends upon what he calls the 'harmonic' view of character, society, and indeed of all reality whatsoever. Everything that is true and valid is mutually reinforcing. This is the golden thread of Hobhouse's thought, from his most ephemeral articles in the *Nation* or *Manchester Guardian* to his densest general philosophy in *The Theory of Knowledge*.[20] The growth of personality is possible only in society, and the fulfilment of personality is possible only in a society composed of fulfilled personalities. Development of character involves not merely absence of conflict, but mutual support. Hobhouse does not assume a pre-existing harmony, waiting only to be revealed with the removal of the excrescences of authority. There is only a *possible* harmony which partly by discipline, partly by the improvement in social conditions of life, men might ideally attain. Passion comes easily to the 'terrible simplifiers'. It is more difficult to hold and propagate with passion the doctrine of self-restraint and mutual respect. There was the fanaticism of the sectarian. What is needed is the fanaticism of the unifying mind.[21]

THE TRACTABLE PROBLEM OF POVERTY

That their material standard of living was too low for many of his fellow citizens to develop their full potential was the starting-point of Hobhouse's political philosophy. But for how many and by how much 'too low'? Since the 1960s 'relative deprivation' has been used almost exclusively as a concept with which to draw new sections of the population into the category of the intolerably poor. But in itself the concept cuts one way just as sharply as the other. Hobhouse's use was that of his contemporaries. It was repeatedly demonstrated in his time that the poor were both better off than they had ever been before, and better off than their equivalents

[20] L. T. Hobhouse, *The Theory of Knowledge* (1896–1905) (London, 1921). From 1896 to 1902 Hobhouse worked for the *Manchester Guardian* in Manchester under C. P. Scott, and was a main contributor thereafter. Scott had told Hobhouse that 'the relations of Liberalism and Labour must govern the future of politics'. (C. P. Scott, *C. P. Scott* (London, 1946), 85.) Returning to London he worked on the *Nation* with J. L. Hammond (also the son of a vicar) and Graham Wallas. They held the same view as Hobhouse about the socialist tendency of true liberalism in the modern world.   [21] *Liberalism*, 128–30, 250.

elsewhere. Certainly there was propaganda about relative deprivation in the modern sense but, as he saw it, only from the ill-
informed or ill-disposed. There was liberty of discussion
in England, and a strong temptation to exaggerate grievances
recklessly. That was no reason for tolerating abuses or neglecting
any means for the amelioration of the poor. But it was a reason
against telling the labouring classes of England that they were the
most wretched people on the face of the earth. As Hobhouse
succinctly put it: 'wages on the whole have increased, the cost of
living has diminished, housing and sanitation have improved, the
death rate has fallen'.[22]

But what of the inhabitants of the slums whose plight had been
so vividly portrayed in the 1880s? Lurid pictures had been
painted—on a curtain, said Charles Booth. Contrary to received
opinion today, Booth did not then go out and find to his surprise
that the agitators and malcontents were correct after all. Even in
East London, he said, by far the largest class (42 per cent) were
labourers with a regular income and a good deal of property.
Above lay a higher grade of labourer and artisan (13.5 per cent).
Both classes lived in comfort or even affluence. The standard of
living of these two classes was fairly secure. If their opportunities
were improved to even a small extent, 'we, or succeeding
generations, should see a glorious structure arise, to be a stronghold
of social progress'. Above them lived the hardworking, sober, and
energetic lower-middle class (4 per cent) and above them in turn the
upper-middle class (5 per cent).

Below all these classes were the 'poor'. By 'poor' Booth explicitly
did *not* mean 'in want'. The poor were 'neither ill-nourished nor ill-
clad, according to any standard that can be reasonably used'. Their

[22] Ibid. 161. Hobhouse seems to depend upon the findings of Robert Giffen,
given in his 1883 Presidential Address to the Statistical Society. (Republished in P.
Abrams, *The Origins of British Sociology 1834–1914* (Chicago, 1968), see esp. 158,
163, 166, 171.) Long-term comparisons of crime are beset with many problems, but
in 1861, when the population of England and Wales was 20 million, indictable
offences known to the police numbered 88,000. By 1891 the population had
increased to 29 million, yet the number of known indictable offences had fallen to
80,000. The rate per 100,000 fell from 438 in 1861 to 249 in 1901. The rate then
tended to rise. By 1929, the year of Hobhouse's death, the rate stood at 340 per
100,000 population. (By 1950 the ratio had risen to 1,094, and in the 1960s, 1970s,
and 1980s showed rapid and substantial growth to 5,119 in 1980 and 6,885 in
1985, i.e. the increase 1980–5 was five times the total in 1929.) (Home Office,
Criminal Statistics England and Wales (published annually).)

income, though barely so, was sufficient for decent independent life. Life for the two sub-classes of the poor, namely, those with small regular earnings (14.5 per cent) and those with intermittent earnings (8 per cent), was an unending struggle. They would be better off if they had more of everything. But, said Booth, 'I do not know that they lack happiness'. Booth insisted that, in order to avoid the danger of 'understating the evils with which society has to deal', he painted the picture too darkly rather than too brightly.[23] When Hobhouse first became acquainted with Beatrice Potter, she was working with Booth on his London survey. The summary of her findings was the same as Booth's. They disproved the assertions of the marxian socialists, she said. Manual workers were *not* in a state of chronic destitution and the poor were *not* getting steadily poorer. She deplored the tendency to exaggerate the penury, helplessness, and incompetence of working people. The independent working class was overlooked, she wrote, and when there was talk about hardships of the 'people' the subject was really the 'ne'er-do-wells'.[24]

Alfred Marshall was another powerful source of Hobhouse's opinions. By 1907 Marshall was protesting that Booth's statistics themselves were being carelessly read and brought into use by the same scaremongers Booth had refuted. The one thing that every German now knew about England was that one million Londoners lived in poverty. 'But they open their eyes when they learn that under this misleading title are included all families with less aggregate income than 21 marks all year round. For twenty-one marks will buy much less food than 21*s* will . . .' Not one-third, as in London, but nearly three-quarters of working-class families in Germany lived on less.[25]

What, then, of the remaining 13 per cent of the population of East London, the 'very poor'? Booth says he deliberately chose the East End because it was acknowledged to contain 'the most destitute population in England'.[26] He found to his satisfaction, however, that the ragged and starving horde of barbarians emerging from the abyss to overwhelm civilization simply did not exist. There was a stage-army of the bad: the battered figure who

[23] Booth, *Life and Labour*, i. 5, 33, 51, 62, 131, 162.
[24] Webb, *My Apprenticeship*, 171, 254–5.
[25] Marshall, *Memorials*, 328.
[26] Webb, *My Apprenticeship*, 233.

slouched conspicuously through the streets, the beggar, the bully, the loafer, and the criminal. They provided the ready material for civil disorder when occasion served. They rendered no useful service, created no wealth. They degraded all that they touched and fouled the reputation of the unemployed and the whole working class. But for Booth his most significant finding relating to this category was the fact that it formed only a tiny proportion of his population, 1.25 per cent.[27]

But there was another section of the population, much larger (11.5 per cent), which did present a problem of poverty. Only some of these, 'and not, I think a very large percentage', Booth said, would be described by anyone, 'including themselves' as being in *distress*. This was the population in want—ill-nourished and poorly clad. Mainly, they were incapable of earning their own keep by productive labour. Some suffered from mental or physical handicaps. Others were shiftless and idle, lacking 'prudence and sobriety'. 'It may with some reason be regarded as not so very bad that a tenth of the population should be reckoned very poor in a district so confessedly poverty-stricken as East London.'[28] Rowntree found that there was also a 'submerged tenth' in York at the turn of the century: the total cost of feeding them at workhouse standard entirely at public expense would have involved a weekly sum of less than £228.[29]

The main sources of information considered reliable by Hobhouse, therefore, showed him that a solid material basis for his society of abstemious, self-improving citizens was already present. The problems of poverty that existed were bitterly sharp, and an exceedingly urgent and important task for the reformer. But they were not of such daunting proportions as to postpone amelioration to the distant future. Even less did they justify all hope being cast upon the uncertain consequences of a violent revolution followed by a hazardous reconstruction of all social institutions.

[27] Booth, *Life and Labour*, i. 38–9, 131. For Marx and Engels's similar view of this group, see, e.g., Marx and Engels, *Selected Works*, i. 295, 646. Some modern Marxists are distressed by these opinions. See, e.g., F. Bovenkerk, 'The Rehabilitation of the Rabble: How and Why Marx and Engels Wrongly Depicted the Lumpenproletariat', *Neth. Journ. Sociol.* 20 (1984); R. Miliband and J. Saville (eds.), *Socialist Register* (London, 1972), 207.

[28] Booth, *Life and Labour*, i. 177–8.

[29] Rowntree, *Poverty*, 67–8.

A BENIGN WORKING-CLASS CULTURE

Hobhouse derived his perceptions of working-class culture partly from Mill and Marshall, and partly from Comte, through one of Comte's ablest disciples, J. H. Bridges (whose sister-in-law Hobhouse married).[30] But he drew them mainly from the observations of such researchers as Booth and Beatrice Potter, and from his own experiences of a certain type of earnest and able working man during his years in the north with the *Manchester Guardian*.

A crucial question was whether an improvement in the conditions of the workers would make it possible for them to become refined characters. If their conditions were bettered, would the workers take advantage of the opportunities for self-cultivation and contributions to the common good? Mill had reported favourably on 'The Probable Future of the Working Class'.[31] Marshall had argued that as skilled workmen came to enjoy more humane circumstances of employment, many of them did indeed become more courteous, gentle, thoughtful, and able. They were accepting private and public duties. They were 'steadily becoming gentlemen'.[32] Toynbee spoke of the very great moral advances in the manufacturing areas, manifested 'in temperance, in orderly behaviour, in personal appearance'. The working class was entering the 'citizen' stage, and the gospel of rights was being transcended by the gospel of duties.[33]

Beatrice Potter's visits to Bacup in the 1880s deeply impressed her with the qualities of the industrial workers in late Victorian times. Already, she said, they were 'more refined in their motives and feelings than the majority of the money-getting and money-inheriting class'. The views of the ordinary Bacup workman, with his fair-mindedness and the kindliness of his view of men and things

[30] The Comtians believed the workers and philosophers were alike in their realism, utilitarianism, generosity, and unconcern with material prospects. Bridges was Comte's English translator—see n. 1.

[31] J. S. Mill, *Principles of Political Economy* (London, 1848). Two years later Charles Kingsley wrote that 'the morals of the working-tailors, as well as other classes of artisans, are rapidly improving'—due mainly to the Chartists, 'the great preachers and practisers of temperance, thrift, chastity, self-respect, and education'. (C. Kingsley, *Alton Locke: Tailor and Poet* (1850) (London, n.d. [1892]), 18–19.) George Eliot similarly wrote, in 1866, of the 'departed evils' of the 1830s. (G. Eliot, *Felix Holt the Radical* (1866) (London, 1965), 13.)

[32] Marshall, *Memorials*, 105, 116.

[33] A. Toynbee, *Lectures on the Industrial Revolution in England* (1884) (Newton Abbot, 1969), 147.

were overshadowed in politics by the 'idler sort of people' and those who selfishly and stridently called for change for everyone if something did not happen to suit themselves.[34]

The later autobiographies of the self-improving working man throw light on those Hobhouse admired as the rare but sure tokens that the society for which he was striving was humanly possible.[35]

When Hobhouse looked at particular aspects of conduct, he saw confirmation that the qualities necessary for his desired society were gaining ground. 'The wave of temperance is rapidly spreading through all classes in our own time.'[36] Criminal conduct was abating. Taking into account changes in the law and other possible sources of error in the statistics, there had been a smooth and steep fall in criminal offences, in spite of a large increase in population. Booth took for granted that his readers would agree that the numbers of criminals in gaol had decreased 'in a marked way'. This was part of Booth's case that morality had been rising in English society in the previous decades.[37] As there was a submerged tenth of those in poverty, so there was a submerged fraction of the industrially degraded.[38] But to Hobhouse these conditions were residues or anomalies, partly disappearing with the advance of modern industrialism, partly problems capable of solution by public intervention. The modern industrial workers of the north, as they were perceived by Beatrice Potter, were the true products of the modern age.

Family life was seen as sound and improving. Their own experience, Blatchford said, tells working people that socialist conduct is a possibility, because it is already there in their own families.[39] Booth lived incognito as a boarder in the East End on three occasions. 'I can only speak as I have found: wholesome, pleasant family life, very simple food, very regular habits, healthy

---

[34] Webb, *My Apprenticeship*, 171, 179.

[35] See, for example, J. Lawson, *A Man's Life* (London, 1932). He gives a vivid account of two young miners engaged down the pit in the discussion of the work of Ruskin and George Borrow. (Ibid. 90–1.)   [36] *Liberalism*, 180–1.

[37] Giffen showed a fall of from 24,000 persons committed for trial in 1839 to 15,000 in 1883, even though the population had doubled. (Abrams, *Origins of British Sociology*, 172; Booth, *Life and Labour*, i. 175 n.)

[38] See, e.g. R. H. Sherard, *The White Slaves of England* (London, 1897) and *The Child Slaves of Britain* (London, 1905); and Beatrice Potter's contributions in Booth, *Life and Labour*.

[39] R. Blatchford, *Merrie England* (London, 1894), 114. Blatchford's newspaper, *The Clarion* had a wide working-class readership.

bodies and healthy minds—affectionate relations of husbands and wives, mothers and sons, of elders with children, of friend with friend.' This 'very agreeable picture' reflected the state of family affairs, in his opinion, in the classes immediately above the submerged tenth and the odious remnant of loafers and penurious criminals. Responsibility in family life meant that one of the arguments against providing working people with the means of self-development had been driven from the field, said Hobhouse.[40]

Beatrice Potter frequently remarks on the importance of the chapel in accounting for the capacity for moral self-government and the warm-hearted integrity of the workers of Bacup. 'It is the only society I have ever lived in, in which religious faith really guides thought and action, and forms the whole basis of life of the individual and the community.'[41] Lawson gives an account of the chapel which may be taken as indicative of the impression Hobhouse would have received from such working men of his acquaintance. 'We talked pit work, ideals, the Bible, literature, or union business. The piano rattled, the choir was in action.' Above all, he recalls, there was about the people of the chapel, whose fine lives gave strength to the working-class communities in which they lived, a 'beautiful humble helpfulness'.[42] Friendly Societies were an important and growing feature of working-class life in Hobhouse's formative years, and he took great interest also in the co-operative movement of his day, regarding its powerful growth and its ideology as portents of the future for which he was striving.[43]

[40] Booth, *Life and Labour*, i. 158; *Liberalism*, 181. See also Lawson, *Man's Life*, 29, 36–7; Webb, *My Apprenticeship*, 183.

[41] Webb, *My Apprenticeship*, 179.

[42] Lawson, *Man's Life*, 65–6, 68–9. As late as 1980 the aspirations of chapel-and-temperance socialism were recorded by one of its surviving adherents, Ernest Armstrong, who was MP for the mining constituency of Durham North West and became Deputy Speaker of the House of Commons. He contrasted the miner-Methodists' emphasis on personal responsibility, persuasion, and consensus with the belief in historical necessity, 'dogma, slogans and control', and class war. 'They won more converts to socialism than all the booklets about Marxist dogma.' (*The Times*, 27 Sept. 1980.)

[43] See, e.g., Rowntree, *Poverty*, 417, 422–3; Booth, *Life and Labour*, i. 109; Hobhouse, *Labour Movement*, 60. See also D. G. Green, and L. G. Cromwell, *Mutual Aid or Welfare State* (Sydney, 1984). Looking today at even the neglected structures erected in provincial towns by the organizations of the late Victorian or Edwardian working class now sold, perhaps, and converted into night-clubs (as the chapels have been turned over for use as carpet warehouses) Cobbett's protest seems to apply: that yet there be those who swear that our dark and ignorant fathers were incapable of such things. (W. Cobbett, *Rural Rides* (1821–32) (London, 1912), ii. 97.)

Until shortly before the First World War the trade unions were developing in strength and conduct in a direction favourable to Hobhouse's aims. This was obviously true of the 'new model' unions of the skilled workers dating from the middle of the nineteenth century. Their leaders condemned 'outrages' unambiguously and immediately. For them, even peacefully conducted strikes were like wars between nations—crimes unless justified by absolute necessity. Unionists were engaged in the task of 'building with care and vision a co-operative commonwealth'.[44] The orderly meetings in which workmen in general expressed their will in late Victorian times was in marked contrast to the 'ignorant crime' that accompanied labour disputes in previous generations.[45]

Such events as the Featherstone riot were quite exceptional,[46] and to a continental observer like Sombart, England at the end of the nineteenth century was the home of a working class that before 1850 had been disorderly, but was now persistent, businesslike, calm, and above all self-confident. Lasalle, the father of German socialism, had taught that to treat an opponent fairly was the first duty of man. The German workers should look to England to see that lesson put into practice; for there, 'opposing forces fight like gentlemen'.[47]

When unskilled labour roused itself in the late 1880s it appeared to Hobhouse to be proceeding along the path already taken not only by the new-model trade unions, but by the miners as well.[48] *The Times* reported that in the speeches of the leaders of the dock

---

[44] A. Briggs, *Victorian People* (Harmondsworth, 1965), 204.

[45] Marshall, *Memorials*, 115.

[46] The Miners' Federation immediately condemned the rioters as 'the worst enemies of the miners' cause'. (R. P. Arnot, *The Miners: A History of the MFGB 1889–1910* (London, 1949), 239.)

[47] W. Sombart, *Socialism and the Socialist Movement* (London, 1909), 287.

[48] In 1841 Martin Jude's Miners' Association of Great Britain with its Newcastle-based journal, *The Miners' Advocate*, committed itself to securing reform through the House of Commons and justice through the courts. The Durham miners' gala was instituted to demonstrate that the miners were a civilized section of the community. At the second gala in June 1872, 180 Durham collieries and 32,000 miners were represented. Adequate precautions were taken against 'almost the worst contingency' of this gathering of thousands of workmen. 'No fewer than forty policemen' were present! (J. Wilson, *A History of the Durham Miners' Association 1870–1904* (Durham, 1907), 60–1.) Lawson, writing in 1932, said, 'Now the business people . . . request those in authority to grant special privileges', so impressed had they been over the years with the 'splendid self-discipline' of the families from the colliery villages. (Lawson, *Man's Life*, 119.)

strike of 1889 there was no reference to revolution 'except in the peaceful spirit of Thomas More'. 'Now, lads', was John Burns's style of oratory to the assembled dockers, 'are you going to be as patient as you have been?' (*Yes!*) 'As orderly as you have been?' (Shouts of *Yes!*) 'Are you going to be your own police?' (*Yes!*) 'Then march off five deep past the dock companies' offices and keep to the left hand of the street.'[49]

At the time of the dock strike, Hobhouse was staying at Toynbee Hall, the university settlement set up in Whitechapel after Barnett's campaign of 1883. The sight of the hitherto ill-organized among the unskilled showing these tendencies towards self-discipline and solidarity—solidarity not merely to their sectional interests but with regard to the national interest as a whole—made him see the strike as a turning-point in the history of labour.[50] In writing *The Labour Movement*, he consulted one of the leaders, Tom Mann. Mann turned later to anarcho-syndicalism. But judging from the third edition of *The Labour Movement*, which takes into account events up to the miners' strike of 1912, Hobhouse does not seem to have taken syndicalism as a serious blow to his optimism. The conduct of the miners, he said, gave no substance to the vague alarm felt that society may be some day arbitrarily put at the mercy of a combination of workers who controlled some vital instrument of production.[51]

To summarize Hobhouse's views prior to the First World War, trade-unionists were the cream of the working class in intellect, and of the community in morality. The influence of trade-unionism, he wrote, was an effect, 'not of quantity, but of quality'. In their characteristic social relationships they did not engage in conflict. Trade-unionists worked by the steady pressure of persuasion, by the 'delicate tact of skilled negotiation', and in all the other 'quietly effective ways about which newspapers are silent'.[52] In 1904 Hobhouse wrote that there was no sign of the kind of class war to which the workers' movement in Germany appealed. In England

[49] G. S. Jones, *Outcast London* (Oxford, 1971), 315–16.
[50] Hobson and Ginsberg, *Hobhouse*, 59.
[51] *Labour Movement*, 6; R. P. Arnot, *The Miners: Years of Struggle* (London, 1953), 114–16. Mann led the dockers' strike of 1911 which brought gunboats and cavalry to the Mersey. He was active in the Cambrian Combine strike of 1911, and his 'Don't Shoot!' leaflet to the troops led to his arrest for incitement to mutiny.
[52] *Labour Movement*, 22, 40.

there was too general a feeling for the common weal to make it likely.[53]

The emerging Labour party made a similar impression on Hobhouse. The earliest working-class MPs were bent upon self-refinement and the elevation of their class through their own self-sacrificing dedication to constitutionally achieved reform. Thomas Burt's spirit is exactly caught in a letter he wrote to Alfred Marshall, praising him for deploying his case in such a way that there was 'not a word of censure applied to man or institution'. Keir Hardie upheld the ideal of a unified and harmonious nation as passionately as Hobhouse. 'We want to awaken in the worker a consciousness of his manhood, not of his class.' Class hatred could not transform society for the better. The political leaders of the Labour movement were upholders of parliamentary democracy. Parliamentary institutions were of overriding importance to the Labour party. MacDonald wrote that to weaken respect for even a bad House of Commons was therefore a heinous crime for socialists.[54]

Hobhouse believed that true socialism was built upon the victories already won by Liberalism. It did not destroy, but completed, the leading Liberal ideals.[55]

THE STATE AS LIBERATOR

As soon as the freedom of action of more than one person is involved, liberty as such and control as such cease to be opposing concepts. In society, people can be free to direct their own lives only in so far as others are prevented from molesting and interfering with them. Each liberty rests on a corresponding act of restraint.

[53] L. T. Hobhouse, *Democracy and Reaction* (London, 1904), 237. The Webbs, in their *Industrial Democracy*, had argued that the most powerful unions had even discarded picketing, 'with its intangible annoyance and early transition into breaches of public order'.

[54] Marshall, *Memorials*, 378; F. Bealey (ed.), *The Social and Political Thought of the British Labour Party* (London, 1970), 62–3, 68–9.

[55] Hobhouse, *Democracy and Reaction*, 225, 229. Socialism coincided, he said, with the Liberalism that sought to 'apply the principles of Liberty, Equality and the Common Good to the industrial life of our time'. (L. T. Hobhouse, *Contemporary Review*, 93 (1908).) L. A. Atherley-Jones named those who aimed at 'a wider diffusion of physical comfort' and 'a loftier standard of morality' the New Liberals. (*Nineteenth Century*, 26 (1889).) See P. Weiler, 'The New Liberalism of L. T. Hobhouse', *Victorian Studies*, 16 (1972); M. Freeden, *The New Liberalism* (Oxford, 1978).

The restraint may be self-restraint in the form of self-imposed duties. But the feeling of duty is not always sufficient. Supplementing duty, there must then be externally imposed obligation. Hobhouse quotes Locke:

Freedom of men under government is to have a standing rule to live by, common to every one in that society, and made by the legislative power erected in it. A liberty to follow my own will in all things where that rule prescribes not, not to be subject to the inconstant, uncertain, unknown, arbitrary will of another man.[56]

It was Hobhouse's contention that the state, which had been opposed by Liberals as the foe of liberty, should be recognized as one of the principal means of securing it. He greatly extended the notion of coercion by private individuals against which the state should protect its citizens. 'If we curtail the liberty of one side, and so obtain an eight hour day for a group of workers', he asks, 'do we add or subtract from it upon the whole?'[57] Left to itself the system of unlimited freedom of contract and casual acts of charity did not raise a degraded part of the population. A degraded population perpetuated and increased itself. To the extent that it was used to redress inequalities of bargaining power the state rendered contract free in a deeper and more genuine sense than ever before. The possibilities of arguing for state intervention on the grounds of the *expansion* of liberty were thus indefinitely extended.

He saw the state, furthermore, as the means for the exercise of compulsion on individuals themselves to raise them to the point at which they became capable of using liberty. Only when they had fully developed all their own harmonious powers of body and mind were they really free people. To some extent it is simply a matter of the state providing the conditions which allow the individual to reach that point. But certain sections of the population, in Rousseau's famous words, must be 'forced to be free'. Thus the state, in the name of a child's liberty as an adult, compels so much education as puts it in a position in which it has all the best thoughts that have been expressed in its mother tongue at its command.[58] Ignorance makes a person unfree. But so do other

---

[56] J. Locke, *The Treatises of Civil Government* (1690) (London, 1924), 127. A key notion was the hindrance of hindrances to freedom. (I. Kant, *The Philosophy of Law* (Edinburgh, 1887), 47.)   [57] *Labour Movement*, 153.

[58] Ibid. Hobhouse would have had in mind such books as Amy Barter's *A Treasury of Prose and Poetry for Learning by Heart* (London, 1912) which, with its

internal conditions of the personality. Hobhouse therefore advocates the use of the state to curtail certain freely chosen lower-grade activities in the interests of higher activities. Higher activities are those which widen the range of choices subsequently open to the individual, and bring the process of choice increasingly under the control of his reason, not his impulse. The true opposition is between the control that cramps freedom and the control that expands it. The individual is more free, the more his life is under rational self-control. On these grounds the state's supervision of the traffic in drink—the drug problem of his time—was not an attack on personal liberty but its defence.[59]

How can controls of different tendency, those that liberate and those that enslave, be distinguished? Hobhouse's answer is that there is no easy formula. It can only be a matter of evidence and the best prediction that can be made. Who claims to offer more is a charlatan. All people are fallible. No world can be envisaged in which that would cease to be true. But the best arrangements that happen for the time being to be available for making the distinction from case to case are the institutions of English parliamentary democracy. The more careless, selfish, hedonistic, ignorant, or irresponsible the population, the worse liberty and growth will be served by them. What can be looked for is the nearest approach to prudent, altruistic, knowledgeable, trustworthy, and wise collective judgement on collective interests, abreast of the wisdom exercised by individuals in their private lives; wise, that is, in tending to a fuller life for all.[60]

How can harmony within the community of free individuals be gained? Once again, the state is a major means. The idea of the neutral state acting for the liberty and equality of all, anathema to Marxists, is put by Hobhouse in its most unadulterated form.

When a properly constituted state intervenes between employer and employee, the weaker party gains the protection of the law, and can no longer be made to accept conditions to which no one, unless driven, would accede. The state can be used to impose rules of the game intended to secure fair play, and limit the conditions to which people might agree in such matters as safety at work; provision

extracts from the work of More, George Eliot, Ruskin, Matthew Arnold, Jane Austin, and Carlyle, reads as though it were Hobhouse's own commonplace book.

[59] Ibid. 154.   [60] Ibid. 157.

against sickness and accidents; and maximum hours and minimum wages.[61] Those elements in the rights of property which give one individual dominance over another should be restored to the state, as the harmonizing agent of the society as a whole. The state would be granted 'eminent' ownership of all things necessary for the production of wealth, as well as 'direct' ownership of some of those necessary things.[62]

As between the trade union, the employer, and the consumer, a close combination of workmen might be inspired by all the ambitions of a narrow ring of monopolists, and take undue advantage of their ability to make the public suffer. The recurrence of disputes of this nature, Hobhouse writes, would probably lead the state to assume close control of conditions of employment in some vital industries, and quite possibly the direct control of the functions of labour management in them. But he believed that the activities of trade unions typically did not need to be brought by the state into harmony with the interests of the rest of society. They were already penetrated by a wide, unselfish, and enlightened view of their duties and interests. In relation to all lesser communities, each of which had its sectional interest, the power of the state was needed not to supersede but to balance and harmonize them, especially as the ability to pursue their sectional interests grew with the strength of organization.[63]

The role of the state, in Hobhouse's view, was to secure harmony within as well as between associations. Within the family (as indicative of the proper role of the state) the relation between husband and wife was being turned by law into one between equal partners, each of whom was a person 'in the full ethical sense'.[64] The task of the state, in this respect too, was not to replace subordinate groups, but in the interests of their internal harmony to guide and supervise them.

The modern state was reforming itself into a suitable agency for

----

[61] Ibid. 89.

[62] C. Gore (ed.), *Property: Its Duties and Rights* (1914) (London, 1915).

[63] *Labour Movement*, 80–1, 91. One of Hobhouse's greatest objections to syndicalism was that it was blatantly sectional, and represented merely a form of collective egoism—the antithesis of social harmony. It was anti-intellectual, and because of its commitment to organized violence it was incapable of producing desired results even in its own terms. (Clarke, *Liberals and Social Democrats* 152.) Labour leaders were more hostile still, see, e.g., J. R, MacDonald, *Syndicalism* (London, 1912), 70–2.   [64] *Labour Movement*, 90.

the tasks Hobhouse wished to assign to it. Adam Smith and his followers, though devoted to the well-being of the people, had looked askance at those who invited the government to undertake new enterprises for the public weal. Experience had taught them that their real motive was private gain. But Hobhouse shared a common view that Britain in the nineteenth century had seen a vast increase in the probity, unselfishness, and resources of government. The movement had been promoted by the achievement of universal male suffrage, which enabled the people to check class abuse of power; by the spread of education; by the increasing zeal of the churches; by the improvement in the moral no less than the intellectual quality of literature; by the writings of Dickens, Tennyson, Ruskin, Newman, and Maurice; by the personal influence of giants of practical morality like Gladstone; and by the rise of the democratic working-class organizations. The honest, competent, and democratic state was for Hobhouse already in existence, and the working basis of practical socialism.

Green had restricted the term 'state' to that set of agents in the society *who by the consent of the members* exercised supreme coercive power. That is, such agents were the only approved users of physical violence, and were approved because their function was to maintain an overall system of rights in such a way that no one gained at the expense of another.[65] It was this ideal democratic state that Hobhouse saw emerging in England. Rowntree and Booth wrote glowingly of the work of the new School Boards in York and London. The Liberal government of 1906–10, and to a lesser extent its successor, instituted many reforms endorsed by Hobhouse's ethical-socialist philosophy. The powers and activities of the new local authorities, created in 1888, pointed for Hobhouse to a rebirth of municipal life. There was now to be found that civic patriotism 'which takes an interest in the local university, which feels pride in the magnitude of the local industry, which parades the lowest death rate in the country, which is honestly ashamed of a bad record of crime'. The democratic city which in late Victorian and Edwardian times was providing art galleries, museums, town halls, and parks, filled Hobhouse with hope. Here were the citizens who would make their own town as desirable, as full of comfort, and as free from all that offends the eye and ear 'as the housewife makes

[65] Green, *Lectures*, 132.

her private home'. This, and no other, he said, was the way to return to 'Merrie England'.[66]

THE STATE'S ROLE IN PRODUCTION AND ALLOCATION

Citizens of a political democracy can be regarded as simply members of a large co-operative society.[67] In Hobhouse's view it had been one of the greatest services of voluntary co-operation to have set up the model of the control of production by communities of consumers. In the democratic state and local government 'we get the true principle of association worked out, namely, that all citizens are called upon to serve the common weal, and, on the other side, that the state shall serve not the interests of the few, nor even of the many, but the interests of all'.[68]

Which industries would Hobhouse make public? First, the democratic state or local authority was preferable to the capitalist firm or voluntary association where there were natural monopolies: a single set of possible tram lines (an obvious example in his day), a single possible water works or gas works. Secondly, there were the goods and services where the demand was constant and predictable, and where the consumers were nearly unanimous in the quality of the provision they desired. They could therefore be supplied by a stable, bureaucratic, non-innovative, utterly reliable organization. All that was needed was honesty and good sense. These virtues were to be found in abundance in the modern public services of Britain. Unlike the co-operative society, which cannot legally make anyone pay for its services, the state and the municipality are compulsory associations. They have the ability to ban competitors and extract payments, from non-users as well as users, in the form of unavoidable rates and taxes. But Hobhouse minimized the element of coercion. Public authorities could provide hospitals, schools, parks, libraries, or trams. They need not require anybody

---

[66] Booth, *Life and Labour*, i. 129–30; Rowntree, *Poverty*, 393, 396; *Labour Movement*, 132.

[67] *Labour Movement*, 67; *Liberalism*, 191–2; *Nation*, 7 June 1913. Here Hobhouse was following the argument suggested to Beatrice Potter by Sidney Webb, that what applied to the voluntary co-operative movement could be extended to the state and local authority. (Webb, *My Apprenticeship*, 390–2.)

[68] *Labour Movement*, 86. Equality was therefore the theme of the first Hobhouse Memorial Lecture. (J. A. Hobson, 'Towards Social Equality', *Hobhouse Memorial Lectures 1930–40* (Oxford, 1948).)

to use them, nor need they prevent the private provision and private purchase of alternatives.[69] The compulsory element in payment, where this appeared, Hobhouse justified by his doctrine of the 'surplus', a matter dealt with below.

These considerations rightly understood, said Hobhouse, also put a limit to state and municipal activity, even though no hard and fast line could be drawn between the proper sphere of socialist and capitalist production. The state had to justify itself in practice (as it had done so far). His hostility to 'mechanical socialism' (the Marxism preached by H. M. Hyndman, and the socialism of the Fabians) lay partly in what he perceived as their doctrinaire preference for the state.[70] Before the First World War the Labour movement appeared to agree with Hobhouse. Keir Hardie managed to have an amendment adopted by the TUC at Norwich in 1894 calling for the nationalization of the 'whole means' of production, distribution, and exchange. But this was rescinded at the 1896 congress and replaced by a Hobhousian list specifying the nationalization of land, mines, minerals, royalty rents, and railways, and the municipalization of water supplies, artificial light, and tramway undertakings.[71] It was not until after the Great War that Labour committed itself to comprehensive collectivization. (The vague terms 'common ownership' and 'socialization' had meanwhile come into fashion out of deference to the co-operators and syndicalists respectively.) Not until the Russian Revolution was credence given to Lenin's view that capitalism had *generally* brought the 'simple functions' of workmen and manager (though not the technical expert) within the capacity of the average city dweller, so that the whole national economy was capable of being organized 'on the lines of the postal system'.[72]

On the side of the allocation of goods and services, Hobhouse embraced a theory of a 'surplus' which some received in excess not only of the modest levels required for the full and free development of their personalities, but also above the levels required, even in strictly self-regarding terms, to attract an adequate supply of

[69] *Liberalism*, 189–92.
[70] H. M. Hyndman, *England For All* (London, 1881), 467; *Labour Movement*, 97–100.
[71] H. Tracey (ed.), *The Book of the Labour Party* (London, n.d. [1925]), i. 115–16.
[72] V. I. Lenin, 'The State and Revolution', *Selected Works* (Moscow, 1947), ii. 174, 210.

labour. Others were underpaid to such an extent that their
personalities were stunted. On the side of both overpayment and
underpayment, Hobhouse agrees with the bourgeois version of
Marx's 'surplus value', as put forward in its most recent authoritative form by Alfred Marshall and expanded by J. A. Hobson.[73]

Economists had generally held (and in this matter they were
joined by otherwise extreme opponents of interference with free
contractual relations) that the 'pure rent' of land was surplus value.
It did not act in any way as an incentive to effort or reward for
achievement. Pure rent is the difference in money terms between, on
the one hand, the costs of production from land of given natural
fertility and, on the other, the costs of production from the less
fertile land which at a given price it is just worthwhile to bring into
cultivation (land 'at the margin'). The same principle was applied to
the sub-soil: royalties were also surplus value. Site value was in the
same category. 'The value of a site in London is due essentially to
London, not to the landlord.'[74] The injustice of one person taking
riches which had been created by myriads of others, including those
now dead who had contributed to the building of all the institutions
of civilization, was a central feature of Hobhouse's thought. In
other cases a site had a raised value, again, not due to the
action of the owner, but because of some special advantage
conferred by the public authorities, in the form of (say) a licence to
trade.[75]

Using Alfred Marshall's concept of 'quasi-rents', Hobhouse
extended the range of the surplus. In the short run the costs of
production of an article or a service (including the production of
labour-power) bear no necessary relation to the price. Whatever the
costs of production, goods can be disposed of only at the prevailing
price in the market. But in the long run the price will fluctuate
around, but always tend towards, the costs of production incurred
by those sellers coming to the market under the greatest dis-
advantages. They are said to be at the margin of production,

[73] A. Marshall, *Principles of Economics* (1890) (London, 1920); J. A. Hobson,
The Economics of Distribution (1900) (London, 1907).
[74] *Liberalism*, 197.
[75] Given his hostility to the liquor traffic, it is not surprising that Hobhouse
frequently gives public-house licences as an example. By contrast, Marx and Engels
had long before, in the *Communist Manifesto*, dismissed the temperance fanatics
with contempt, along with other cranks who adhered to 'conservative socialism'.
(Marx and Engels, *Selected Works*, i. 60.)

because any fall in price will lead to their withdrawing their supply. All other producers, with lower costs of production than the marginal producer, find their costs covered by the price, and enjoy a surplus above their costs. Only part of this surplus has attracted them to develop skills, to take responsibility, and to intensify their efforts. Part of the surplus is like pure rent. It is attributable to the fortuitous difference between whatever happens to be the given price, equal to the high costs of the marginal producers, and whatever happens to be the non-marginal producer's lower costs. The surplus is that portion of the cost-savings that cannot be attributed to any efforts of or incentive to the non-marginal producer. 'Quasi-rents', that is, are all those *incentiveless* elements in income which exceed, in the long run, the costs of the marginal producer. There thus exists a large fund which furnishes no stimulus to voluntary industrial energy, and which can be taken for public service without injury to industry.

In addition to this 'producer's surplus' are inherited fortunes. Some part of the wealth allocated to an heir does provide an incentive to effort, and is a reward for effort expended—for it provides an incentive to the accumulator of the fortune, and it may even provide some incentive to the legatee to develop originality and provide disinterested public service. But part of inherited wealth does not act as incentive or justified reward, and is therefore also part of the surplus. The gains of gamblers and stock-exchange speculators seemed to Hobhouse to be wholly surplus. He doubted whether a tax on such sources would actually hamper any of the processes of production at any stage.

Because of the inequalities of human and non-human nature, sellers' surpluses—rents and quasi-rents—are bound to appear. That is a 'categorical or unconditional generalization', writes Hobhouse. But the *disposal* of the seller's surplus is a different matter. It would be the purpose of democratic control 'to divert every element of economic rent from private to public coffers'.[76] The manner in which the state would exercise this power would be learnt by experience and cautious experiment. The effects of taxation on the supposed surpluses would have to be closely monitored to ensure that the personal element in production was rewarded sufficiently to elicit the required abilities and endeav-

---

[76] *Labour Movement*, 97–100, 119.

ours.[77] Hobhouse's disdain for 'luxury' meant that he was untroubled by the problem of the possible loss of hitherto unsuspected talents and products (pen and ink being replaced by word processors, for example) which would be outside the scope of experiment, being by definition beyond the knowledge of the experimenters.

Another element of surplus consisted of 'forced gains'. The sale of goods, land-use, capital-use, or labour-power in the various markets are conducted by a series of bargains. In a very large proportion of the bargains one side is notoriously stronger than the other. A sale is thus forced upon conditions which give to one side almost the whole gain of the bargain, leaving to the weaker side only a minimum inducement. The share of the gain of a bargain is a prize to be fought for and can therefore stimulate good work; but it also cherishes 'sinister arts' and in its train comes repeated disorganization of industry—and in particular the deterioration of labour. *Laissez-faire* economists had themselves advocated measures to improve equality of bargaining power, but did not approve of redistribution where inequality remained. In Hobhouse's view it was the task of the state to redress such inequality by redistributive taxation. Where that in turn proved too difficult, then the private holders of predominant power in the market should be simply replaced altogether by the agents of the state.[78]

It was the duty of the person who believed in the efficacy of fact and logic, the man or woman of reason, to attempt to convince other people, not to force them, to take the right path. In *The Rational Good* he set out his ethical theory. In *The Elements of Social Justice* he applied it to social affairs as a 'reasoned ethical basis for political reform'.[79] The person dedicated to the rule of reason had to be ever ready to consider new facts and inter-pretations. But that was not a justification for the self-indulgence of permanent indecision, nor for the abandonment of reason under the banner of reason. Because no one can be certain he is right, it does not follow that everybody's version of the empirical world was just as true as everybody else's, and one ethical code just as valid as any other. 'The duty of having convictions is correlative and

[77] *Liberalism*, 209–10.
[78] See also, e.g., Hobson, *The Economics of Distribution*, 115.
[79] See n. 17; L. T. Hobhouse, *The Elements of Social Justice* (1921) (London, 1949), 14.

supplementary to the duty of tolerance and open-mindedness.'[80]

For the transformation of society Hobhouse believed also in the efficacy of altruism. The creation of altruistic personalities was his goal. 'We want a new spirit in economics—the spirit of mutual help, the sense of the common good. We want each man to feel that his daily task is a service to his kind, and that idleness and anti-social work are a disgrace.'[81] Altruism, however, also provided the *means* to further advances towards an altruistic society. The consent of mankind has always honoured the soldier, Ruskin wrote, not because his trade is slaying (that is true of the cut-throat and the pirate) but because his trade is to be slain. The spirit of the soldier existed in business, where there were already, said Hobhouse, people who would 'rather starve than engage in socially noxious traffic'. It was present in the co-operative movement. Every advance in trade-unionism involved progress in the 'public spirit and intelligence of the workers', and thus added to the available means for the progress towards ethical socialism.[82]

Hobhouse also directed his rational and altruistic appeals directly to possessors of the surplus. His contribution to Gore's *Property: Its Duties and Rights* was explicitly designed to influence them in terms strongly taken up by Tawney. Deriving the distinction from Aristotle, he argued that 'property for use' was indeed an integral element in an ordered life of purposeful activity; but 'property for power' enabled the possessor to deprive another or many others of such a life. The argument of the defenders of property, that it was necessary for self-realization, was thus turned upon themselves; for it was precisely the property that was capable of fulfilling this role that had been stripped from many members of modern society, and all were the poorer in personality for it.[83]

THE STATE AS EQUALIZER

The obverse of a surplus for some was deficient income and wealth for others. Orthodox economics no longer recognized an iron law of wages. Alfred Marshall argued that the erroneous theory that

---

[80] *Labour Movement*, 158. As Weber said at about the same time, it was the 'damned duty' of the reasonable person to make up his mind. (Weber, *From Max Weber*, 145). [81] *Labour Movement*, 75.
[82] Ruskin, *Unto This Last*, 20; *Labour Movement*, 74, 85–6.
[83] See n. 62.

wages must inevitably be forced down to starvation level originated with the Physiocrats, who had based their views on the peculiar circumstances of France in the eighteenth century: there was no universal law of subsistence wages. But there were certainly strong *tendencies* for wages to be pressed to or below subsistence in a capitalist society.[84] Hobhouse followed Marshall precisely. In the first place, the labourer as seller of labour-power exists for a very long time in the 'short-run' situation. As a seller he must take what price he can get, whatever his costs of production (food, clothing, shelter). If a low price—a low wage—is spread over many trades, the supply of the marginal increment can only be withdrawn in the form of the death of the seller. The labourers, in the 'long run' of economic theory, are quite literally 'all dead'.

The seller of labour-power under capitalism has a second peculiarity, already alluded to in the discussion of the forced gain. He is regularly at a vast disadvantage as a bargainer against the employer. The employer can more easily wait for a favourable moment to conclude the bargain. He can more easily pick and choose between sellers of labour-power than can the labourer pick and choose between buyers.[85] There is a third peculiarity. If the price of coal or eggs goes down, the commodity does not deteriorate. But if the price of labour-power goes below a certain level, debility lowers the marginal productivity of the labourer. 'We have in fine one of those cases of cumulative action', Hobhouse writes, 'to which Professor Marshall has carefully drawn attention.' Below that level, the tendency of free competition will be, not to raise the labourer to the level of healthy activity, but to depress him further below it.[86]

There was therefore scope to benefit society in general by raising wages so that they lay within the discoverable limits of benign social effects. One means of doing this was the trade union. By eliminating some of the employer's forced gain, the workman as seller wins a better deal. The employer as buyer also gains through the improvement of the quality of the marginal labourer. This was not enough for Hobhouse. His main interest was in the material conditions not of a physically healthy life only, but of a full life of

---

[84] Marshall, *Principles*, 422. Marshall was concerned about the limitations on self-interest as a prompter to public benefits. See also A. Marshall, *Industry and Trade* (London, 1919).

[85] *Labour Movement*, 109–10.   [86] Ibid. 111.

citizenship. In raising wages towards a level that made such a life possible by acting in concert (with officials appointed to watch the market and thus putting the workman more on a footing of equality in securing the gains of bargaining) unions were fulfilling a vital social need.

But it was uncertain how far the mass of unskilled labour above the bottom tenth of the population would prove themselves capable of forming durable combinations. The promise of the New Unionism of the late 1880s and early 1890s had soon faded, and up to the time of the First World War the outbursts of energy from the unskilled, even when successful, had been spasmodic. Hobhouse was an enthusiast for the Trade Boards for fixing wages in the lowest paid industries, and took a prominent part in their work when they were established. Where the requirements of civilized life could not be obtained by trade union action, he argued, 'they must be secured by means of the deliberate action of the state'. Using figures supplied by Rowntree, Hobhouse calculated that one-third of the eight million men employed in regular work earned less than was necessary for 'full civic life'. Using the figures of Rowntree, Bowley, and Chiozza Money, he calculated that to bring the wages of all workers in Britain to this standard would cost a mere £100 million annually. This would take at most one-third of the surplus. The worker would still have to labour in order to qualify for this minimum. His income remained his, therefore, by right of independent effort. It would now simply include a share (and not even his full rightful share) in the surplus.[87]

Others not in receipt of employment incomes carry out vital tasks for other people. Hobhouse wanted a wage for the widowed or deserted mother. Instead of earning outside the home to the detriment of her children, and eventually of others in the society, she should be paid to keep her home respectable and bring up her children in health and happiness.

There are periods in everyone's life when income cannot come directly from employment. When such periods occur it is not just a matter of whether individuals can or do provide from private insurance or savings for their own old age, sickness, invalidity, or unemployment. For the surplus essentially results from their previous efforts which, along with the unidentifiable contributions

[87] *Liberalism* 205; *Labour Movement*, 32–3, 147.

of countless others, has been privately appropriated. It is available to be reappropriated by the state through taxation. The beneficiaries are then only reclaiming their own share in the social inheritance which is to fall to them as citizens.

Thus old-age pensioners remain free and independent men and women because the state gives them what is theirs by justice: their own portion of 'private property in public funds'. For the normally productive who are unemployed due to temporary incompetence, in the sense that their wage-level is for the time being in excess of their marginal productivity, the state is the means of allocating them part of the surplus in the form of 'definite benefits as a matter of indefeasible right'.[88] This applies also to the temporarily sick. Hobhouse welcomed the state insurance scheme of 1911, but criticized it for being only in part based upon a charge upon the surplus. Upon such resources so provided individuals could and would build according to their own abilities and tastes through such organizations as commercial insurance companies and Friendly Societies. The experience of life, he said, suggests that hope is a better stimulus than fear, and confidence than insecurity.

The handicapped may partly rely on the family, neighbours, and private philanthropy to secure the means for leading as full a life as possible. But here too the doctrine of the surplus led Hobhouse to assign a large role to the state. It is not merely a matter of plugging the gaps left by private effort—all citizens are entitled to their share in the socially created wealth which has temporarily fallen into the hands of particular undeserving individuals. The mentally handicapped would be subject to such degree of tutelar restraint by the state as would be appropriate to the development of their capacity for self-control. The provision should be so conceived as to render the handicapped person as nearly as possible independent, and the costs should be charged to the surplus.

SQUEEZING OUT THE RESIDUUM

The incompetent able-bodied would be the object of the state's control. No one put this view more firmly or influentially than Booth. The social problem lay primarily in the submerged tenth of incompetent labour. 'My idea', he wrote, 'is that these people

[88] *Liberalism*, 209; *Labour Movement*, 91, 139.

should be allowed to live as families in industrial groups, planted wherever land and building materials were cheap—being well housed, well fed and well warmed.' They would be employed from morning to night. They would be taught and trained. A family that built up a positive balance of account (on their admittedly subsidized labour) by hard work and good conduct would be free to return to the open society. But no one would be allowed to live in the open society at below a given standard of living; that would be the only compulsion involved.[89]

Hobhouse followed Booth closely. Not everyone, he argued, can produce the income necessary for even bare physical existence. Those who could not, however, would not be allowed to sell their labour at below cost price on the basis of (in the terminology of the economics of the market) the short run. There would be a wage 'befitting a civilized being'. No fringe of incompetents would be permitted to depress wages generally by bidding themselves into jobs for less. They would be detached from the labour force and dealt with on principles other than the equation of function and reward. They would be treated as a particular class of the infirm, and those who could work would be made to work.[90]

In addition to the incompetents in the above senses there were also the morally defective. Hobhouse's paramount aim was the formation of character through the provision of non-coercive conditions of self-development. Drunkards were, therefore, for him, fit objects of tutelar restraint by the state with the intention of restoring their capacity for the growth of personality under rational self-control.

In the case of certain recalcitrant individuals these conditions were ineffectual, and their character resulted in conduct that threatened the common good. These, the morally uncontrollable, required punitive discipline. The incorrigible idler would be regarded as a social pest. It would be only the incompetent, and not also the idle—of whatever class—who would be allowed to live on the surplus products of other men's industry.[91] The Labour party applied this to the poor in its Unemployed Workmen's Bill (introduced year after year from 1906) which proposed to give

---

[89] Booth, *Life and Labour*, i. 165–7. See also Marshall, *Memorials*, 144; Jones, *Outcast London*, 317–8.
[90] *Labour Movement*, 38.   [91] Ibid. 140.

unemployment authorities permission to enforce, as it said, 'the performance of reasonable work from a wastrel'.[92]

Punitive discipline was also appropriate for the treatment of the declining number who by their conduct put themselves at war with their neighbours. These included the members of Booth's savage semi-criminal class who preferred to be outcasts from society, and sought in some undisturbed sanctuary of the city the 'mutual protection of each other's character of evil'. But, Booth said, their golden age was over; and Hobhouse, too, saw them as a marginal and diminishing problem for his ethical-socialist society. Whether or not punishment did the rich or poor criminal any good was certainly something to be weighed. But also to be weighed was the efficacy of deterrence. The criminal selects himself as the means by which others can be encouraged to be law-abiding, even if the damage to him is great.[93]

Hobhouse, like More, was sometimes carried a long way into language shared by totalitarians. A community of mutually-developing individuals was Hobhouse's ultimate aim: personal liberty was only a means to its realization. The supreme requirements are those of the common good. He insists on perfect freedom in the direction of mental and spiritual development but also the perfect organization of the material basis of society—and perfect personal freedom does not extend to the right to drink when and where you please or even, on occasion, to 'the right to free labour'.[94] Nevertheless, he attacked all authoritarians of his day: Fabians, 'advocates of national efficiency', and all those who wanted to use compulsion as a master key to open all doors. He feared that humane intentions without a vigilant commitment to liberty would end by putting the citizen at the mercy of the inspector and expert. For welfare without liberty, like liberty without equality, was a concept of noble sound but squalid results.

THE SICKNESS OF AN ACQUISITIVE SOCIETY

Would such an ideal ever become a full reality? Hobhouse's rejoinder is that there is no need to answer that question. All that needs concern us is the practical value and immediate promise of existing tendencies as contributions towards it. If anyone claims he

[92] Tracey, *Book of the Labour Party*, i. 170.
[93] Booth, *Life and Labour*, i. 174–5; *Labour Movement*, 158.
[94] *Liberalism*, 178; *Labour Movement*, 154.

can foretell the future, let us in platonic fashion crown him with garlands as the wisest and most far-seeing of men, but promptly ban him as unfit for responsible office.[95] Tawney later said exactly the same.

'Hobhouse was as persistently led by his intellect to hope as by his temperament to despair.'[96] He had reason to take satisfaction throughout his life in the continuing strength of neighbourhood, family, and trade-unionism among the earnest working class, based as they were on the chapel, the co-operative movement, adult education, and Friendly Societies. The rhetoric of some socialist writing continued to be moralistic and inspirational, still carrying to mass audiences the ethical fervour of Green's Oxford. Socialism, wrote Bruce Glasier, 'consists not in getting at all, but in giving; not in being served, but in serving; not in selfishness, but in unselfishness; not in desire to gain a place of bliss for one's self or one's family, but the desire to create an earthly paradise for all'.[97]

Some of the new working-class leaders of local government conformed splendidly to Hobhouse's model of the gentlemanly man and woman: frugal, sober, self-sacrificing, and against all the odds deeply respectful of the Oxford Greats type of learning. Peter Lee was an example of the type, the first chairman of the first ever Labour county council in 1919. He was born in the same year as Hobhouse, 1864, in Duff Heap Row, Trimdon, the son of a miner, and started work underground in the pits as an illiterate boy of ten. At the age of twenty he decided to learn to read and write. When President of the Miners' Federation of Great Britain, he opened his address to the annual conference at Edinburgh with remarks which reflected his acquired culture. 'There is nothing, at least in a poor man's experience, whether bitter or sweet, which can happen to him', he told the assembled miners' delegates, 'but a line of Burns springs to his mouth and gives him courage and comfort if needed. It is like a second Bible.'[98]

To Hobhouse, rival forms of socialism seemed for many years to be diminishing threats to his own preferred political outcomes. The

---

[95] *Labour Movement*, 128.

[96] Clarke, *Liberals and Social Democrats*, 117.

[97] J. B. Glasier, *The Meaning of Socialism* (1919), 2nd edn. (London, 1925). Hobhouse considered that since about 1908 the Labour party represented true Liberalism better than the Liberal party. (S. Collini, *Liberalism and Sociology* (Cambridge, 1979), 24.)

[98] J. Lawson, *Peter Lee* (London, 1936), 25–6.

'wild deep poetry' of socialist Utopianism, the revolutionary threat of the Marxists, and the unlimited state control of bureaucratic socialism seemed to him to be all on the retreat. But in 1917 the Bolshevik Revolution gave renewed impetus to revolutionary Marxism. In the same year the Labour party, already fast growing in affiliated membership, experienced a snub (the so-called 'door-mat incident') ending in the Labour party adopting, for the first time, a party programme. For the programme, Henderson turned to a body of doctrine 'which had been long in decline',[99] Fabianism—the socialism of élite officials which Hobhouse had execrated in *Liberalism*. Emphasis on class in Labour politics, instead of weakening, strengthened. In the 1920s Fascism conquered in Italy, and National Socialism grew in Germany.

In 1913 Hobhouse had written that the impulse to harmony dominated the entire evolution of mind, and that the rationality of the process was the guarantee of its ultimate success. In 1927, not long before his death, he concluded that the conception of human development moving towards a maturity of self-direction could be still legitimately retained. He always insisted on the fact that there had been and might be again 'long ages of stagnation or regression' within the general trend.[100] Nevertheless, he was undoubtedly shaken profoundly by the Great War. While it did not strike 'directly at the foundation of this thought', as his biographers allege, it made an old man of him at the age of fifty.[101] The war had been produced by a generation that had not after all matured further towards greater rationality, altruism, consensual legality, and self-discipline—the virtues of George Eliot's time and his own youth. With Nietzsche and Bergson leading the revolt against reason, conscience, and law, and with syndicalism attacking the same values, the moral world had changed to one more favourably disposed to violence and the exaltation of the human will.[102]

To many of those who survived the war, the moralistic assumptions of Hobhouse's generation seemed laughable. 'The

---

[99] S. H. Beer, *Modern British Politics*, 2nd edn. (London, 1969), 138.

[100] *Development and Purpose* (1913), p. xxix; *Development and Purpose* (1927), p. xxxvi; *Morals in Evolution*, 634.

[101] Hobson and Ginsberg, *Hobhouse*, 91. For Hobhouse and the war see S. Collini, 'Hobhouse, Bosanquet and the State', *Past and Present*, 72 (1976).

[102] Hobhouse admired George Eliot's work because she exalted self-sacrifice as a means to social harmony in this world. (L. T. Hobhouse, *The World in Conflict* (London, 1915), 29, 43–4, 46.)

value of self-sacrifice, the importance of striving to attain an ideal, the belief in progress, and the duties owed by one class to another— all this', Richter writes, 'the younger generation considered to be inflated and diffuse hypocrisy.'[103] Stephen Spender, the son of Harold Spender (Hobhouse's old Oxford friend), described his own generation as one which publicly scorned the imperatives of discipline, purity, and duty.[104] Gilbert Ryle wrote with contempt of the 'philosopher missionaries' of his youth and their 'intermittent rosy visions of some acts of edification and inspiration issuing out of the philanthropically-unbolted doors of our philosophy departments into the homes and hearts of the Common Man'.[105] This is such an accurate sketch of Hobhouse if one is unsympathetic to his objectives that it may be that he was the model for Ryle's despised type. A recent biographer is equally dismissive of Hobhouse's moralizing (and indeed of his whole life's work). Hobhouse's thinking, Collini writes, 'was embedded in a set of assumptions which no longer command our allegiance, and addressed to a range of problems which no longer command our attention'.[106]

In *Liberalism* Hobhouse had expressed the fear that under modern conditions the civic sense was under threat. People might be inclined to take too much for granted what they owed to the community. They might use the personal security and freedom of speech provided them by the state in order to recklessly denounce its works and repudiate its authority. They might assume the right to be in the social system when it suited them, and to emancipate themselves from it when in some particular it did not. The year before his death he felt that his fears were being realized in the 'unmitigated selfishness' of the times.[107]

After the First World War, therefore, his ideals had on balance lost out, at least temporarily. In his worst moments, he said, he felt that there was going to be more machinery and more ugliness.

---

[103] Richter, *Politics of Conscience*, 376.

[104] S. Spender, *World Within World* (London, 1951), 7, 9. A milieu of homosexual hedonism already existed prior to the First World War among Cambridge undergraduates who later became famous and influential. 'Even womanizers pretend to be sods', Keynes wrote to Duncan Grant, 'lest they shouldn't be thought respectable.' (Clarke, *Liberals and Social Democrats*, 132.)

[105] G. Ryle, '50 Years of Philosophers', *Philosophy*, 51 (1976), 386–7. Ryle had seen Hobhouse in action.

[106] Collini, *Liberalism and Sociology*, 253.

[107] *Liberalism*, 150; Hobson and Ginsberg, *Hobhouse*, 69.

Some form of class war would end in the triumph of Fascism, and probably an international war would then destroy urban life. Basically he still felt that what he had to say was worth saying, and that it would be a betrayal of his ideas and ideals to remain silent. A better society had been germinating; what had been, could be. Perhaps he did not express very well the arguments for what was empirically true and ethically valid, he said. Yet it was better for him to put them badly than they should not be put at all.[108] He continued to write. But the final stanzas of Housman's *The Shropshire Lad* must in the end serve also as Hobhouse's epitaph:

> I hoed and trenched and weeded,
> And took my flowers to fair;
> I brought them home unheeded;
> The hue was not the wear.
>
> So up and down I'll sow them
> For lads like me to find,
> When I shall lie below them,
> A dead man out of mind.
>
> And fields will yearly bear them
> As light-leaved spring comes on,
> And luckless lads shall wear them
> When I am dead and gone.[109]

---

[108] Hobson and Ginsberg, *Hobhouse*, 259.
[109] A. E. Housman, *A Shropshire Lad* (1896) (London, 1940), 95.

5

THE LAST SOCIALIST IN EUROPE
George Orwell (1903–1950)

INTRODUCTION

Though Orwell never knew it he had a contemporary at All Souls College, Oxford, who remembered from his youth an aged life-fellow who in turn could remember from his early days having seen Napoleon. Apparently it was the occasional sport of after-dinner conversation to persuade the ancient Georgian to tell the company what sort of man was Napoleon. And the old fellow would begin his discourse with the remark, 'Well, you could tell at a glance that he was not a Varsity man'.

The same can be well said in any introduction to the writings of George Orwell. He fashioned for himself a style of simple and direct prose which gives him a high place among the masters of the mother tongue. He thus built a defensive landmark of plain meaning in the menacing twentieth-century swamp of polysyllables, evasions, and jargon of political literature. Geroge Orwell is the outstanding modern exemplar of the virtues which oppose pedantry and portentousness in political science.

We shall treat Orwell here in the way that we discuss others, i.e. in the manner of Weber's *verstehende Soziologie*. Just as we asked of More, Cobbett, and Hobhouse, so we shall again put the question, what were his intentions? What sort of world, physical, social, and cultural, did he believe he was operating in and on? What means did he believe were efficacious to realize his ideals? And what results emerged from his efforts?

Our first unqualified answer must be that his intention was to promote 'common decency' as a way of life. He called this way of life socialism and, like Tawney, he saw the result not as a permanent and mechanical state of social virtue but as a set of personal and public moral principles to be constantly struggled for and defended against tendencies towards cruelty and tyranny. He was, like Charles Dickens whom he much admired, a moralist rather than a political philosopher or social engineer. His guiding end of common humanity was not deduced from academic political theory. It was the outcome of an unremitting drive towards personal autonomy and of observation of the ideal elements of the culture of the traditional working class. The labour leaders Thomas Burt and Peter Lee exemplified the citizens of the country Orwell wanted to create. Decency prescribes no exact and detailed political programme: it is a general touchstone for all personal conduct in any political order. Where it becomes the dominant culture the resultant political order will be socialist, meaning a manifestation of the radical tradition we describe in this book. Decency is first and foremost a personal ethic: in concert with others it becomes a moral culture: as expressed in organized politics it makes a socialist country.

Orwell's Britain was not, but could become, such a country. His appraisal of the state of affairs—the initial conditions from which he set out to achieve his ends—contained elements of both hope and despair. He saw around him a physical world of marvellous beauty (he loved the surface of the earth, especially that of rural England). Now it was threatened by the machine age. He also saw a social world of incalculable human potential. Now it was threatened by totalitarianism, whether communist or fascist or some combination of the two. He saw Britain as a family 'with the wrong members in charge'. He identified a cultural inheritance of liberalism in the sense of love of freedom and the rule of law. He believed in 'the English genius' as that of a people with unfanatical and inarticulate conviction that the individual conscience was the final identifier and arbiter of good and evil.

The contemporary ideological orthodoxies of Marxism, Fascism, and economic liberalism were all in effect enemies of the truth, subverters of decency, and instruments of oppression. The hope for the future lay in the development of the Labour party, socialist planning, and above all an autonomous, free, intelligent democracy of citizens whose political wisdom descended more from the experience of the working class than from the theories and enthusiasms of the middle-class intelligentsia.

Hope and despair still contended for possession of Orwell's soul at the end of his days. He lived to see a tired but triumphant Labour party embark, as the Attlee government, on reforms that he had himself vigorously advocated during the Second World War. He was an enthusiastic Labour party supporter but, true to his vocation, a candidly critical one. Hope, he might well have insisted, is impossible without doubt; and his doubts were continually renewed out of the nature of his socialism—the conviction that no social institution, including the socialist planning he persistently recommended, could achieve the desired socialist end unless continually driven forward by the personal moral commitment and the honest criticism of informed citizens. Before his life was cut short and his efforts exhausted by tuberculosis his attention was fixed on what he saw as 'the last man in Europe' (the alternative and, we think, better title of *Nineteen Eighty-Four*) who was really the last socialist in Europe in the sense of the ordinary citizen whose freedoms and decencies, if not vigorously defended, could be defeated and obliterated from history by the development of three totalitarian super-states in stable conflict with each other.

ANTECEDENTS AND AIMS

The tradition of ethical socialism requires of all its adherents an unusual integrity of private and public life. Perhaps its central feature is a belief that, in contemporary phrasing, agency is prior to structure, that individual will is indispensable to the creation of a political commonwealth. Orwell was never far from preoccupation with maintaining personal moral integrity at the same time as political engagement. These two sets of rights and duties defined for him his vocation as a writer.

In politics one can never do more than decide which of two evils is the lesser, and there are some situations from which one can only escape by acting like a devil or a lunatic. War, for example, may be necessary, but it is certainly not right or sane. Even a general election is not exactly a pleasant or edifying spectacle. If you have to take part in such things—and I think you do have to, unless you are armoured by old age or stupidity or hypocrisy—then you also have to keep part of yourself inviolate. For most people the problem does not arise in the same form, because their lives are split already. They are truly alive only in their leisure hours, and there is no emotional connection between their work and their political activities. Nor are they generally asked, in the name of political loyalty, to debase themselves as workers. The artist, and especially the writer, is asked just that—in fact, it is the only thing that politicians ever ask of him. If he refuses, that does not mean that he is condemned to inactivity. One half of him, which in a sense is the whole of him, can act as resolutely, even as violently if need be, as anyone else. But his writings, in so far as they have any value, will always be the product of the saner self that stands aside, records the things that are done and admits their necessity, but refuses to be deceived as to their true nature.[1]

Such a man and such a writer was George Orwell.

ERIC BLAIR AND GEORGE ORWELL

How then was such a man formed? How did he join the ethical-socialist tradition? We shall argue that England made him: but, again like Tawney, he was not born in England. They were both children of the Empire but they both felt a deep love of country in conjunction with a passionate rejection of imperialism. For Orwell this was expressed not only in engaging essays on the common toad, in defence of English cooking or umpteen different ways of making tea but also in a sustained derision towards the intelligentsia of his day—'bearded fruit-juice drinkers'—whose nationalism had been transferred elsewhere, typically to Moscow, and whose common consistency was an always predictable disloyalty to Britain. The transformation of Eric Blair into George Orwell turned an expatriate into a patriot, a child of imperial Britain into a man of the British people.

Orwell first drew breath on 25 June 1903 at Motihari in Bengal where his father was an agent of the opium department of the government of India. Name in his case was more important than place for he was born Eric Arthur Blair. Name and place together ascribed a *persona* which was later transmuted into the loyal if eccentric champion of a different England. Eric Blair inherited a social position in the English imperial administrative class. He descended from colonial civil servants, anglican priests, and merchants on both sides of his family. His paternal grandfather was the last son of a rich and aristocratically connected family (he was a godson and cousin of the Earl of Westmorland). He was ordained into the Church of England in 1839 in Calcutta, illustrating Cobbett's jibe that the empire was 'a system of outdoor relief for the indigent sons of the aristocracy'.[2] He returned to England in 1854 to become a vicar in Dorset. In the next generation his son

---

[1] G. Orwell, *Collected Essays, Journalism and Letters*, ed. S. Orwell and I. Angus, (Harmondsworth, 1970), iv. 469–70.
[2] B. Crick, *George Orwell: A Life* (Harmondsworth, 1982), 46.

Richard, Eric's father, chose to enter the secular services rather than the Church. These were the two broad alternative professional careers for men born into what Orwell later dubbed the lower-upper-middle class.

Richard Blair belonged to what was probably the last generation of boys who could enter imperial administration without attending a 'public' school. In the fourth quarter of the nineteenth century the upbringing and career for this class—typically birth in an imperial outpost, schooling outside the normal domesticities in a boarding school, and return to the Empire through the military, administrative, or clerical professions—became a set pattern into which Eric Blair was conventionally launched and habituated during his first twenty-five years. He was sent to a private preparatory school in Sussex at the age of eight until he was thirteen and then on to Eton for four and a half years via a term at Wellington. And thence, not yet out of his teens, back to the Indian Imperial Police in 1922 to be trained in Burma.

Thus Eric Blair was, in any social and statistical sense, an extraordinary English man. The vast majority of those at the beginning of the twentieth century with him in England were in fact born in England and into the familistic culture of the English working class. He was born overseas and never underwent the normal experiences of English family life. He hardly saw his father before the latter retired in 1912. He spent most of his childhood in the peculiar institutional life of the dormitory houses of schools designed to bring up the metropolitan and imperial classes. His was an upbringing not in a family or even a nation so much as in a ruling-class network in which he was a subordinate rather than a dominant member.

Raymond Williams[3] puts great emphasis on the background we have described, atypical as to class and family, so as to dramatize the translation of identity from Eric Blair to George Orwell. Williams makes on the one hand a distinction between the imperial and the domestic (England in the context of Empire and England as a parochial island); on the other hand he distinguishes between the ruling class and the working class. Eric Blair belonged to the imperial ruling class. He could have moved in three possible directions. He could have gone native in Burma (imperial working

---

[3] R. Williams, *Orwell* (London, 1971).

class). He could have rejected the Empire but remained in the dominant class as a don or teacher or writer or in some other island-based profession (domestic ruling class). In fact Orwell emerged pseudonymously out of excursions into the domestic working class. As V. S. Pritchett put it, 'he might be described as a writer who has "gone native" in his own country'.[4]

From the time he returned on leave from Burma in 1927, Blair sought a life as a writer and affiliation with the exploited and the ordinary, away from imperialism and from the ruling class. He spent time in spikes, lodging houses, and hotel kitchens, living with tramps and hop pickers, washing dishes. Out of it came his *Down and Out in Paris and London* (perhaps better described under its French title, *La Vache enragée*). Discussing its publication with his agent in 1932, he asked for it to be published under a pseudonym and gave a list which included his preference for George Orwell— the reference being to a river in Suffolk near his parents' home. Blair the person continued in his family, his marriage, and some of his literary and professional connections. But George Orwell the writer, journalist, and developing political moralist was now established. How far Orwell is to be 'explained' by Blair's desperate search for identity with an acceptable family, class, and nation is probably an unanswerable question. Nor need it detain us, for Orwell's arguments in favour of a radical and pessimistic socialism must stand on their own merits, not on his personal vicissitudes.

ORWELL'S SOCIALISM

During the 1930s Orwell completed his self-tutelage as a socialist. By the time he returned from Barcelona and the Spanish Civil War in 1937—a decade, that is, after resigning from the Burma police— his political and moral character was mature. And from the mid-1930s he was able to make a meagre living by his writing, augmented by a bit of shop-keeping and growing vegetables. He had committed himself to the cause of the ordinary working people of England. He was not so unrealistic or simple-minded as to suppose that 'going native' made him personally a proletarian. Notice, for example, his description of an incident on entering 'the spike' in 1931:

[4] G. Phelps (ed.), *Living Writers* (London, 1947).

The terrible Tramp Major met us at the door and herded us into the bathroom to be stripped and searched. He was a gruff, soldierly man of forty, who gave the tramps no more ceremony than sheep at the dipping-pond, shoving them this way and that and shouting oaths in their faces. But when he came to myself, he looked hard at me, and said: 'You are a gentleman?' 'I suppose so,' I said. He gave me another long look. 'Well that's bloody bad luck, guv'nor,' he said, 'that's bloody bad luck, that is.' And thereafter he took it into his head to treat me with compassion, even with a kind of respect.[5]

Moreover, Orwell remained aware of his early training in class attitudes. The lower classes were ignorant, stupid, sub-human, and they stank. After a decade of proletarian experience from the hop fields of Kent through Yorkshire coalfields and the Spanish trenches, he was derisory towards middle-class illusions about the working class. He wrote to Jack Common (his proletarian friend) in 1936 as follows: 'Yes, this business of class-breaking is a bugger. The trouble is that the socialist bourgeoisie, most of whom give me the creeps, will not be realistic and admit that there are a lot of working-class habits which they don't like and don't want to adopt. E.g. the typical middle-class socialist not only doesn't eat with his knife but is still slightly horrified by seeing a working man do so. And then so many of them are the sort of eunuch type with a vegetarian smell who go about spreading sweetness and light and have at the back of their minds a vision of the working class all T. T. [tuberculin tested], well washed behind the ears, readers of Edward Carpenter or some other pious sodomite and talking with B.B.C. accents.'[6]

Orwell claimed, somewhat disingenuously, to have no knowledge of socialist theories before he set out on the road to Wigan Pier in 1936 or even before he went to Spain. Writing in 1937 he records what he learned from his anarchist comrades in Barcelona about the spirit or mystique of socialism. 'For several months large blocks of people believed that all men are equal and were able to act on their belief. The result was a feeling of liberation and hope that is difficult to conceive in our money-tainted . . . atmosphere.' He illustrated this from *Red Spanish Note Book* by Mary Lowe and Juan Brea: a bootblack refusing a tip, a notice in the brothels saying, 'please treat the women as comrades', to show that in

---

[5] Orwell, *Collected Essays*, i. 59.   [6] Ibid. i. 245.

Barcelona at that time human beings were 'trying to behave as human beings and not as cogs in the capitalist machine. No-one who was in Spain during the months when people still believed in the revolution will ever forget that strange and moving experience. It has left something behind that no dictatorship, not even Franco's, will be able to efface.'[7]

For a brief interlude Orwell had seen the socialist vision of people bound together in a shared life of optimally balanced freedom and equality; a life of dignity and purposefulness for each individual granted by the goodwill of all; a life not determined by material circumstance nor dominated by selfish scramble under conditions of scarcity.

One had been in a community where hope was more normal than apathy or cynicism, where the word 'comrade' stood for comradeship and not, as in most countries, for humbug. One had breathed the air of equality. I am well aware that it is now the fashion to deny that socialism has anything to do with equality. In every country in the world a huge tribe of party-hacks and sleek little professors are busy 'proving' that socialism means no more than a planned state-capitalism with the grab-motive left intact. But fortunately there also exists a vision of socialism quite different from this. The thing that attracts ordinary men to socialism and makes them willing to risk their skins for it, the 'mystique' of socialism is the idea of equality; to the vast majority of people socialism means a classless society, or it means nothing at all.[8]

To the experience of the Barcelona mystique must also be added the experience of Paris, London, and Wigan in which Orwell noticed that he never met a genuine working man who accepted Marxism. Orwell was thus fixed in the radical tradition as an ethical socialist. He knew that socialism was a way of life, a personal moral code governed by the individual conscience following self-evident rules of good conduct towards others. He had picked up a few marxist bad habits of thought such as the idea that pacifists were 'objectively' pro-fascist because they opposed war against Hitler and Mussolini. But this kind of distorted perception was unusual and transient in him. By the mid-1940s he had the full measure of such evasive moral sophistries. He could deal sharply with Professor Bernal who had written in 1945 that

[7] Ibid. i. 321.
[8] *Penguin Complete Longer Non-fiction of George Orwell* (Harmondsworth, 1983), 375–6.

'many of the basic virtues—truthfulness and good fellowship—are, of course, as old as humanity and need no changing, *but those based on excessive concern with individual rectitude need re-orienting in the direction of social responsibility*'.[9] Orwell, translating into plain English, insists that the passage emphasized 'means that public spirit and common decency pull in opposite directions; while the paragraph as a whole means that we must alter our conception of right and wrong from year to year, and if necessary from minute to minute'.[10] He would have none of it. Once given the assurance of honest observation as the method of access to individual conscience and given further the tempering of absolute values by a readiness to allow kindness to override rigid rectitude and persuasion to take precedence over compulsion, then honest and decent individuals would make a society of justice, of liberty, and of equality—in short a socialist society.

ORWELL AND SOCIOLOGICAL THEORY

'Not a Varsity man.' The ethical-socialist tradition owes more to the experience of work and politics than to the academy. Nevertheless most of the writers we discuss belonged self-consciously to a philosophical or political school of thought with systematic scholarly expression. Thomas More was an Oxford graduate and a theologian as well as Henry VIII's Chancellor. Tawney, T. H. Marshall, and L. T. Hobhouse all held university chairs if somewhat eccentrically. In this context Orwell is more directly descended from Cobbett than from the academic succession, though even in Cobbett's case it must be noted that the intelligentsia and the organization of science and letters were still on a scale small enough to be encompassed competently by all those who claimed to advance general views on the constitution of society. V. S. Pritchett, reviewing *The Road to Wigan Pier*, complimented Orwell by placing him in the line of distinguished British pamphleteers and compared him with Swift and Cobbett. Swift was (along with Dickens, Samuel Butler, Flaubert, and D. H. Lawrence) one of Orwell's acknowledged heroes. Cobbett seems not to have engaged his attention. Yet, however unconsciously, the inherited *Geist*, including fierce personal independence, the love of rural tradition, and a radical patriotism, is remarkable. What is

[9] Orwell, *Collected Essays*, iv. 185–6.   [10] Ibid. iv.

difficult for us in codifying Orwell's thought by comparison with that of Hobhouse or T. H. Marshall is that Orwell never systematically read or discussed his intellectual forebears.

Bernard Crick tells us that there is nothing in the papers he left behind or in the papers he possessed to indicate that he ever read the standard marxist sources systematically. He absorbed his knowledge of marxist theory out of the air and the conversation of endless political meetings and encounters. He became aware of R. H. Tawney only after he had written *The Road to Wigan Pier*. He knew about Sidney and Beatrice Webb but again through conversation, some of it no doubt with Malcolm Muggeridge. He had not read G. D. H. Cole. He knew H. G. Wells's novels and had absorbed and admired the sociological essays as well as the novels of D. H. Lawrence. But he cannot be discussed in the ordinary academic way. Like the larger radical tradition his own learning was autodidactic and from an oral tradition fortified by direct experience and personal moral reflection. He was against Shaw and the Webbs because they were authoritarians and he rejected Wells as one who equated socialism with order and efficiency. Orwell himself was a Cobbettian radical. He would have sided with Wilkes against Samuel Johnson, with libertarians and against authoritarians everywhere.

Orwell was Cobbettian also in his willingness to indulge in wild generalizing disparagement of social stereotypes even though his view was based on passionately felt and honestly reported personal experience. For example he was, rightly, taken to task by Victor Gollancz (in a foreword to *The Road to Wigan Pier*, 1937) for suggesting that almost every socialist is a crank, i.e. 'anyone holding opinions not held by the majority—for instance, any feminist, pacifist, vegetarian or advocate of birth control'. Orwell had permitted himself to be carried away by his own rhetoric to the point of writing that 'one sometimes gets the impression that the mere words "socialism" and "communism" draw towards them with magnetic force every fruit-juice drinker, nudist, sandal wearer, sex-maniac, Quaker, "nature cure" quack, pacifist and feminist in England'. This tendency in Orwell is undeniable. Raymond Williams points to the contradiction between the sneering labels ('little fat men', 'dull, empty windbags', 'that dreary tribe of high-minded women') and Orwell's equally passionate devotion to plain words and accurate description.

Zeal for action on behalf of a socialist ideal frequently led Orwell, whether as writer or soldier, into emotional evaluation of both the allies and the enemies of the socialist movement. At the same time his intellectual interests, though formally unschooled, played with enthusiastic frequency over the general problems of social philosophy which must challenge anyone, socialist or anti-socialist, who seeks either to justify or to condemn or to change the existing social order. As we pointed out in Chapter 1, the early socialists (English and French) formulated theories of human nature so as to establish the possibility of socialism, and theories of history so as to demonstrate the possibility or even inevitability of its genesis.

Orwell, too, though he nowhere discusses those like Marx, Thompson, Owen, Proudhon, Saint-Simon, or Fourier, from whom he descends, can be theoretically placed in the socialist tradition of thought. He, like them and unlike Hobbes or Locke, was acutely aware of a place in history. He believed that the war against Fascism made an English revolution in the direction of socialism both possible and urgent. He shared with the early socialists a distrust of the bureaucratic state: but he had inherited from the New Liberals, and to some extent from the Marxists, a belief that the control of production was a necessary state function under socialism. He shared too with the early socialists a dislike of violence, despite his strictures on many contemporary pacifists and his realistic appraisal of the armed threat from Nazi Germany. His preference and his optimism were rooted in an admiration for the blend of gentleness, courage, and anti-militarism which he saw as the deep grain of English culture, explaining both hypocrisy about the Empire and stubborn defence of the individual against authority. He is close to Owen, Thompson, Fourier, and Saint-Simon and distinguished from Marx in rejecting the idea that the ills of society could be purged by violence.

Finally, he again balanced hope and despair in his view of the universals of human nature. While claiming that socialists were all unfairly assumed to believe in the perfectibility of man, he dismissed the stock argument of pessimists that people in their original sinfulness could never be made virtuous by Act of Parliament. His grounds were in part 'materialistic'. Socialism would ease scarcity. But greed for wealth was not a permanent human attribute. It would disappear with the abolition of poverty.

'We are selfish in economic matters because we all live in terror of poverty. But when a commodity is not scarce, no-one tries to grab more than his fair share of it.'[11] This is a moment of optimism (in 1944) which was to be put to severe test, not so much in the austerities of the immediate post-war years, but in the 'revolution of rising expectations', after Orwell's death, in the 1950s and 1960s. He dismissed the socialist illusion that material progress would solve all moral issues. He knew the paradox that people with full bellies rather than empty bellies were confronted with more difficult problems about the meaning and purpose of life. He recognized the problem of social order under socialism and had pointed to it during the war as a consequence of class inequality. In other words, demand and supply, consumption and production, could only be brought into consensual equilibrium through a just distribution of the fruits of labour, that is, in a classless society.

HIS ANALYSIS OF ENGLAND

Orwell's analysis of the initial conditions from which he had to start in pursuit of the social aims he espoused was never an exercise of academic detachment. We must now review his diagnosis of what his predecessors called 'the condition of England' knowing that his commitment partly influenced the aspects of life to which he gave selective attention. The political and social scene changed as the century advanced to its middle point. Orwell had lived from the Edwardian autumn of British imperialism through the slaughter of the First World War, the years of slump at home and the encircling threat of Fascism and Communism abroad. He had experienced the renewed promise for socialist patriots like himself of the Second World War which might be turned into a peaceful social-democratic revolution in England and even a united federation of democratic-socialist states in Europe.

As the scene shifted Orwell's analysis was adapted. He had begun as the repatriated Burmese policeman sensitive to imperial exploitation and seeking an English social identity with the oppressed. He became an anti-Fascist and Independent Labour party revolutionary. As a mature democratic socialist he saw hope for a peaceful

---

[11] Ibid. iii. 222.

political transformation by a new and enlarging class of industrial workers by hand and by brain. But he also developed a fear of a new age of tyranny under the heel of a political class—more likely to be called communist than fascist—using control of communication and the state apparatus to eliminate freedom and even able, through media technology, to control the future by, to an unprecedented degree, controlling the past. For Orwell the enemy was always both to the Right and the Left. The analysis starts in other words from Orwell's classic essay on English social structure *The Lion and the Unicorn* written in the aftermath of Dunkirk, and his *Homage to Catalonia* written in 1938 after the disaster of fascist and communist intrusion into Republican Spain. It then moves through his many essays, pamphlets, broadcasts, reviews, and columns in *Tribune* during the war, setting out both diagnoses and prescriptions for an English socialist future. Towards the end, in *Animal Farm* (1945) and *Nineteen Eighty-Four* (1949), he produced his vivid allegories of the threats to democratic socialism in the past and in the future.

There are two continuing threads running through Orwell's social analysis: class inequality, which Tawney had labelled England's 'hereditary curse', and patriotism, of which we may claim that Orwell is the most illuminating commentator since Cobbett. It is in the interplay of these twin staples of British economy, polity, and culture that Orwell finds his distinctive explanation of social change and his prescriptions and proscriptions for advance towards his version of the New Jerusalem.

We have already seen that George Orwell was committed to the profession of writing and saw himself as living in a period in which the plain duty of a writer was to use plain prose to further the proletarian cause. He tried without cease to link the method to the aim. On the one hand 'so long as I remain alive and well I shall continue to feel strongly about prose style, to love the surface of the earth, and to take pleasure in solid objects and scraps of useless information. The job is to reconcile my ingrained likes and dislikes with the essentially public, non-individual activities that this age forces on all of us.' On the other hand 'every line of serious work that I have written since 1936 has been written, directly or indirectly, *against* totalitarianism and *for* democratic socialism, as I understand it. It seems to me nonsense, in a period like our own, to think that one can avoid writing of such subjects. Everyone writes of them in one guise or another. It is simply a question of which side one takes . . .'[12]

Orwell identified with the working class: he tried to contribute to 'proletarian writing' but he did not see this as a new and permanently different type of literature; 'it is founded on the revolt against capitalism, and capitalism is disappearing'.[13] The advent of socialism would mean the end of class. He maintained that the class distinctions in a country like England were so unreal that they could not last much longer. Before the First World War or even before the Second World War a factory worker and a small professional man, for instance, were very different kinds of class creature. 'Nowadays they are very much alike, though they may not realise it. They see the same films and they listen to the same radio programmes, and they wear very similar clothes and live in very similar houses. What used to be called a proletarian—what Marx would have meant by a proletarian—only exists now in the heavy industries and on the land.'[14] This was Orwell broadcasting in 1940.

The Stalin–Hitler treaty and the Second World War had shifted Orwell's perception. In September 1938 he had written, in criticism of Franz Borkenau's *The Communist International*, that he did not believe in 'an orderly reconstruction through the cooperation of all classes'. He did not believe that a man with fifty thousand pounds a year and a man with fifteen shillings a week could or would co-operate. 'The nature of their relationship is quite simply, that the one is robbing the other, and there is no reason to think that the robber will suddenly turn over a new leaf. It would seem, therefore, that if the problems of western capitalism are to be solved, it will have to be through a third alternative, a movement which is genuinely revolutionary, i.e. willing to make drastic changes and to use violence if necessary, but which does not lose touch, as communism and fascism have done, with the essential values of democracy.'[15]

Orwell's identification with writing for the working class as a revolutionary socialist was therefore complex and contextual. He shifted his responses in intelligent reaction to political events. He joined the Independent Labour party in 1938 on the basis of his experience of imperialism in Burma, of poverty and unemployment

---

[12] Ibid. i. 128.   [13] Ibid. i. 257.   [14] Ibid. i. 256.
[15] Ibid. i. 388.

in Britain, and of Fascism and Communism in Spain, believing at that time that the ILP was the only British party aiming at what he regarded as socialism. But even then he never intended to imprison himself in a fixed party-political position. 'I do not mean that I have lost all faith in the Labour Party. My most earnest hope is that the Labour Party will win a clear majority in the next General Election. But we know what the history of the Labour Party has been, and we know the terrible temptation of the present moment—the temptation to fling every principle overboard in order to prepare for an imperialist war. It is vitally necessary that there should be in existence some body of people who can be depended on, even in the face of persecution, not to compromise their socialist principles.'[16]

In an autobiographical note written in April 1940, Orwell recorded the 'horror of politics' given him by his Spanish experience and what he subsequently learned of the workings of left-wing political parties. He left the ILP at the beginning of the Second World War because 'they were talking nonsense and proposing a line of policy that could only make things easier for Hitler'. A writer, he believed, could only remain honest by avoiding party labels. But Orwell was none the less an increasingly committed man of the Left. Within a couple of years his view had been crucially shifted by the outbreak of war with Germany. The English revolution had begun, though characteristically sleepily and unwillingly. English socialism had failed because of the timid reformism of the Labour party, the transfer of nationalism abroad by the intelligentsia and the stupidity of the rentier upper class.

Nevertheless capitalism had failed still more conspicuously— physically debunked by Nazism which had constructed the greatest military machine the world had ever known by instituting state planning to that end. Capitalism did not work. We could not win the war against Fascism 'without introducing socialism, nor establish socialism without winning the war'. England could not survive with its present social structure. Orwell was clear what was needed: 'A socialist movement which can swing the mass of the people behind it, drive the pro-Fascists out of positions of control, wipe out the grosser injustices and let the working class see that they have something to fight for, win over the middle classes instead of antagonising them, produce a workable imperial policy

[16] Ibid. i. 374.

instead of a mixture of humbug and utopianism, bring patriotism and intelligence into partnership—for the first time, a movement of such a kind becomes possible.'[17]

War had turned socialism from a theoretical end into a practical policy. War had in part sharpened class resentments. Orwell was biting in his scorn of advertisements for butlers and domestic servants while ordinary families were bombed into homelessness. Yet more important, war, especially total war, was a class solvent, facilitating or necessitating such elements of siege socialism as rationing, billeting of evacuees, or the communal use of the Underground as air raid shelters.

THE NATION AS FAMILY

Orwell, or at least Orwell the revolutionary socialist, believed in the inevitability of class antagonism. But he equally believed in the more profound relationship of emotional unity of the nation. In the final analysis of British society, and not only in the desperation of a war almost lost, he gave priority and dominance to national feeling over class consciousness as the paramount force for collective response to collective danger. By comparison with patriotism, Christianity or international socialism are 'as weak as straw'.[18]

In *The Lion and the Unicorn* Orwell subjects his own interpretation of English culture to extended scepticism. Is not England notoriously two nations, the rich and the poor? And were there not other nations or races in the Welsh or the Scots or the Ulstermen? He readily concedes the reality, subjective in the case of regions, both objective and subjective in the case of classes, of distinct differences. But, he insists, these differences fade away the moment that any two Britons are confronted by a European.

And even the distinction between rich and poor dwindles somewhat when one regards the nation from the outside. There is no question about the inequality of wealth in England. It is grosser than in any European country, and you have only to look down the nearest street to see it. Economically, England is certainly two nations, if not three or four. But at the same time the vast majority of the people *feel* themselves to be a single nation and are conscious of resembling one another more than they resemble foreigners.

[17] 'The Lion and the Unicorn' (1941), Ibid. ii. 117.
[18] Ibid. ii. 78.

Patriotism is usually stronger than class-hatred, and always stronger than any kind of internationalism. . . .

In England patriotism takes different forms in different classes but it runs like a connecting thread through nearly all of them.

England is not the jewelled isle of Shakespeare's much-quoted passage, nor is it the inferno depicted by Dr. Goebbels. More than either it resembles a family, a rather stuffy Victorian family, with not many black sheep in it but with all its cupboards bursting with skeletons. It has rich relations who have to be kow-towed to and poor relations who are horribly sat upon, and there is a deep conspiracy of silence about the source of the family income. It is a family in which the young are generally thwarted and most of the power is in the hands of irresponsible uncles and bedridden aunts. Still, it is a family. It has its private language and its common memories, and at the approach of an enemy it closes its ranks. A family with the wrong members in control—that, perhaps, is as near as one can come to describing England in a phrase.[19]

ORWELL'S CLASS THEORY

The metaphor of the family is the one which enabled Orwell to reconcile his revolutionary marxist perceptions with his appreciation of the deep-rooted British tradition of individualism combined with patriotism. His writing shows a notable shift of emphasis on to these forces of fusion rather than fission in the period after Dunkirk. The commonplace of sociology that external threat diminishes internal division is here heavily applied to assert that the emotional unity of the nation surmounted the class antagonisms of the first capitalist-industrial nation.

Raymond Williams is hostile in his rejection, claiming that Orwell thereby formulated a new mythology of England and trivialized into family quarrels what were in reality the deep structural contradictions and antagonisms of a capitalist society. Williams rejects Orwell's view as a special one which remained influential right through to the Labour governments of the 1960s. 'The old system, with its aristocratic and parvenu stupidities, is seen as a top layer, to be replaced with "new blood, new men, new ideas". The spread of the middle class is seen as having made the old class analysis almost obsolete, and the working class anyway is believed to be rapidly acquiring middle-class habits and ideas. The ruling class is seen as having become mere owners, their work done

[19] Ibid. ii. 84, 88.

for them by managers and technicians. All that is then needed, it seems, is for all the decent members of the family—middle class and working class alike, to get rid of the outdated old fools in charge.' Williams prefers a more full-blooded marxist analysis. He seizes on the weakness of Orwell's description of the ruling class. To argue as Orwell did that the privileges of the bourgeoisie and the aristocracy had long ceased to be justifiable presupposed an original justification 'when the aristocracy was not bumbling and stupid but able, daring, and ruthless'.[20] For Williams this is an illusory rhetoric 'which in its sentimental and indulgent underestimate has always weakened the British Left'.

The difference of view expressed here brings us to the centre of the division between revolutionary and reformist socialism. Orwell was in the end a subscriber to the idea of transformation by piecemeal social engineering rather than violent revolution. Revolution for him was at the level of ideas: action was reformist.

Orwell's class analysis is commonsensical rather than theoretical. Certainly he never systematically read the sociological literature. Some of his ideas about the impotence of the dominant class seem to derive from D. H. Lawrence. In Britain 'an entirely functionless class, living on money that was invested they hardly knew where . . . they were simply parasites, less useful to society than his fleas are to a dog'.[21] Or in looking back on H. G. Wells's *The Sleeper Awakes* and Jack London's *The Iron Heel*, he makes the generalization that societies with hedonistic élites do not survive and refers to Aldous Huxley's *Brave New World*: 'No society of that kind would last more than a couple of generations, because a ruling class which thought principally in terms of a "good time" would soon lose its vitality. A ruling class has got to have a strict morality, a quasi-religious belief in itself, a mystique.'[22]

Why then was the effete upper stratum not replaced? Orwell thought that by 1930 millions were aware of its functionlessness. But he advances the dubious explanation that the upper class survived through the only escape available to them—*stupidity*. 'They could keep society in its existing shape only by being *unable* to grasp that any improvement was possible. Difficult though this was, they achieved it, largely by fixing their eyes on the past and

---

[20] Williams, *Orwell*, 26.
[21] Orwell, *Collected Essays*, ii. 90.
[22] Ibid. ii. 46.

refusing to notice the changes that were going on round them.'[23]

As an explanation of the continuity of power and advantage this can hardly suffice. Yet Orwell's refusal to substitute a marxist analysis cannot on that ground be condemned. His sociological instinct is sound in that the coexistence of inequality and patriotism and even the possible prospect of a socialist Britain could not be encompassed within the marxist framework of thought.

Moreover the concept of motivated stupidity or trained incapacity does illuminate some aspects of the history of stratification in Britain. For example it is true that certain regiments in the Army were traditional preserves for upper-class sons and comprehensively incompetent because prepared always to fight the previous war. But, as Orwell remarks,[24] the Navy had only partially and the Air Force had hardly at all been drawn within the ruling-class orbit: and both services had a history of high competence in the hands of men typically drawn by merit from the less-advantaged classes.

The underlying conception, which is at once powerful and difficult to assimilate into the language of political science, is his idea of decency. Orwell is always implicitly searching for a definition of the conditions under which decency can triumph over class interests. On occasion he despairs: 'it would seem that what you get over and over again is a movement of the proletariat which is promptly canalized and betrayed by astute people at the top, and then the growth of a new governing class. The one thing that never arrives is equality. The mass of the people never get the chance to bring their innate decency into the control of affairs, so that one is almost driven to the cynical thought that men are only decent when they are powerless.'[25] On other occasions he is more cheerful. For example he was struck by an encounter in 1930 in which the district magistrate of Rangoon had to try Sen Gupta, one of the leaders of the Congress Party and at that time Mayor of Calcutta. The imperialist judge faced the Indian Nationalist and gave a sentence of ten days' imprisonment. 'Afterwards the two men were able to meet privately and talk the affair over. The description of the Indian and the Englishman meeting in perfect amity, each fully aware of the other's motives, each regarding the other as an honourable man and yet, in the last resort, as an enemy, is strangely

[23] Ibid.   [24] Ibid. ii. 91.
[25] Review of Jack Common's *The Freedom of the Streets* in *New English Weekly*, 16 June 1938, Ibid. i. 372.

moving and makes one wish that politics nearer home could be conducted in an equally decent spirit.'[26]

Orwell's class analysis is also weak because, in academic terms, it is confined to status analysis. He does not in other words address seriously the problem of class 'objectively' as the outcome of market relations. To him in his time the problem of economic classes was easily soluble. All people of good will, he thought, knew perfectly well that class could be eliminated. 'The world, potentially at least, is immensely rich; develop it as it might be developed and we could all live like princes, supposing that we wanted to.' At no point in his writings does the analysis of class in relation to economic scarcity go any further. His interest is almost exclusively in what he calls the social side of the question, i.e. status attitudes. Here his sophistication is great and includes an observation which has since been given great emphasis by writers like Raymond Williams, that working-class status forms the common people into communities which are forced to live to some extent against the existing dominant order. They have their own distinctive values as well as those they may share with the dominant classes.

Orwell fully appreciated the obstacles to classlessness and, as he put it,

To abolish class distinctions means abolishing a part of yourself. . . . All my notions—notions of good and evil, of pleasant and unpleasant, of funny and serious, of ugly and beautiful—are essentially middle class notions; my taste in books and food and clothes, my sense of honour, my table manners, my turns of speech, my accent, even the characteristic movements of my body, are the products of a special kind of upbringing and a special niche about halfway up the social hierarchy.

Orwell in other words understood that status was not simply a matter of private snobbishness but that its elimination would involve the surrender of a much wider range of tastes and acquired habits and prejudices.

These differences of status attitudes could not be eliminated for example by the then Duke of York's yearly summer camps where public-school boys and children from the slums were supposed to mix on equal terms. Orwell wrote that they did mix for the time being but rather like the animals in the circus cages 'where a dog, a cat, two ferrets, a rabbit and three canaries preserve an armed truce

---

[26]   Ibid. i. 341.

while the showman's eye is on them'. And so after all the sharp talk about socialists and socialist propaganda in the second half of *The Road to Wigan Pier*, Orwell ends by advising the socialists 'to go easy and not frighten more people than can be helped . . . if you belong to the bourgeoisie, don't be too eager to bound forward and embrace your proletarian brothers . . . and if you belong to the proletariat, by birth or in the sight of God, don't sneer too automatically at the old school tie'.[27]

Orwell's conception of the dynamics of the class structure began in the 1930s as a marxist one. He accepted the idea of polarization and particularly believed that people who had been brought up with middle-class status but in fact had working-class incomes had 'nothing to lose but their aitches'. It is a view, common to Marxists and Weberians, in terms of which the analysis of stratification since before the Second World War could be written as a debate on an aphorism: 'class dominates status'. But in the mean time we must treat Orwell's analysis in the context of his own time.

That context necessarily involves recognizing that the attitudes of middle-class socialists to the working class were fraught with ambivalence. Orwell himself is no exception. Subsequent commentators have sometimes been impressed by Orwell's insistence on the autonomy of the working class as the best judge of their own interests, which is really an application of the fundamental liberal principle that a person is his or her own best expert. Orwell was well aware that the best contribution possible for a middle-class socialist was to join the proletarian cause and fight alongside working-class activists giving any technical or professional assistance that might otherwise be lacking but never under any circumstances assuming a dictatorial or dirigiste role.

Others, by contrast, have seen Orwell, for all his honesty and personal wish for self-sacrifice, as essentially patronizing towards working-class people and working-class culture. Raymond Williams is implicitly scathing in his selective excerpts from Orwell—working-class people as 'natural inferiors . . . like animals' and (from *Nineteen Eighty-Four*, p. 227) as those 'out of whose mighty loins a race of conscious beings must one day come'. Williams, writing in 1971, then goes on, 'this stale revolutionary romanticism is as insulting as the original observation. It is the rising of the animals as

[27] *The Road to Wigan Pier* (London, 1937), 191. By 1984 this work had been reprinted by Penguin Books no fewer than 23 times.

in the fable . . . if the tyranny of 1984 ever finally comes, one of the major elements of the ideological preparation will have been just this way of seeing "the massess" . . . the 85 per cent who are proles. And nobody who belongs to this majority or who knows them as people will give a damn whether the figure on the other side of the street sees them as animals to be subjected or as unthinking creatures out of whose mighty loins the future will come. The incomplete humanity will be too clearly visible in the gesticulating observer himself.'[28]

The first judgement is too celebratory and Williams's harshly unfair. Together they demonstrate the quite extraordinary tension and guilt of those with origins in the advantaged classes who have tried to come face to face, like Orwell, first with imperialism and then with poverty and injustice in the English class system.

We could argue endlessly as to whether Williams accurately represents Orwell's view of the working class. But at least it would be difficult to reconcile Williams's representation with the following observation of the family life of a manual worker in steady work and drawing good wages in the 1930s.

His home life seems to fall more naturally into a sane and comely shape. I have often been struck by the peculiar easy completeness, the perfect symmetry as it were, of a working-class interior at its best. Especially on winter evenings after tea, when the fire glows in the open range and dances mirrored in the steel fender, when Father, in shirt sleeves, sits in the rocking chair at one side of the fire reading the racing finals, and Mother sits on the other side with her sewing, and the children are happy with a pennorth of mint humbugs, and the dog lolls roasting himself on the rag mat—it is a good place to be in, provided that you can be not only in it but sufficiently of it to be taken for granted.[29]

Mythology and sentimentalism or honestly observed ethnography? Certainly it is not vacuous and we can testify personally to its reality—and not only from our own childhood. Nor was Orwell sentimentalizing about some timeless stability of respectable working-class family life. He is at pains to stress that the scene can—but by no means must—abruptly shift where there is unemployment. He is well aware that moving back into the middle ages would bring us to a world of grim deprivation for ordinary people. 'A windowless hut, a wood fire which smokes in your face because

---

[28] Williams, *Orwell*, 79.
[29] Orwell, *The Road to Wigan Pier*, 104–5.

there is no chimney, mouldy bread, "Poor John", lice, scurvy, a yearly childbirth and a yearly child-death, and a priest terrifying you with tales of hell.'[30] And Orwell was equally alive to the possibilities and the dangers of a technological future which would inevitably transform the material conditions to which working-class respectability had been in so many ways an admirable, civilized adaptation.

Whatever picture of the 'condition of England' we ultimately accept, and whatever changes we may diagnose in the second half of the twentieth century, Orwell's analysis can never be brushed aside. A marxist class analysis has never adequately explained patriotism or the state. Orwell, Right or Left and right or wrong, offers us a marvellously observed and patently honest account. Class inequality is counted and castigated again and again. But in the end Orwell was convinced that there were deeper forces, and most particularly a belief in constitutionalism and legality, which knitted together the socially unequal England of his day. 'It is not that anyone imagines the law to be just. Everyone knows that there is one law for the rich and another for the poor. But no-one accepts the implications of this, everyone takes it for granted that the law, such as it is, will be respected, and feels a sense of outrage when it is not.'[31] Orwell notices that there are letters to the papers from eminent marxist professors pointing out that this or that is a 'miscarriage of British justice'.

Everyone believes in his heart that the law can be, ought to be, and, on the whole, will be impartially administered. The totalitarian idea that there is no such thing as law, there is only power, has never taken root.[32]

In England such concepts as justice, liberty and objective truth are still believed in. They may be illusions, but they are very powerful illusions. The belief in them influences conduct, national life is different because of them.[33]

The hanging judge, that evil old man in scarlet robe and horsehair wig, whom nothing short of dynamite will ever teach what century he is living in, but who will at any rate interpret the law according to the book and will in no circumstances take a money bribe, is one of the symbolic figures of England. He is a symbol of the strange mixture of reality and illusion, democracy and privilege, humbug and decency, the subtle network of compromises by which the nation keeps itself in familiar shape.[34]

---

[30] Ibid. i. 105.   [31] Orwell, *Collected Essays*, i. 82.
[32] Ibid.   [33] Ibid.   [34] Ibid. i. 82–3.

That was the England from which Orwell projected his hopes and fears for the future.

HOPES AND FEARS OF THE FUTURE

Orwell set out his programme in *The Lion and the Unicorn* under six headings, three dealing with domestic and three with foreign policy. They were:

1. Nationalization of land, mines, railways, banks, and major industries.
2. Limitation of incomes, on such a scale that the highest tax-free income in Britain did not exceed the lowest by more than ten to one.
3. Reform of the educational system along democratic lines.
4. Immediate dominion status for India, with power to secede when the war was over.
5. Formation of an imperial general council, in which the coloured peoples were to be represented.
6. Declaration of formal alliances with China, Abyssinia, and all other victims of the fascist powers.

Such a programme was consciously intended by Orwell to turn the Second World War into a revolutionary war and England into a socialist democracy.

Hope for the future lay in socialism, fear in totalitarianism. Those like Paul Johnson who in the 1984 celebration of *Nineteen Eighty-Four* wanted to claim Orwell for any kind of anti-socialist party were engaged in the characteristic exercises of self-justification proper to spiritual descendants of the Vicar of Bray. As Crick remarks, in a biographical footnote, 'doubts as to where Orwell "really stood" ' in his last years and 'speculation that he was abandoning socialism [are] only plausible in the slightest if his minor writings are not known or ignored'.[35] Crick quotes to the point from an article in the *Manchester Evening News* of 31 January 1946 where Orwell was reviewing a group of books on socialism. He distinguishes between socialism as the search for human brotherhood and the abolition of poverty and war, and socialism as 'a new kind of caste society in which we surrender our individual rights in return for economic security'. He also made a

[35] Crick, *Orwell*, 633.

threefold distinction among those who believe in the possibility of human progress—Machiavellianism, bureaucracy, and Utopianism. And this led him to a succinct statement of his own position in the tradition of socialism that we have been tracing in this book. He opted for a set of ideas

> . . . leading back through Utopian dreamers like William Morris and the mystical democrats like Walt Whitman, through Rousseau, through the English Diggers and Levellers, through the peasant revolts of the Middle Ages, and back to the early Christians and the slave revolts of antiquity.
>
> The pamphlets of Gerrard Winstanley, the Digger from Wigan whose experiment in primitive Communism was crushed by Cromwell, are in some ways strangely close to modern Left Wing literature.
>
> The 'earthly paradise' has never been realized, but as an idea it never seems to perish, despite the ease with which it can be debunked by practical politicians of all colours.
>
> Underneath it lies the belief that human nature is fairly decent to start with, and is capable of indefinite development. This belief has been the main driving force of the Socialist movement, including the undergound sects who prepared the way for the Russian revolution, and it could be claimed that the Utopians, at present a scattered minority, are the true upholders of Socialist tradition.[36]

Hope in practical terms lay still in a determined pursuit of the Labour party programme. He had outlined his six-point programme early in the war with economic, fiscal, and educational measures to prevent the re-emergence of a capitalist class structure, and a foreign policy designed to end imperialism and to usher in a new international contract between nations in Europe and races in the Empire. Some steps in both directions had already been taken by the Attlee government. But meanwhile Orwell's mind had turned to reflect pessimistically the possibility of anti-socialist developments. He focused in his last book on the threat of totalitarianism, not so much from the defeated fascist countries nor even from the Stalinist regimes but from the spread of totalitarian ideas (especially among the intelligentsia) in the capitalist democracies.

It must be recognized that in the immediate post-war years, the publication of *Animal Farm* and *Nineteen Eighty-Four* probably gave more help to the enemies than to the friends of the Attlee government that Orwell supported. *Animal Farm* was less open to misuse because, though allegorical, was clearly aimed at the

[36] Ibid. 507.

betrayal of socialism which is the soviet system ruled by Stalin. Even so it was used in the Cold War as propaganda against any kind of socialism, including Orwell's own. *Nineteen Eighty-Four* was intrinsically prone to the same misuse and was undoubtedly so misused. The tense relations between the USA and the USSR immediately after the war (and the fear that the next war would be atomic) made this Ingsoc allegory an inevitable weapon in the war of words. Crick's judgement is surely correct. 'Orwell was at best incautious, at worst foolish.'

Nevertheless, avoiding the distortion of hindsight as well as the temptations of contemporary dispute, we must reiterate that Orwell was voicing his pessimism about the possible perils of British and American society, not simply and savagely satirizing the Soviets. He meant what he said in his anguished reply to a cable from the American United Automobile workers.

My recent novel is NOT intended as an attack on Socialism or on the British Labour Party (of which I am a supporter) but as a show-up of the perversions to which a centralized economy is liable and which have already been partly realized in Communism and Fascism. I do not believe that the kind of society I describe necessarily *will* arrive, but I believe (allowing of course for the fact that the book is a satire) that something resembling it *could* arrive. I believe also that totalitarian ideas have taken root in the minds of intellectuals everywhere, and I have tried to draw these ideas out to their logical consequences. The scene of the book is laid in Britain in order to emphasize that the English-speaking races are not innately better than anyone else and that totalitarianism, *if not fought against*, could triumph anywhere.[37]

LAST RITES

What then had Orwell achieved? Certainly not all that was possible, for he died at the age of forty-six. *Nineteen Eighty-Four*, though a great book, assuring him of the mantle of Swift and a permanent place among satirical pamphleteers, was not a final political testament. Orwell in the 1950s, 1960s and 1970s (into which he would most likely have lived if streptomycin had come earlier into medical practice) might have been expected to exercise major influence on British and European socialist thought, warding

[37] Ibid. 569.

off Marxism but strengthening the determination of ethical democratic socialism.

Orwell's life and work stand for us as a most impressive recent monument to that tradition. He knew, as the democratic socialist must know, that the good society must have its foundation in a commitment to decency among its members. The code of conduct denoted by that essential word—love of truth, respect for persons, and hatred of injustice and inequality—must then run as the working principle of all human institutions.

Socialism so defined is the Utopia to be sought. Orwell believed that the idea and the energy would stem from humanism and in this way departed from the faith of his moral forerunners. He was not a Christian—or perhaps better he may be thought of as post-Christian—strong in the ethic but weak in the faith of the tradition that sustained him. He had been confirmed into the Anglican Church by the Christian-socialist Bishop of Oxford, Charles Gore. And he paid his last respects to the 'poor old unoffending Church of England' by asking in his will to be buried in accordance with the established anglican rites. In 1932 he had written:

> So shall we in the rout of life
> Some thought, some faith, some meaning save,
> And speak it once before we go
> In silence to the silent grave.[38]

In his last years he saw that 'one cannot have any worthwhile picture of the future unless one realizes how much we have lost by the decay of Christianity'. He recognized that the socialist would not salvage civilization 'unless he can evolve a system of good and evil which is independent of heaven and hell'.[39] He did not live to work out a modern answer to the problem of social order under socialism. But he left us an exemplary individual life.

[38] *Adelphi*, Mar. 1933.   [39] Quoted by Crick, *Orwell*, 228.

6

THE THEORY OF CITIZENSHIP
T. H. Marshall (1893–1981)

If the London School of Economics ever brought a 'light-leaved spring' for successors to Hobhouse it was especially in the first years after the Second World War. In the inter-war period R. H. Tawney had established himself as the outstanding tiller of fertile socialist soil. The tradition of moral and political radicalism remained abundantly productive in Houghton Street with Evan Durbin in economics and Harold Laski in politics. Richard Titmuss became the high priest of the welfare state after the war. T. H. Marshall lived through both periods. But he was no 'luckless lad'.

Marshall's writing was in one sense heavily dated by the political debate of the 1980s. He was the subtle advocate of the British version of the welfare state, legitimizing it by placing it in the long march of British history. He eventually described and approved of a tripartite, hyphenated society, democratic-welfare-capitalism. The three spheres, political, social, and economic each represented a dominant value, equality, fraternity, and freedom, which had to coexist in integrated balance to form a viable society. One consequence was that, in his view, as in that of most analysts of the modern Western European political democracies, the market has a necessary place in welfare-capitalism. Neither Marshall nor any of the rest of us fully realized at that time how far economic liberalism had the power through governmental action in a democratic society to shift the balance between welfare and market principles. It was hardly conceivable that an occupant of No. 10 Downing Street would even rhetorically announce an intention of eliminating 'socialism' from the political agenda.

Nevertheless, writing in the early 1970s, Marshall demonstrated his firm grasp of the central issue. Looking back over developments in the post-war period he saw that the democratic-welfare-capitalist society had been expected to bring with it consensus over basic issues and values. His view of the history of Western Europe during the 1960s was that though the principles and practices of democracy, capitalism and welfare were the objects of much criticism, this did not reflect battles being waged between them, but dissatisfaction with the whole of which they were the parts. Materialism, profit-seeking, quantity-worship and growth-mania are not characteristics of capitalism, but permeate the whole of modern technological mass society. Bureaucratic excesses and rigidities are not a political malady only but are found also in the economy, the universities and even in welfare. The transformation sought by the more purposeful and less destructive sections of those voicing our present discontents is one of attitudes and values rather than of basic structure, though institutional changes are sought as a means to this end, as is also the protection of the physical environment. I see no reason why their aims should not be achieved—if they can be achieved at all—within a social framework that includes representative government, a mixed economy and a welfare state. The only alternative is something more totalitarian and bureaucratic, and that is not at all what the more novel and significant elements in the movement of protest are seeking.[1]

Then, in the very last thing he wrote just before he died in 1981, he noted that

there is a disposition today, when considering what more should be done, to imagine that the desired effect can be obtained by attaching a framework of scaffolding of welfare services alongside the market economy, matching its operation and engaged to patch cracks, fill holes, press wounds and generally to make up, as far as is considered necessary, for the inability of the economy to meet its social obligations. Already there is too much of this, and to put still greater reliance upon it would lead to the gradual degradation of the welfare principle. There will always be casualties to be cared for and it will be part of welfare's task to care for them, but, it is to be hoped, more as a personal social service than as poor relief. Welfare fulfils itself above all in those services which are its own in every sense—health, education, the personal social services and, with increasing emphasis, community services for the preservation and development of the physical, social and cultural environment. It is by strengthening these that the civilising power of welfare can be most effectively increased.[2]

It is this passage and its final, now unfashionable, affirmation that dates Marshall. Yet we can begin to place him in the tradition of ethical socialism by reminding ourselves of a generalization about the distributions which result from market and welfare institutions in Western European political democracies.

[1] T. H. Marshall, 'Value Problems of Welfare-Capitalism', in *The Right to Welfare* (London, 1981), 120–1. [2] Ibid. 135.

If we divide a nation into households and order the households into quintiles by income it typically turns out as follows. The top fifth of households takes about half of total market income and the bottom fifth approximate to zero. Then if we look at welfare benefits the mirror image appears—the bottom fifth gets half and the top nothing (actually not quite nothing because educational grants in particular tend to go to the better-off families). But then putting all income together, because market incomes typically make up over three-quarters of all the income generated, the net result is a markedly unequal distribution of income between families in democratic-welfare-capitalist society.

The British case illustrates the generalization. Trends in the decade after Marshall wrote were towards greater inequality. Between 1976 and 1984 the original or market income of the bottom fifth of UK households dropped as a share of all market income from 0.8 to 0.3 per cent while the top fifth moved up from 44.4 to 48.6 per cent. The redistributive activity of the state modified this inequality but did not change the direction of the movement. The bottom group had final household incomes amounting to 7.4 per cent of the whole in 1976 reduced to 7.1 per cent in 1984 while the top fifth raised their share from 37.9 to 39.0 per cent.[3]

We use this example simply to illustrate that T. H. Marshall's concern about the capitalist or market sphere in its balance with the other two spheres, welfare and democracy, is more, not less, problematic a decade after he expressed it. Citizenship was the key to a balanced society.

Marshall is important to us not so much because he offers yet another personal example of one born to advantage who lived and worked to better the lot of his less fortunate compatriots. He was indeed a private cultivator of friendship and a dutiful public servant: but exculpation from middle-class guilt, if present at all in his conduct of life, was certainly never dramatized in the manner of an Arnold Toynbee or a George Orwell. It is rather that he offered a theory of ethical socialism, conceptualized as citizenship, which is sociologically more defensible than the Hobhousian theory of progress, for while it gives due weight to the autonomously moral, it corrects Hobhouse's overemphasis on it.

In Marshall's sense of the term, all the writers we have reviewed

---

[3] *Social Trends No. 17* (London, 1987), Table 5.19, p. 98.

have in common a search for the theory and practice of citizenship. The word citizenship is often narrowly associated with the ideology of the French Revolution, but carries older radical concerns than those of nineteenth-century and twentieth-century socialists, and belongs to a vocabulary of class anterior to that disseminated by Marx and Engels. In T. H. Marshall both citizenship and class receive an analysis which advances their historical and sociological usefulness. Marshall, unlike T. H. Green, Bosanquet, and Hobhouse was able to explain the development of both the welfare state and class equality in terms of the progress of society through the moral sense of the individual.

Marshall's work is also of more immediate political significance for the interpretation of the post-war period and for the debate over welfare-state capitalism led by economic liberals since the mid-1970s. By adding a social dimension to the idealist theory of citizenship advanced by T. H. Green,[4] the Oxford school in the second half of the nineteenth century eventually had a spectacular and divisive impact on liberalism in British theory and practice. Its impact on the twentieth century Labour party was also impressive. But its validity was disputed and undermined by criticism of its metaphysic. It always had the debilitating weakness in political argument that its propositions could not be falsified by empirical enquiry. For those who accepted the Christian faith it had few problems as a general guide to social obligation. But few modern philosophers accept its metaphysic and few practical politicians can agree with Green that it can be rooted in the implicit social consciousness of ordinary people.

Moreover social, especially marxist, historians such as Gareth Stedman Jones[5] or John Foster,[6] challenge or reject the account of ordinary consciousness which the ethical progressivists (George Eliot, Arnold Toynbee, Hobhouse) offered. Writers in the ethical-socialist tradition have, to be sure, found that decency, the habit of solidarity, the conviction that we are here for a purpose beyond egotistical calculation, can be established as at least part of the

---

[4] On which see the excellent discussion by A. Vincent and R. Plant, *Philosophy, Politics and Citizenship: The Life and Thought of the British Idealists* (Oxford, 1984).

[5] G. S. Jones, *Languages of Class: Studies in English Working Class History 1832–1982* (Cambridge, 1983).

[6] J. Foster, *Class Struggle and the Industrial Revolution: Early Industrial Capitalism in Three English Towns* (Cambridge, 1974).

description of English culture, including the culture of the English working class. Cobbett found this consciousness among agricultural labourers, Beatrice Potter among her kin who were factory operatives in Lancashire. Hobhouse and Charles Booth observed it among trade union leaders and working-class families in the East End of London, Orwell on the road to Wigan Pier, and Richard Hoggart remembered it, albeit nostalgically, as a residual social outlook from Leeds in the 1920s.

Yet marxist historians of working-class movements offer a fundamentally different emphasis. It is not so much that they point to the failure of evangelism or temperance movements to enfold working peoples' lives in sober and thrifty adherence to the Christian churches, as that they insist on tackling the class relations of industrial society as the central determinant of culture, morals, and politics.

Citizenship theory before T. H. Marshall paid little attention to, indeed from the pens of many liberals denied, the great fact of class in industrial society. A class structure of inequality impedes the exercise of citizenship, and appeals to common membership may even be used for the ideological subordination of the disadvantaged classes. From the 1860s a working-class party aspiring to dominate decision was on the political agenda. 'The young academic liberals of the day, like T. H. Green, A. V. Dicey, James Bryce, and Leslie Stephen took the hopeful view that the working class could be safely accommodated within the national community and would make a fruitful response to political leadership of the right calibre.'[7] And Gladstone's populism managed to run the democratic Liberal party by excluding class issues. 'The Gladstonian style of politics made a transcendental appeal to conscience, but one seldom directed towards social evils at home.'[8]

In the twentieth century, as a restricted franchise moved towards universal adult suffrage, industrial economy towards high productivity, and industrial society towards suburban mobility and prosperity, the problem of citizenship became more, not less difficult. The bases of social integration in Christian belief, national and imperial success, localized kinship, and the collective self-help institutions of the urban proletariat were all to decay. Erosion was slow and could be reversed, as during the Second World War when

---

[7] P. Clarke, *Liberals and Social Democrats* (Cambridge, 1978), 5–6.
[8] Ibid. 7.

a form of siege socialism knit the nation together, widened social sympathies, and gave popular appeal to the possibility of a future classlessness. In his remarkable history of war-time social services R. M. Titmuss argued a logic of social solidarity, class reconciliation, and communal altruism in response to external military threat.[9] Total war with its food rationing, conscription, and evacuation justified the limitation of egoism and demonstrated the practicality of social planning. Tawney, reviewing Titmuss, saw the whole experience as a universal socialist education.[10] T. H. Marshall is the outstanding interpreter and advocate of the central development of an alternative social solidarity—the welfare state.

THE MAKING OF A GENTLEMAN

Marshall was born in 1893.[11] His life and work extended virtually over the whole period of the development of sociology as an organized academic discipline in Britain. He was a schoolboy at Rugby when the first Chair of Sociology was instituted in 1907 at the London School of Economics and occupied by Hobhouse—a Chair of which he was to be the third incumbent from 1954 to 1956. He began his career as a Cambridge historian, translated to the London School of Economics in 1925, emerged formally as a sociologist in 1929, and alternated thereafter between academic and public service. Formal retirement in 1960 did not diminish his sociological writing, and he was an influential figure in the frantic national recruitment of the 1960s as well as a guiding hand in the establishment of sociological teaching at Cambridge where he lived for his last twenty years until he died in 1981.

He was a child of Victorian prosperity and a youth in the confident autumn of imperial Britain. The high culture of the metropolitan professional classes was his by inheritance. He was a textbook offspring of the characteristic blending of the bourgeoisie and the gentry in nineteenth-century England with its roots and sentiments in the country, its official place in London, its investments in industry, and its occupation in the major professions and higher officialdom. His great-grandfather had made an

---

[9] R. M. Titmuss, *Problems of Social Policy* (London, 1950).

[10] R. H. Tawney, 'The War and the People', *New Statesman and Nation*, 22 Apr. 1950, 454–6.

[11] From this point this chapter is for the most part extracted from A. H. Halsey, 'T. H. Marshall Past and Present', *Sociology*, 18 (1984), 1–18.

industrial fortune in the north a hundred years before. His family
had settled in the Lake District and retained this connection to
arcadian affluence from its later London home. His father was a
successful architect, and Tom was the fourth of six children.

His childhood was one of calm, ordered, and assured, if
unostentatious, privilege. The Adam ceiling and chandeliers of an
elegant drawing-room, William Morris wallpapers, and 'good
pieces' of furniture, nanny, governess, chauffeur, servants: these
were the accepted features and figures of a Bloomsbury home,
constantly visited by famous friends and titled relatives. And the
seasons and stages of growing up were no less typical of the upper-
middle class to which the Marshalls so securely belonged. There
was a country house at Hindhead in Surrey—a fashionable country
settlement among families of similarly elevated status. There were
frequent visits to the Lake District or to relatives in Ireland. The
future was an assumed combination of private cultivation and
public duty. The home was educative, not to any narrow vocation,
but for a life of gentlemanly culture. Conversation, chamber music,
and charades fitted easily into the weekly and seasonal round of
town and country. Formal education launched the children into the
public domain through select preparatory boarding schools and, in
Marshall's case, into Rugby and Cambridge. The elements of a
conventional upbringing into the ruling class of Edwardian
England were thus complete.

The Marshall family was established in Bedford Square long
before the Bloomsbury Set. A younger sister, Frances (who married
into the centre of that avidly discussed circle of British Edwardian
and inter-war proprietors of contemporary standards in art,
literature, and elevated life) has elaborated Marshall's own terse
description of his home as 'intellectually and artistically cultured
and financially well-endowed'.[12]

Frances's autobiography appeared,[13] as it happened, at the same
time as Angela Hewins's account of the life of George Hewins—a
slum dweller in Stratford. Marshall and Hewins were contemporaries in two worlds of the same country. George Hewins's
reminiscences record another and a different England at the turn of
the century. In 1899 George married Emma:

---

[12] T. H. Marshall, 'A British Sociological Career', *Intern. Soc. Sci. Journ.* (1973),
88–100.   [13] F. Partridge, *Memories* (London, 1981).

She was clean as a new pin, swilled herself in the basin morning and night, all over, kept her hair smelling sweeter 'n any wench I'd knowed. She had long light-coloured hair—it fell down to her waist when she let it out a-nights—and tits like cooking apples! We had to share a bed with her mother. There was us at one end, and her mother's feet a-sticking in our faces! But I was lucky—the old lady generally dropped off afer a day's charring and a couple o'stouts . . . It was three hundred, four hundred years old, that cottage . . . However much the missus scrubbed the flags, however much I limed the walls, we couldn't keep it clean. Bugs and fleas, it was one long battle, and we was on the losing side . . . There was one room downstairs with an open fire, where the missus did the cooking and the washing and the ironing, two tiny rooms upstairs—the one we slept in was over the passage . . . [14]

To understand how people of such contrasted fortunes could be held together in one nation—especially a nation which boasted of its political liberties and in which the ruling class governed with minimal use of armed force—was an obvious challenge to any intelligence of Marshall's time. He responded through a British sociological career, and we must remind ourselves that, for all the stark complementarity and conflict of social conditions between Bedford Square and George Hewins's Pimms Court, this class polarity was easy for the high-born to ignore and difficult to traverse.

Peter Clarke has neatly posed the dilemma involved in the bourgeois socialism of the liberal intellectuals of this period. 'What they yearn for is peace of mind. Commitment to a radical critique of capitalism may be quite inappropriate as a strategy of social change, but functional as adaptation for the individual. If it becomes an ethic of alternate ends it needs no utilitarian justification; and since it will not in fact be realised, it can give the intellectuals not only the material satisfactions of membership of a privileged class but also the psychic satisfaction of rejecting the morality of the system which sustains them.'[15] We have seen how Eric Blair sought redemption as George Orwell. We now look at a different strategy of confrontation with the two English nations.

The young Tom Marshall 'knew nothing of working-class life, and the great industrial north was a nightmare land of smoke and grime through which one had to travel to get from London to the

---

[14] A. Hewins (ed.), *The Dillen: Memories of a Man of Stratford-Upon-Avon* (London, 1981), 64–5.   [15] Clarke, *Liberals and Social Democrats*, 5–6.

Lake District'.[16] Before the great trauma to his class of the outbreak of war in 1914, he was (as his sister describes him) 'a charming and clever nineteen-year-old, my mother's favourite child and destined for the Foreign Service. . . .'[17] It was at this point, in the spring of 1914, that the easy unfolding of a successful career was arrested and turned to new direction. He spent the next four years as a civilian prisoner-of-war in a camp outside Berlin, having been in Weimar learning German. He received, one might say, an abruptly involuntary and unconventional pre-education in sociology. Marshall recognized his enforced sojourn at Ruhleban as 'undoubtedly the most powerful formative experience of my early years'.[18] His attitude to the world around him was 'deeply affected by having lived through this real-life social experiment'.[19]

Ruhleban was also an enforced escape for Marshall from the narrow social confines of his upbringing in the English bourgeois intelligentsia. A prison camp being non-producing cannot be a class society in the ordinary sense. But the merchant seamen and fishermen, the 'camp proletariat', introduced Marshall to an unfamiliar sub-culture of class. As David Ketchum described it, 'without its seafarers Ruhleban would have been a very different camp, softer, less virile, top-heavy with intellectuals. It was their courage that set the first high standards, and their healthy philistinism that kept the cultural life in balance.'[20]

Of course, in a formal academic sense, it was an unknowing introduction to his future profession, just as was the medieval history which he studied at Cambridge under Gaillard Lapsley, and which gave him his first acquaintance with the study of social systems as understood by Vinogradoff, Maine, and Maitland. Marshall's later conception of capitalism, socialism, and democracy was built on the foundations of the analytical construction of estate society fashioned by these historians. The greater significance of Ruhleban lay in personal confrontation with an unexpected, uncharted, to-be-constructed world. It is a widely observed characteristic of most, if not all, notable sociologists that they negotiate social marginality. The generalization rests on a commonplace: disjunctive personal experience is likely to induce curiosity about

[16] Marshall, 'Brit. Sociol. Career', 88.
[17] Partridge, *Memories*, 42.
[18] Marshall, 'Brit. Sociol. Career', 89.
[19] For a detailed account of Ruhleban see David Ketchum, *Ruhleban: A Prison Camp Society* (Toronto, 1965).   [20] Ibid. 126.

society. Sociologists have typically lived and moved between at least two social worlds, be it Jewish and Gentile, rural and urban, colonial and metropolitan, or some other margin of national, ethnic, or class identity. For Marshall at Ruhleban it was a temporary marginality thrust upon a most unmarginal young man.

At all events the experience was morally and intellectually crucial, generating in him a new dimension of social sensibility reaching beyond the civilities of his upbringing in the style of life of Victorian London and Edwardian Cambridge. Superficially and initially, however, it was not so. Marshall returned to Cambridge to compete successfully for a Trinity Fellowship on the basis of a dissertation on seventeenth-century guilds, suggested by Clapham. He formed an understanding of post-feudal or post-estate society, especially in England, and most especially from the point of view of the legal basis of the institutions of class and status which interacted to produce equalities and inequalities.

He was thus embarked on what would have been a career entirely appropriate to a young man of his class, that of a Cambridge historian. But he soon made a diversion, at least temporarily, from the normal path of the don into another encounter with working-class people. He stood as a Labour candidate for a safe Conservative constituency in Surrey at the General Election of 1922. He was beaten and returned to Cambridge knowing that he was not suited to a career as a politican. Campaigning did not fit his temperament. Though politics engaged his deep interest, he decided at that point that the academic cloister must be his base. He went on with his historical studies but here, too, was a limitation of personal character. For he also knew that it was not in his nature to spend his working life 'pouring over original documents to the extent demanded by reputable historical research'.[21] As the end of his Fellowship approached he realized that he must get away from Cambridge and, accordingly, he applied for the first post he saw advertised, that of a tutor to students of social work at the London School of Economics. Beveridge appointed him in 1925. Thus his formal journey into sociology began.

What intellectual and moral baggage did he take with him from

[21] Marshall, 'Brit. Sociol. Career', 91.

Cambridge? The answer is not simple: for it turns not only on Marshall the man but also on sociology the subject. Neither the man nor the subject were yet firmly established in British culture and society. But both had significant antecedents in Victorian Cambridge. Readers of Marshall's brief autobiographical sketch[22] will have noticed that, in his detached and economical manner, he allocates a single sentence to the fact that at Rugby he was a sincere and devout Christian and that by the end of his first year as an undergraduate at Cambridge he had totally lost his faith. Nowhere else in his writing is there a discussion either of this personal event or of the more significant social fact of declining religious belief, despite his sustained preoccupation with the determinants of social integration in the society to which he eventually attached his 'democratic-welfare-capitalism' label.[23] It is true that in the same essay he asserts that 'welfare decisions . . . are essentially altruistic and must draw on standards of value embodied in an autonomous ethical system'. He finds it 'impossible to say how these ethical standards arise in a society or are recognised by its members', and he veers away from this unanswered fundamental question with the observation that 'total consensus with regard to them is unthinkable, outside a devout religious community, but without a foundation of near-consensus, no general social welfare policy would be possible'.[24]

How, then, are we to explain the transition from the Victorian order of class inequality, evangelical religion, and social deference to the consensus which produced the welfare state and the 'Butskellism' that Marshall spent his life in analyzing? His answer was to emerge as sociology—a subtle unravelling of principles of social action and reaction between institutions and classes in the specific historical context of British industrialization and modernization. Yet it was rooted in the intellectual culture of Cambridge. Marshall's sociology, is, first, an extension of Maitland's view of history. But, second, it can be described as the further development of a corpus of work in the 'moral sciences' in Cambridge from the middle of the nineteenth century—with Henry Sidgwick, Alfred Marshall, and Leslie Stephen as the founding fathers—which aimed to produce a secular substitute for the traditional theological

[22] Ibid.
[23] T. H. Marshall, *The Right to Welfare and Other Essays* (London, 1981), 104.
[24] Ibid. 109.

justifications of social morality and explanations of social integration.[25]

The task was to produce 'authoritative doctrine'—authoritative
in the sense of being able to command what Sidgwick called the
'unconstrained consent of experts'.[26] The movement recruited such
notable authorities as Russell, Whitehead, Keynes, G. E. Moore,
the Stracheys, the Woolfs, and the Bells. T. H. Marshall was drawn
into the circle by birth, education, and affinity. This is not to
suggest that he was of quite the same high scholarly stature or
worldly influence as either his more famous namesake or Keynes.
He was not admitted to the close and closed circle of 'the Apostles';
he belonged neither to the school of philosophy nor of economics;
and his later public offices in the Foreign Office, the Control
Commission in Germany and UNESCO were minor compared with
those of Keynes. Nevertheless, he certainly belonged to the still
select, if slightly wider, circle of Trinity, Cambridge, and Bloomsbury. And that circle sought to define the nature and substance of a
high secular civilization in its social and its professional forms.

How far, apart from his historical training, Marshall was
systematically aware of his intellectual inheritance from the
Cambridge he was leaving is doubtful. What is certain is that, at
that time, he had little or no idea that modern European sociology
since Comte and Saint-Simon could be properly thought of as a
similar, if wider, movement in search of a secular alternative to the
Judaic-Christian tradition of social thought. As we have already
pointed out, sociology was, and still is, described as the European
reply to Marxism: but viewed more widely and deeply, both have
clear theological antecedents; and both, like Cambridge's anxious
agnosticism, have been essentially concerned with the problems of
social order and social change in industrial society, whether as an
outcome of new class struggles (Marx), new divisons of labour
(Durkheim), or new patterns of authority (Weber).

Another aspect of his Cambridge experience had been deeply and
permanently learned. He was a gentleman: and the meaning of that
persona, which is now largely lost, had significant professional as
well as distinctive personal consequences.

The personal consequences are perhaps best conveyed by
reference to the Bloomsbury Set. As Keynes put it, 'our religion

---

[25] See the bold sketch of this theme in R. Skidelsky, *John Maynard Keynes*, i,
Hopes Betrayed 1883–1920 (London, 1983), ch. 2.   [26] Ibid. 28.

closely followed the English puritan tradition of being chiefly concerned with the salvation of our own souls'.[27] These heirs to Victorian evangelism were not a group in the *Gesellschaft* sense. They are more exactly if less precisely defined as an interlocking network of friends who sought personal and secular salvation, not social transformation. G. E. Moore's *Principia Ethica* was the 'Bloomsbury Bible'. The typical social outlook was felt to be individual even though shared to the extent that Frances Partridge could label the members as left-wing First-World-War pacifists, atheists, Francophiles, and lovers of the arts and travel. Marshall was an accomplished amateur violinist and shone as an actor in the Marlowe Society.[28] There was endless talk: conventions were constantly challenged and rational intelligence exalted. Above all friendship was valued, and James Meade and Donald McRae both remember the practice of friendship as Marshall's especial gift.[29]

The professional consequences stemmed more from Cambridge than from Bloomsbury. They owed a particular debt to Alfred Marshall's effort to establish economics as the intellectual engine of moral progress. What Keynes said of his intimate friends is also true of Tom Marshall, 'We were among the last of the Utopians, or meliorists as they are sometimes called, who believe in a continuing moral progress by virtue of which the human race already consists of reliable, rational, decent people . . .'[30]

Robert Skidelsky has argued cogently that the Cambridge movement to which we have alluded was closely related to Victorian university reform. The abolition of the Test acts, the opening of Fellowships to merit, and the reform of curricula and examinations had transformed Oxford and Cambridge in such a way as to prevent the emergence of a rival or dissenting intellectual class. 'In this it was successful: with the exception of the small group of Fabians, no-one who had not been to Oxford or Cambridge made much impact on English thought over the next sixty years (after 1860) . . . Undoubtedly the relatively inclusive character of the English notion of a gentleman helped this

[27] J. M. Keynes, *Two Memoirs* (London, 1949), 84.

[28] Partridge, *Memories*, 64.

[29] At the LSE Memorial Meeting in February 1982 Meade spoke of Marshall's modesty, unselfish interest in others, and intellectual honesty. But above all was his 'genius for deep, natural undemonstrative friendship'. And MacRae described how 'Tom had lived with music and friendship and affection'.

[30] Keynes, *Two Memoirs*, 99.

consolidation of intellectual property.'[31] Sheldon Rothblatt has traced the transformation of the idea of a profession in the same period when, in the minds of dons, it became securely linked to the idea of social service and clearly distanced it not only from brutalizing manual toil but also from the profit motive of business or commercial pursuits.[32]

T. H. Marshall absorbed these ideas and preferences into his personal life. They were also later to appear in his sociology, in his writing on the professions, and most cogently when he revisited Cambridge in 1949 to deliver the Marshall lectures. By that time a mature sociologist, he found it natural to expound his theme— *Citizenship and Social Class*—from Alfred Marshall's equally characteristic phrasing in 1873 of the question 'whether progress may not go on steadily, if slowly, till, by occupation at least, every man is a gentleman'.[33] Alfred Marshall had held that it would. T. H. Marshall was to go on to show how, and to what extent, it actually did—through the development of citizenship. Deferring sociological consideration of his thesis, the point here is that Marshall's bridge to his proletarian compatriots was thrown from the position of a Cambridge gentleman. His method was that of the detached and civilized observer from the study and the library rather than the party activist on the hustings. R. H. Tawney (his senior by thirteen years) had gone from Balliol to Toynbee Hall in the East End of London and to the Workers' Educational Association in Rochdale. George Orwell (ten years his junior) went to the slums of Paris, the spike, and Wigan pier. Marshall never moved far from the Cambridge and Bloomsbury connection. Except that he went to Houghton Street.

He went to London stamped with the personal and professional morals and manners of the Cambridge élite. But he was not merely a representative of that high culture, however excellent. His assured gentlemanliness was more than convention: it was expressed exquisitely by a shy and physically beautiful man of critical but generous sympathy towards others. His austere blend of irony, diffidence, and duty made him a delightful colleague and a punctilious public servant. His quiet passion for justice took him momentarily to the hustings, made him a co-signatory of the

[31] Skidelsky, *Keynes*, 27–8.
[32] S. Rothblatt, *The Revolution of the Dons* (London, 1968).
[33] A. Marshall, *Memorials of Alfred Marshall*, ed. A. C. Pigou (London, 1925).

memorial to the Master of Trinity college in favour of reinstating Bertrand Russell to a lectureship,[34] and impelled him to a lifetime's study of class inequality and social policy. His awareness of his own limitations tended to draw a modest veil over what we can now see as a genuinely original sociological mind.

THE MAKING OF A SOCIOLOGIST

So Marshall moved from Trinity to the London School of Economics. If anywhere, it was at this Fabian institution, creation of the Webbs and Shaw, that a nascent alternative intellectual élite was to be found. It was a brilliant and passionate place, the home of sociology and the London bastion of the secular search for understanding of the movement of modern society. Its sociology was an amalgam of two elements—the evolutionism of Hobhouse and Ginsberg and the social amelioration survey methods of the Webbs, Booth, and Rowntree. Marshall was later to draw on both, taking his central concept of citizenhip from Hobhouse (whom he admired as 'the most famous and original of British sociologists since Spencer'[35]) and his understanding of the 'conditions of the poor' from the ameliorationists. At the LSE he eventually forged elements of both London sociology and Cambridge history into a new analysis of the relation between social stratification and social integration and so made significant advances on the earlier work of Weber and Durkheim.[36]

Marshall, however, was no instant sociologist. He came to 'the School' to teach economic history and, in his first year, to tutor aspiring social workers on the writing of essays about what was still called 'the social question'. Not until Hobhouse died in 1929 did he join the sociology department. He became the Reader in 1930, replacing Ginsberg (who succeeded to the Martin White chair). His task was to teach comparative social institutions. As he remembered it in the 1970s he was still at that time 'quite ignorant of sociology in the professional sense': but he had developed (partly in Ruhleban) a sociological curiosity and had acquired in his historical studies 'some skills in the analysis of social systems and the interpretation of social change'.[37]

[34] See G. H. Hardy, *Bertrand Russell and Trinity* (Cambridge, 1942).
[35] Marshall, *Right to Welfare*, 159.
[36] This is also Lockwood's judgement. D. Lockwood, 'For T. H. Marshall', *Sociology*, 8 (1974), 363–7.   [37] Marshall, 'Brit. Sociol. Career', 91.

Nevertheless, Marshall did not at this time make a systematic attempt to master the classics of sociological theory. In retrospect he saw this as 'a mistake which I have regretted ever since'.[38] Though his writing in the 1930s shows a detailed familiarity with German and French social and political affairs, he did not confront the theories of conflict and consensus put forward by Marx or Durkheim. As it turned out he was able, through his own originality, to use Hobhousian sociology and Cambridge history as a framework within which to throw new light on the relation between class and citizenship. Had he also explicitly related his analysis of Britain to the work of the continental masters the task of comparative analysis of the advanced societies would have been accelerated and his own achievement recognized earlier and more widely. Instead the connections were left to be observed by later writers, notably Bendix,[39] Lipset,[40] Giddens,[41] and Room.[42]

During the 1930s Marshall came to identify himself whole-heartedly as a professional sociologist, with developing interests in social stratification and social policy. In neither of these fields, however, did he equip himself with the statistical skills which might have been available to him from his colleagues—Bowley or Hogben or, later, D. V. Glass or R. G. D. Allen. Such expertise would have been well within his competence. It is clear from his essays and reviews that he thoroughly understood the methods of survey, the powers and limits of social measurement, and the logic of multivariate analysis. But he remained a sophisticated consumer and did not become a professional practitioner of the statistical techniques, advancing the dubious rationalization, by analogy with his experience as a violinist, that a sociologist must not only learn to use instruments but also 'learn to grow them on the tips of his fingers'.[43] This also, we believe, was a mistake by the man and a lost opportunity for his subject. It was, for example, James Meade

[38] Ibid.
[39] R. Bendix, *Nation Building and Citizenship* (New York, 1964) and *Kings or People* (Berkeley, 1978).
[40] S. M. Lipset, 'Tom Marshall—Man of Wisdom', *British Journal of Sociology* (1973), 412, 417. See also Lipset's introduction to the American edition of T. H. Marshall, *Sociology at the Crossroads* (New York, 1973).
[41] A. Giddens, *Profiles and Critiques of Social Theory* (London, 1982), esp. chs. 12, 9.
[42] G. Room, *The Sociology of Welfare* (Oxford, 1979).
[43] T. H. Marshall, *Sociology at the Crossroads and Other Essays* (London, 1963), 42.

who wrote *Equality, Efficiency and the Ownership of Property* (1964) and Meade's pupil, A. B. Atkinson, who explored the fate of the first children of the welfare state (i.e. the children of the 1950 survey of York by Rowntree) in his *Parents and Children: Income in Two Generations* (1983). Works of this kind, at once theoretical and statistically empirical, might have been undertaken by Marshall and, if they had, the connection between sociological theory and policy-orientated investigation would have been made earlier and the relationship would have been stronger and more central to the discipline of British sociology.

For better or worse, Marshall never acquired the driving puritanical dedication to research and writing which might have been possible in the ethos of Houghton Street. His professionalism was never so narrow. Teaching was at least as important as research. Administration, burdensome as he found it, especially as head of the social work department (1944–9), was a compelling duty. Public service, though never sought, was always felt as a call to be unstintingly answered. He served in the Foreign Office Research Department from 1939–44, with the British Control Commission in Germany 1949–50, and as director of the social sciences division of UNESCO from 1956–60. And beyond both professional and public duty there remained the constant pull of a highly civilized private life of music and friendship where he expressed perhaps his greatest gifts of character.

So it was that as a professional sociologist he somehow remained deceptively amateur, always amenable to the wishes of his colleagues, and characteristically delivering his written work, even the excellent best of it, as a *pièce d'occasion*. One of his most valuable and least noticed essays illustrates the point. Karl Mannheim had undertaken to lecture on the professions at an International Summer School at Santander in Spain in the year before the outbreak of the Civil War, but decided he could not go. Marshall agreed to take his place, read up the subject, and produced a brilliant analysis of the idea and evolution of professionalism in the nineteenth and twentieth centuries[44] which bears favourable comparison with the much more widely cited essay by Talcott Parsons.[45] Neither refers to the other.

[44] Ibid. 150–70.
[45] T. Parsons, 'The Professions and Social Structure', *Essays in Sociological Theory Pure and Applied* (Chicago, 1949).

Marshall may be said to have completed his idiosyncratic formation as a sociologist by the outbreak of the Second World War. His subsequent career brought together both sides of the biography we have sketched—the upbringing of a Cambridge gentleman and the education of an LSE sociologist. The styles then merged. In his writing there is elegance and economy: sociological jargon is avoided, and meticulous citation shunned. In his teaching there was a personal style of clear, cool analysis dominating a lightly-carried but wide erudition. In his public and administrative work there was the rigorous honesty of a Leonard Woolf combined with no less rigorous standards of professional skill. Courtesy and competence, diffidence and dedication marked all his activities. Thus David Lockwood refers to Marshall's qualities of mind as 'a finely balanced tension of opposites'.[46]

In his extra-academic excursions from 1939 and his retirement to Cambridge from 1960 Marshall applied his sociology. He did so in the analysis of German war propaganda, in planning the post-war reconstruction of German education, and in directing the UNESCO effort towards applying the social sciences to the problems of development. In his retirement, and almost entirely in that period,[47] he devoted himself to social policy and administration, writing and revising the standard text on that subject[48] as well as a series of occasional papers which Robert Pinker persuaded him to put together and publish in the year before he died.[49] Again the work is applied sociology, indebted to, yet independent of, the definition of social policy and social administration which was so strongly advanced after 1950 by Richard Titmuss and the productive group of academically passionate advocates of welfare at the LSE.[50]

Professor Pinker's introduction to these last papers is nicely balanced. He sets Marshall's work on social policy in the broader context of his sociology. As Pinker says, 'the sequence of his publications gives the misleading impression that Marshall's career as a scholar can be conveniently divided between the period when he worked mainly as a sociologist and the period after his retirement in which he (wrote) books on social policy and

[46] Lockwood in Rothblatt, *Revolution of the Dons*, 363.
[47] But see his 'The Basic Training for All Types of Social Work' (1945) in *Training for Social Work* (Oxford, 1946).
[48] T. H. Marshall, *Social Policy* (1965), 4th edn. (London, 1975).
[49] Marshall, *Right to Welfare*.
[50] Notably Brian Abel-Smith, Peter Townsend, and David Donnison.

administration'.[51] In fact the story is one of 'unity and continuity'.[52] It is the story of a man who balanced scholarly detachment with social attachment to understand himself and the society in which he lived.

Unquestionably central to the outcome was what David Lockwood has described as 'the most outstanding British contribution to the analysis of the structure and dynamics of capitalist society as this has taken shape in the last two decades'.[53] Lockwood was writing in 1974 and referring primarily to *Citizenship and Social Class*, the Marshall lectures of 1949. He would now, no doubt, also include Marshall's later essays, and specifically his analysis of 'Value Problems of Welfare-Capitalism' and the 'After Thought' to it which was added in 1980.[54] Lockwood's eulogy has not been, and is unlikely to be, challenged. Even Marshall's severest critic to date, Anthony Giddens, also admires and has been influenced by the work. He recognizes the 1949 lectures as 'a famous analysis' in 'a very short book but its influence has been deservedly quite disproportionate to its size'.[55] Lockwood's praise rests more interestingly on the theoretical significance of Marshall in relation to Weber and Durkheim. Giddens's blame attaches to Marshall's leaning towards the ethical evolutionism of L. T. Hobhouse and his neglect of Marx. In our terms Marshall's was a crucial contribution to the sociology of ethical socialism.

It is obvious that any twentieth-century contribution to the theory of stratification and social change would have to be assessed against the background of interpretations of capitalism and industrialism handed down by Marx, Weber, and Durkheim. In T. H. Marshall's case L. T. Hobhouse has to be added as the English spokesman of ethical-socialist thought with its antecedents in the work of John Stuart Mill, Alfred Marshall, and the philosophy of the Oxford idealists.

As children of nineteenth-century Europe this quartet shared evolutionist conceptions in their classification of societies—simple

[51] R. Pinker, Introduction to *T. H. Marshall* (London, 1981), 1.
[52] Ibid.
[53] Lockwood, in Rothblatt, *Revolution of the Dons*, 364.
[54] Marshall, *Right to Welfare*, 123–36.
[55] Giddens, *Profiles*, 166.

or advanced, archaic or capitalist, mechanically solidary or organically solidary—even if they differed sharply about the mode and mechanism of transition between them. Hobhouse is the proximate influence on Marshall in this respect. But to assert that Marshall was indebted to Hobhouse is not necessarily to label either as subscribers to the liberal form of historical determinism. It is true that Hobhouse proposed criteria for the comparative scaling of social development (scale of organization, efficiency in control and direction, co-operation in the satisfaction of mutual needs, and freedom for personal development) and that he claimed to have established correlated growth in terms of these criteria which he interpreted as expressions of the growing power of the human mind—so far. It is also true that Hobhouse believed in the underlying drive of the human mind towards unity and social integration. Indeed the conceptual influence of the hope for continued evolutionary progress pervaded Hobhouse's writings, remained wearily in Ginsberg's, and sceptically in Marshall's, who wrote of an 'evolution of citizenship which has been in continuous progress for some 250 years'.[56]

Yet there is little force in Anthony Giddens's comment that Marshall 'writes as though the development of citizenship rights came about as something like a natural process of evolution, helped along where necessary by a beneficent hand of the state'.[57] Hobhouse explicitly disavowed belief in a mechanical evolution, insisting that social development was neither continuous, nor regular, nor assured. 'It does not move with the assured sweep of a planet in orbit on a mechanically determined curve, nor does it resemble the inevitable unfolding of a germ through predetermined stages with harmonious correlation of parts to an assigned maturity of type.'[58] Marshall for his part would never have deemed such a disavowal necessary for he was always reluctant to abstract 'epochs' or revolutionary transitions from the complexities of historical process—at least beyond the convenience of heuristic purposes.[59]

Citizenship and Social Class was in one sense *histoire raisonnée.*

---

[56] Marshall, *Sociology at the Crossroads*, 73.
[57] Giddens, *Profiles*, 171.
[58] Quoted in M. Ginsberg, *Reason and Unreason in Society* (London, 1974), 54.
[59] For example he begins his textbook with a warning against 'how many "epochs" with profoundly significant opening and closing dates historians have discovered, and subsequently, discarded'. (Marshall, *Social Policy*, 9.)

The assumptions and vocabulary of the doctrines of evolution and progress, it must be conceded, may still be discerned in Marshall's writing. There is the persistent tendency in British traditions of social and political thought towards the so-called Whig version of history. Given the influence on him of Alfred Marshall's Cambridge and Hobhouse's LSE, Marshall was prone to accept and propound it. This inclination is particularly dangerous to any understanding of the emergence of the welfare state, not only on the side of political rights but also with respect to what Marshall termed the secondary system of industrial citizenship. But the thrust of his work is towards the importance of contingency in historical explanation and towards openness or voluntarism in any view of the future.

Marshall treated industrial citizenship or economic rights more briefly than either political or social rights. His history in this respect is all the more likely to be misinterpreted as Whig—that is the gradual unfolding of liberal principles through enlightened institutions of bargaining and conciliation, parallel or assimilated to the steady evolution of the institutions of parliamentary democracy. On this view, as Alan Fox describes it, 'the triumph of liberal principles and civilized restraints, with workers coming gradually to "learn" what was required of them in this best of all liberal worlds'. Fox's alternative view is that groups of workers fumbled their way towards collective bargaining 'as the most promising way of reducing the uncertainties of their immediate work experience': employers reacted 'in the light of their particular interests and exigencies'.[60] Marshall would agree, but remains less obviously concerned to stress the contingencies as well as the continuities of history.

Giddens, however, takes his criticism further and remarks on an odd similarity here between Marshall's interpretation of the development of contemporary capitalism 'and that of some Marxist authors who in other respects have very different views from those of Marshall'.[61] These authors interpret citizenship rights (what Marx himself had dismissed as 'bourgeois freedoms') as a form of concessionary social control by the ruling class. In a wider context Frank Parkin takes a similar view when he emphasizes 'how readily an "equality of opportunity" version of socialism can be accom-

[60] A. Fox, *History and Heritage: The Social Origins of the British Industrial Relations System* (London, 1985), ch. 4.   [61] Giddens, *Profiles*, 171.

modated to the institutions and values of modern capitalism' and that 'the allocation of benefits to the less privileged serves to damp down radical or revolutionary movements'.[62]

Giddens's point is that such accounts, Marshallian or Marxist, put too little emphasis on *struggle*. He is empirically justified in insisting that all three elements of Marshall's citizenship rights had to be fought for over a long period in the development of capitalism. And the recent resurgence of market liberalism in Europe and America demonstrates that none of the three elements is either secure or irreversible.

Yet Giddens's criticism cannot be fully sustained when, as he himself notices, Marshall describes class and citizenship as principles or social forces which have been 'at war in the twentieth century'[63] and this conflict of principles springs from the very roots of our social order. Unlike Durkheim and unlike some of his own interpreters, Marshall saw conflict (though he would not have used the marxist term 'struggle') as a permanent and indeed desirable feature of a dynamic society.

'The affluent societies of the mid-twentieth century', he believed, 'contain within themselves elements producing a discord that has not yet been resolved and which . . . could remain unresolved for a long time without disrupting the social order.'[64] In his very last essay he concludes with respect to 'democratic-welfare-capitalism':

The system survives in . . . a precarious and somewhat battered condition . . . It is obvious that an acute incompatibility of values prevalent in different sectors may cause intolerable friction or possibly the destruction of one value system by another. But it would be absurd to assume that the coexistence of different value systems in different contexts must necessarily be on balance 'disfunctional', since this kind of ethical relativity has been a feature of very nearly every society since civilisation began. The question is whether potential conflict can be managed . . . Each case must be judged on its merits.[65]

In the same essay Marshall returns to a personal affirmation of both his devotion to liberty and his belief in the chronic conflict embedded in what Richard Crossman had called 'civilized capitalism':

[62] F. Parkin, *Class Inequality and Political Order* (London, 1971), 30.
[63] Marshall, *Sociology at the Crossroads*, 87, 115.
[64] Marshall, *Right to Welfare*, 61.   [65] Ibid. 129.

I am one of those who believes that it is hardly possible to maintain democratic freedoms in a society which does not contain a large area of economic freedom and that the incentives provided by and expressed in competitive markets make a contribution to efficiency, and to progress in the production and distribution of wealth which cannot, in a large and complex society, be derived from any other source. But I also believe that the capitalist market economy can be, and generally has been, a cause of much social injustice. The vital question whether this is an inevitable outcome of its ethos or a malady which could be treated . . . without destroying all that is of value in the system, has yet to be answered.[66]

The influence of Hobhouse and Alfred Marshall, so obvious in these passages, had been confirmed by both sociological analysis and by direct experience of the post-war vicissitudes of the British welfare state. Struggle is clearly recognized but not thereby assumed to result either in an inevitable class polarization or in ineluctable progress. Past progress is subtly assessed within particular and changing historical contexts. The future is open. Progress is possible—but a hope rather than an expectation. But a hope rationally based on probabilities. As between 'the spirit of acquisitiveness' and 'the pursuit of civilized enjoyment, which has close affinities with welfare', Marshall thought that in the long run the scales may be weighted in favour of the second, partly because it represented the natural reaction of the majority to a rising standard of living and partly because it received the powerful support of collective action in favour of common enjoyment and general welfare.[67]

Of course it is no less rational to put a more pessimistic value on these probabilities. Recent experience, particularly in Britain and the USA, strongly suggests a stable possibility *in a parliamentary democracy* of majority support for 'the spirit of acquisitiveness' and its associated market inequalities buttressed by social and political control of dispossessed and deprived minorities minimally maintained by state charity. Even so Marshall's non-historicist view of history, his weaving together of ideological with institutional factors in a theory of change, and his scepticisim about structural solutions to the problem of inequality still stand as firm contributions to our understanding of the genesis and contemporary state of capitalist society.

Moreover, Giddens's picture of the importance of struggle—'the

---

[66] Ibid. 135.   [67] Ibid. 61.

outcome of the active endeavours of concrete groups of people'[68]—can itself easily be overdrawn. The clash between the interests of capital and labour in the development of the industrial relations system in Britain, though real enough, is no simple story. For example, as Alan Fox reminds us:

Even within the socialist element [of the working-class movement] there was a strong tradition which gave only qualified support to the international Marxist appeal—a strand of indigenous as against exotic socialism, characterized by such names as Morris, Blatchford, Tawney and later Orwell and Edward Thompson, which remained strongly libertarian and shared the old radical love of country.[69]

And the political ruling class was never a mechanically reliable 'executive committee' of the capitalist class. It maintained a commitment to constitutionalism, law, and a not-too-heavy hand on the lower orders (partly no doubt, as Fox points out, because it was not wholly dependent on the domestic economy) but in such a way as to make the struggle for civil, political, and social rights, industrial citizenship, and still more the development of welfare rights, neither a predictable process of liberal enlightenment nor a new set of controls invented out of the cunning of a Fabian ruling class.

None the less Giddens is able to find a weakness in Marshall's *histoire raisonnée* concerning the sequence of the establishment of civil, political, and social rights as they developed from the status hierarchy of feudalism in the capitalist era. Marshall's account gives the impression that civil rights were fully and finally established before the long march of political enfranchisement and the subsequent expansion of social rights in the nineteenth and twentieth centuries. Giddens argues that civil rights, or we might say legal citizenship, established in the courts, always remained at issue, especially in what Marshall treated as their extension into industrial citizenship. These civil rights were at least as much a battle ground of class conflict as the basis for class abatement or amelioration.

Present struggles serve Giddens's view that the separation of the economy from the polity as arenas of conflict between class interests and citizenship principles, which was so characteristic a feature of the history of capitalist society, throws doubt on the

---

[68] Giddens, *Profiles*, 172.   [69] Fox, *History and Heritage*, ch. 9.

classification of economic citizenship as an extension of civil rights. Such struggles have also to be seen as a challenge to the separation of the 'economic' from the 'political' by labour movements. Working-class entry to Parliament was a necessary step towards reforming anti-working-class law. But Marshall well recognized that political rights have been used to gain extended civil rights just as much as civil rights were used as a basis for demanding the extension of the political franchise. The 'political' strike is notoriously controversial. More generally in the analysis of contemporary capitalism we are well advised to think of the three citizenships as in delicate balance, always threatened by class conflict, just as we must think of the civil rights of individuals under state socialism as always diminished by monopolized party political power. Thus the Marshallian analysis, rid of its residual evolutionism, can be turned powerfully against both the tendency of liberal theory towards envisaging a 'post industrial' society in which citizenship has replaced capitalist class conflict and against the shortcomings of marxist theories of the state in both capitalist and socialist societies.[70]

If in these ways Marshall advanced the analysis of conflict as conceived by Hobhouse and, in a different tradition by Marx, his contribution to the analysis of consensus is still more clearly an advance on Durkheim. Durkheim's central question was to identify the basis for 'organic solidarity' in modern societies: his answer was threefold. Such societies were integrated when normative rules emerge from an advanced division of labour, when there is a collectively shared value ('cult') of individualism, and when equality emerges in the conditions of occupational selection and inter-group competition in politics and industry. A 'forced division of labour' stood temporarily in the way of the new social cohesion, resulting in anomic disorder.

Much can and has been made of the Durkheimian perspective. For example, as John Goldthorpe has argued with respect to industrial (and we would add race) relations in Britain, 'within a society in which inequality exists as a brute fact—largely without moral legitimization—"disorderly" industrial relations cannot be

---

[70] Giddens draws attention to the extension of surveillance techniques by the modern state and points out that the resulting threat to civil rights in both western and socialist countries needs urgent analysis, has had little attention from marxist or liberal political theory and can be aided by Marshall's precise specifications of the nature of civil, political, and welfare rights. (*Profiles*, 177–8.)

T. H. Marshall (1893–1981)

147

understood as a particular pathological development which will yield to particular remedies ... this disorder must be seen as "normal"—as a generalized characteristic of societies of this type'.[71] Durkheim saw clearly the need for new institutions to regulate economic life in advanced societies and posed what are now acknowledged as crucial problems for the state in such moral regulation. But Durkheim's corporations have not come into existence and most modern commentators would agree that he did not answer the question he so cogently raised.[72] He postulated a process of change from stable 'moral classification' sanctioned by custom in pre-industrial Europe through 'declassification' or 'deregulation' during the upheavals of capitalism to a new and stable future of reclassification.

As Lockwood remarks, there is a parallel here in Marshall's account of the transitions from estate society through market capitalism dominated by class to modern democratic-welfare-capitalism in which a reconstructed status and class order is established. But whereas Durkheim 'did not differentiate the structural elements of his notion of moral classification or show in a precise way how they contribute to conflict and disorder',[73] Marshall does. He demonstrates the interplay between his three elements of citizenship, status, and change in class formation and economic power at each stage of transition; and his analysis shows, as Durkheim's does not, that such integration or 'uneasy equilibrium' as advanced western societies possess is based on the social relations and ideology of citizenship. To be sure strain, tensions, even contradictions exist between citizenship and class. Amelioration does not imply classlessness. Nevertheless it is in the three elements of citizenship and their less than perfect expression in the courts of law, the political organizations of national and local government, and the offices of the welfare bureaucracy that a national integration is maintained.

As a history of transitions of social integration Marshall's dissection of citizenship adds to Weber's dicussion of the classic

---

[71] J. H. Goldthorpe, 'Social Inequality and Social Integration in Modern Britain', in D. Wedderburn (ed.), *Poverty, Inequality and Class Structure* (Cambridge, 1974), 226.

[72] See S. Lukes, *Emile Durkheim: His Life and Work* (London, 1973); G. Hawthorne, *Enlightenment and Despair* (Cambridge, 1976); and Giddens, *Profiles*, ch. 9.

[73] Lockwood, in Rothblatt, *Revolution of the Dons*, 366.

class conflicts of the capitalist transition as well as to Durkheim's description of the genesis of anomic disorder. Both Weber and Durkheim relied almost exclusively on the rapidity and scale of shifts in economic power as explanations of class polarization and anomic breakdown. Marshall's work offers a more complete set of causal factors behind both of these phenomena. The equality principle inherent in all three aspects of citizenship, legal, political, and social, is set against class inequality in such a way as to explain both class conflict and class amelioration. And the same analysis of citizenship throws light on the role or possible role of the state, of the professions, and of local community organizations in the moral regulation of the distributive arrangements of society and the selection, expectations, and obligations of individuals for places in the social structure.

For Marshall, civil rights are the bulwark of a free democracy. Legal rights as rights of citizenship are dispersed through many institutions: they are intrinsic to all social relations, not simply to the polity; and they refer to citizens as political actors not merely, as with social rights, to people as consumers. They are more than an institution: they are a culture. The rights to freedom of thought, speech, and assembly, and the right to justice and the rule of law are externalized expressions of principles internalized by upbringing. 'They thus become part of the individual's personality, a pervasive element in his daily life, an intrinsic component of his culture, the foundation of his capacity to act socially and the creator of the environmental conditions which make social action possible in a democratic civilization.'[74]

Marshall, the inheritor of high civility and the scholar of high sensibility was here describing his own best self, his ideal for his country, and the ultimate hope of ethical socialists for all societies.

---

[74] Marshall, *Right to Welfare*, 141.

7

SOCIALISM AS FELLOWSHIP
R. H. Tawney (1880–1962)

Richard Henry Tawney has been the crowning figure of ethical socialism in the twentieth century. Though he wrote no systematic philosophy or codified political theory he enjoyed pre-eminence as the source of exemplary wisdom for the British Labour party for forty years from the First World War. The leader of the party, Hugh Gaitskell, led a laudatory chorus of obituaries when Tawney died, describing him as 'the best man I have ever known' and the 'democratic socialist par excellence'.[1] But was he an effective political sage? Three years later a philosopher of the New Left, Alisdair MacIntyre, dismissed Tawney's morals as 'cliché ridden high mindedness' and his political life as 'a monument to the impotence of ideals'.[2]

Tawney was indeed a moralist: he had a vision of society embodying a set of ideals, and he pursued them politically as well as personally throughout a long life. We are accordingly entitled to ask of him what society he desired and how he proposed to achieve it; and we want to understand his life both by tracing the beliefs on which he based his theory and method, and by assessing the results of his political action. These interrogations, followed in the Weberian manner, should lead to more than a 'life and times' of Tawney. They should help us to refine our definition of the ethical-socialist tradition; inform us about the general role of morals in politics; perhaps reveal to us that other social movements may also be monuments to the impotence of politics; and finally allow us a view of the conflicts of value with which we struggle in the political life of the last decades of our century.

Tawney was born in 1880 in Calcutta, an upper-middle-class child of Victorian imperialism. He died in 1962, having seen the

---

[1] R. H. Tawney, *The Radical Tradition: Twelve Essays on Politics, Education and Literature*, ed. R. Hinden (London, 1964), 212.

[2] A. MacIntyre, 'The Socialism of R. H. Tawney', *Against the Self-Images of the Age* (London, 1971), 39.

end of the Pax Britannica and the absorption of the Labour party
into the British establishment, if not its decline as the major vehicle
of political radicalism. The British Labour movement, as a set of
social adaptations to the circumstances of a rapidly created urban
proletariat, was born before Tawney in the industrial towns of the
nineteenth century. A new culture of survival emerged from the
novel conditions of huge dormitory annexes to capitalist factories—
vulnerable to economic insecurities, the hazards to health of high
density, and the threat to 'social harmony' of tenuously regulated
class relations, disorganized religion, and inadequate schooling.
The Labour movement strove to integrate a remarkable apparatus
of collective self-help beyond the family—trade unions, co-
operatives, chapels, pubs, burial clubs, Friendly Societies, football
clubs, and even schools. It was a vast social invention born of
adversity under unprecedented challenge. It was a culture of people,
typified by Tawney's Henry Dubb, whose fundamental relation to
capitalist society was one of moral revolt against the denial of
dignity to human beings. It was a social movement in search of a
right order of life.

But the political arm of the working-class movement was created
in Tawney's lifetime. Neither he nor we believe that it did or could
serve as the sole means of attaining a socialist Britain. Tawney's
socialism was not restricted to a political programme, and he saw
politics as a consequence as well as cause of the structure of society.
He believed in democracy and socialism as both ends and means.
Both were ways as well as destinations. When left-wing intellectuals
in the 1930s followed Stalin, albeit to combat Fascism, Tawney
remained a democrat. When right-wing labour intellectuals in the
1950s adopted revisionism and made economic growth the
spearhead of policy, albeit to fund egalitarian measures, Tawney
remained a socialist. Against both communist and liberal theorists
he refused to accept historical inevitability and hence rejected both
the inescapability of violent revolution and the 'end of ideology'.
The future he held to be open. Socialism was a society fit for human
beings, ordinary free people, neither puppets of history nor rational
angels. Socialism was fellowship in a free society made by people
who recognized each other's equal right to dignity and respect.

Tawney's socialism was above all personal, moral, and religious.
Though his world for more than eighty years was that of the
Church of England, the British upper classes, Rugby, Balliol, the

Somme, the London School of Economics, and the Labour party, he nevertheless lived and died without disillusion as both a Christian and a socialist. This is not to suggest that he was somehow *sui generis*, but rather to emphasize his remarkable charisma. If he was Church of England, his friends were Temple and Gore; if he was Oxford, it was the Oxford of Barnett House and the tutorial classes committee; if he was a gentleman he dismissed the 'honours' system with elegantly ironical prose and earned his living and the respect of others as a professional historian and teacher; if he was a soldier his army was not that of the Guards officer but of the Poor Bloody Infantry in the front line trench and 'the little man beside me, the kindest and bravest of friends, whom no weariness could discourage or danger daunt, a bricklayer by trade, but one who could turn his hand to anything, the man whom of all others I would choose to have beside me at a pinch'.[3]

To take the Sermon on the Mount with calm and almost prosaic seriousness, as he did, is to possess both rare personal freedom and a shattering political critique of profane society. Through his life and writings, Tawney offered socialists a code of personal conduct which dismisses the acquisitive scramble for money and peerages as vulgar trivialities, sets its face against the whole degrading cult of individualistic materialism, and enjoins service and humility as active principles of man's relation to his fellows.

Tawney's conception of the social order began with the morality of the New Testament. He saw capitalism not simply as un-Christian but anti-Christian in that it converted economic means into overriding ends and thus introduced the worship of false gods. In his preoccupation with the three venerable abstractions of western politics—liberty, fraternity, and equality—he was in the tradition of eighteenth- and nineteenth-century radicalism and an immediate descendant of William Morris, Matthew Arnold, and John Ruskin. But he carried their critique of capitalist industrialism further into systematic argument which, while it had continuity with the development of liberalism in the nineteenth century, became and remains, in *The Acquisitive Society* and *Equality*, the best and probably the most widely influential modern statement of democratic socialism.

The foundations of socialism for him were ethical. Socialism was a matter, 'not of quantity of possessions, but of quality of life'. The

[3] R. H. Tawney, *The Attack and Other Papers* (1953) (Nottingham, 1981), 14.

aims of the ethical socialist were, as he said, a society which valued public welfare above private display; which, though relatively poor, made the first charge on its small resources the establishment for all of the conditions of a vigorous and self-respecting existence; which gave a high place among those conditions to the activities of the spirit and to services which promoted them; which held that the most important aspect of human beings was not the external differences of income and circumstance that divided them, but the common humanity that united them; and which strove, therefore, to reduce such differences to their proper position of insignificance.[4]

Against Marxism he sought to maintain that socialism was only possible as an extension of the idea of political democracy with its corollaries of free speech and free assembly. Democracy was not only the sole political method discovered by man of effecting bloodless change but also a style of life, thought, and conduct admirable in itself. Socialism, he similarly argued against liberals, was not the antithesis of democracy but involved, on the contrary, the extension of democratic principles and methods into spheres of life which in the past had escaped them. Thus Tawney summarized a type of society nurturing and nurtured by a moral outlook among ordinary people which in elaboration is the tradition of ethical socialism.

TAWNEY'S EDUCATION

Tawney's father was the Principal of Presidency College—a senior position in education in the Indian Empire at the height of its security and success.[5] The confident sense of benign historic mission felt by such servants of Empire is remote to us now.[6] Others of Tawney's class became socialists through the experience of rejecting the imperialist culture in Eastern service. Tawney's exact contemporary Leonard Woolf did so gently out of Ceylon,[7] the younger Eric Blair did so dramatically as George Orwell out of Burma. It was a culture Tawney never embraced. He was sent to England to be reared in the conventional mode of his class—a

---

[4] Tawney, *Radical Tradition*, 167.
[5] L. Pressnell, *Country Banking in the Industrial Revolution* (Oxford, 1956), 55–6. The Tawneys had a family history of professional service going back to eighteenth-century country banking.
[6] See P. Woodruff, *The Men Who Ruled India* (London, 1953–4).
[7] See L. Woolf, *An Autobiography* (Oxford, 1980), i. 133–301.

preparatory school at Weybridge, followed by Rugby and Balliol. The cult of the English gentleman in his generation was as strong and as laden with commitment to public service at home and abroad as it was ever to be. John Henry Newman had defined it as 'a cultivated intellect, a delicate taste, a candid, equitable, dispassionate mind, a noble and courteous bearing in the conduct of life'.[8] Alfred Marshall had looked forward confidently in 1873 to its dissemination to the working class.[9] Tawney was to live its ethos and to work for its realization in the British Labour movement.[10]

The Oxford ideal of a gentleman in Tawney's youth enjoined a moral character and outlook which preferred public service to private commerce, asceticism to social display. Social obligation was the corollary of privilege. Ruskin, T. H. Green, and Arnold Toynbee were among its founders; Christians and socialists like Scott Holland and Sidney Ball were among its proselytes. The most famous Master of Tawney's college, Benjamin Jowett, had urged idealistic undergraduates to go and 'find their friends among the poor'.[11] Edward Caird, Master in Tawney's day, urged both Tawney and Beveridge in 1903 to discover why poverty coexisted with so much wealth in England. Tawney responded positively, as did Hobhouse, Beveridge, Attlee, and Gaitskell. He lived for three years at Canon Barnett's Toynbee Hall during his Oxford days and after.

Through Barnett's friendship he became secretary of the Children's Country Holiday Fund and in that way faced a contemporary conflict concerning charity, class, and social work. On the one side stood the Charity Organization Society led by Octavia Hill and C. S. Loch. The COS emphasized the importance of character defects as the cause of poverty and squalor, and character-building as the cure. Barring accidents to life and health, any family could maintain its independence were its members only sober and dutiful.

---

[8] J. H. Newman, *The Scope and Nature of University Education* (1859) (London, 1903), 112.

[9] A. Marshall, *Memorials of Alfred Marshall*, ed. A. C. Pigou (London, 1925).

[10] This is not to say that Tawney approved of the pretensions and conduct of every person who claimed to be a gentleman. Precisely because of the importance of the ideal to him—the corruption of the best is the worst—he was merciless in his attacks on those who had either too narrow a conception of what being a true gentleman meant, or who regarded it as an ideal unattainable by the lower orders. In its corrupt form it became for him *das Gentlemanideal*. (See, e.g. R. H. Tawney, *Equality* (1931), 4th edn. (London, 1952), 23–4.)

[11] S. and A. Barnett, *Practicable Socialism* (London, 1915), 97.

To school the poor in industry, honesty, thrift, and filial piety was the principal solution to social problems. On the other side were those, such as the Fabians, who stressed the influence of material circumstances which could throw even the healthiest and most virtuous person into penury or prevent even the most gifted infant from growing into an intelligent adult. They looked for state control within a dual system of, as Charles Booth put it, 'socialism in the arms of Individualism'.[12]

Tawney combined both these influences to emphasize, among social conditions, *the moral climate* within which individuals had to make their way in the world. During his period at Toynbee Hall he had begun to educate himself in practicable socialism by observing working-class life. He noticed the deteriorated moral and religious state of the East End. 'One of the great social forces of history', he wrote, 'is gradually and reluctantly drifting out of the lives of a not inconsiderable part of society.' It was this 'permanent ethical atmosphere' which developed poverty, crime, and crowded tenements.[13]

Tawney's next steps in self-education as a socialist were through practice as a teacher. In 1906, with the help of the Master of Balliol, he secured an assistantship under William Smart, Professor of Economics at Glasgow University (one of the signatories in 1909 of the Webbs' Minority Report of the Royal Commission on the Poor Laws and Relief of Distress). In Glasgow he again saw the spoiled lives of the poor, especially the plight of young school-leavers in dead-end jobs, and expressed his indignation in the editorial columns of the *Glasgow Herald*.

Meanwhile a series of local extension lectures sponsored by the Borough Council of Longton, in the Potteries, proved successful, and this led the organizer, E. S. Cartwright, to ask for tutorial classes to be provided there. At about the same time a similar request came from the Educational Guild of the cotton town of Rochdale, Lancashire, the home of the pioneers of the co-operative movement in Britain.[14] Tawney accepted the tutorship of classes

---

[12] A. Fried and R. Elman (eds.), *Charles Booth's London* (Harmondsworth, 1971), 387–8.

[13] R. H. Tawney, 'The Daily News Religious Census of London', *Toynbee Record*, 16, 6 (Mar. 1904).

[14] L. T. West, 'The Tawney Legend Re-examined', *Studies in Adult Education* (1972); D. J. Booth, 'Albert Mansbridge's Formative Years', *Journal of Education, Administration and History* (1974).

for workers in these two towns. He was immediately immersed in the experience of adult education which was always thereafter his model of the socialist society. At the end of the first year sponsorship of the classes was undertaken by the recently established Oxford University Tutorial Classes Committee, with funds provided in part by New College and All Souls. In April 1909 it was decided that Tawney should take additional classes in Littleborough and Wrexham. He was appointed the first 'All Souls Teacher' of the Tutorial Classes Committee. The archives of All Souls became an important source on the industrial history of the late fifteenth and early sixteenth centuries for a book which Tawney was required to write in lieu of a fifth tutorial class, all royalties to go to the Committee.[15] After his army service in the Great War he returned to tutorial class teaching at Longton, and undertook work as the Workers' Educational Association's general tutor in North Staffordshire.

Tawney travelled the social distance from All Souls in Oxford to the WEA in Rochdale on a distinctive passport. His version of the gentleman's culture denied class—by finding its distinctive qualities of character in all strata of a hierarchical society. Tawney believed from direct experience that both George Eliot's Felix Holt and Thomas Hardy's Jude the Obscure were to be found among the earnest working people of the industrial North-west of England— miners, potters, cotton spinners, iron- and saltworkers. Here were men and women, freely choosing, not the selfish pursuit of superfluous possessions, but the fellowship of learning. They were equals in the sense that differences in class and income were indeed for them 'vulgar irrelevancies'. They were engaged in 'honest and wholesome' communication (Raphael Hythloday had said this of the inhabitants of the island of Utopia) and in exercising the liberty of the mind, and the garnishing of the same, in which consisted the felicity of this life.[16]

Tawney came to know similar people, among whom a prototypic figure was Thomas Burt, the leader of the Northumberland miners, who had been brought up among Primitive Methodists and laboured, man and boy, in various pits in Durham and Northum-

---

[15] This book was published as *The Agrarian Problem in the Sixteenth Century* (London, 1912).

[16] T. More, *The Complete Works of Sir Thomas More*, ed. E. Surtz and J. H. Hexter (New Haven, 1965), iv. 135.

berland.[17] Burt sought to realize those ideals of 'the English gentleman' which were compatible both with his working as a trade union official and with his fidelity to the values of his mining community of north-east England. He assimilated, in other words, those aspects of the ideal of the Christian gentleman that were capable of being democratized. As he wrote of a Bishop of Durham and Christian Socialist, Brooke Foss Westcott, 'wisdom, justice and gentleness—in a word, Love—these are the all-conquering weapons of the reformer. They alone bring ultimate and permanent victory.' When Burt eventually became Father of the House of Commons, a parliamentary correspondent wrote of him that 'gentleness and tact, the incommunicable strength and modesty of a great nature, are independent of station, and unite the highest with the humblest of the land'.[18] And Earl Grey once said that the finest gentleman he had ever known had been a working miner—Burt—'whose gentleness, absolute fairness, and instinctive horror of anything underhand or mean' had raised him to the position of Privy Councillor.[19]

Tawney eased his arduous travelling as an adult education tutor in 1909 by settling in Manchester. He had married William Beveridge's sister, Jeannette,[20] the year before. At Manchester he came into close contact with the New Liberal culture of the *Manchester Guardian*. There, Hobhouse was a prominent figure. Another contributor was J. L. B. Hammond, son of the vicar of Drightlington, Yorkshire. As the editor of the *Speaker* Hammond had been the first to discuss British concentration camps in South Africa during the Boer War, the existence of which had been exposed by Hobhouse's sister, Emily.[21] Tawney himself wrote frequently for the *Manchester Guardian*, especially on educational matters. The moral transformation of Britain to a 'right order of life' as a socialist commonwealth was a process with education at its centre. He seized every opportunity to disseminate socialist

---

[17] T. Burt, *Pitman and Privy Councillor: An Autobiography* (London, 1924), 110–11. [18] *Daily News*, 14 June 1910.
[19] Burt, *Pitman and Privy Councillor*, 316.
[20] J. Harris, *William Beveridge* (Oxford, 1977). Beveridge's wife was one of the Northumberland Shaftoes, neighbours to the Trevelyans, both prominent families in the tradition of public-service gentlemanliness. Beveridge had been sub-warden of Toynbee Hall.
[21] R. H. Tawney, *History and Society: Essays by R. H. Tawney*, ed. J. M. Winter (London, 1978), 229–30.

education and he searched steadily in history and in contemporary Europe for ways to increase its power.

In 1903 he made a long visit to Germany, where the Marburg-school socialists were attempting to introduce explicit Kantian moralizing into the discussions of the—marxist—Social Democratic party. He returned to Germany in the years 1908–10, pursuing his interest both in the particular problems of boy-labour in Glasgow and Beveridge's work at the Board of Trade on Labour Exchanges. Tawney testified before the Poor Law Commission, commending the German approach to the alleviation of unemployment and poverty. He was particularly impressed by the way that the Germans used the state to tackle misuse in the labour market of early-teenage children. He records the remark of a manager of a German Labour Exchange: 'We don't *let* boys become casual labourers.'[22]

These experiences fed his passion for the reform of inadequate education and for an end to the exploitation of the labour of young people. The future policy had to be 'secondary education for all'. In this campaign his influential ally was the Northumberland gentle-man, Sir Charles Trevelyan, who, abandoning his Liberal career in Parliament, presented himself in 1921 as Labour candidate for a Newcastle upon Tyne constituency. President of the Board of Education in the first Labour government, one of his earliest acts was to set up a Consultative Committee on the education of the adolescent. Under Tawney's influence it recommended the abolition of elementary education, and the substitution of a universal system of primary and secondary education.[23]

In 1891 Pope Leo XIII, in his encyclical *Rerum Novarum*, announced to all Catholics that the Church was free from the claims of capitalism, and that some of the ideals of socialism were essentially Christian. During his extended study visits to Germany, Tawney found that Christian interest and involvement in industrial and urban questions was growing strongly. In this period, too,

---

[22] R. H. Tawney, *Economic Journal* (Dec. 1911). Tawney quotes this remark in connection with books he is reviewing. Articles by Tawney on his German experiences are, 'A Report on the Visit to Germany Made by Members of the Rochdale Branch of the W.E.A', *Highway* (Mar. 1910); and 'Municipal Enterprise in Germany', *Economic Review* (Oct. 1910).

[23] *Report of the Consultative Committee on the Education of the Adolescent* (the Hadow Report) (London, 1926). Trevelyan wrote the Preface to Tawney's *Education: The Socialist Policy* (London, 1924).

Weber had published his articles on the influence of Calvinist Christianity on morality, and of Calvinist morality on economic conduct, which (as an English commentator was able to note as early as 1910) had produced 'a remarkable impression' in Germany both among economists and theologians.[24]

TAWNEY AND THE LONDON SCHOOL OF ECONOMICS

In 1913 Tawney returned from Manchester to live in London, having been granted leave of absence to study the causes of poverty as Director of the Ratan Tata Foundation at the London School of Economics. Three strands of thought were represented in the pre-war LSE. One was that of New Liberal philosophy, advocating the use of the state to enlarge and extend the freedom of the individual—the doctrine of T. H. Green. This strand was represented by L. T. Hobhouse, who was Tawney's superior at the Ratan Tata Foundation, and Graham Wallas, the professor of politics who had put forward Tawney's name for the post. The second was that of detailed investigation in aid of social reform, on the model of Booth's studies of the London poor. The third was that of the Charity Organization Society which assumed two classes of poor, as we have seen, those capable of being restored to self-sufficiency by the influence of a person of superior moral character and those who were incorrigible and had to be dealt with by the Poor Law, the prisons, and other agencies.[25] The COS had promoted a School of Sociology under E. J. Urwick to train the staff to carry out the work of redeeming the redeemable poor, and it had been incorporated into the LSE—with some anxiety that in Houghton Street the necessary firm ethical commitment and ethical guidance might be relaxed.[26]

Tawney's work at the Ratan Tata Foundation was empirical study, in the Booth tradition, of conditions in the chain-making and tailoring trades. In this and all his later work, both as a historian and an investigator of current social and industrial issues, Tawney used the philosophical assumptions and conclusions of Hobhouse

[24] P. T. Forsyth, 'Calvinism and Capitalism', *Contemporary Review* (1910), 97–8.

[25] C. S. Loch, *How to Help Cases in Distress: A Handy Reference Book for Almoners, Almsgivers and Others* (1883) (London, 1895).

[26] C. L. Mowat, *The Charity Organization Society, 1869–1913: Its Ideas and its Work* (London, 1961), 107, 112.

to develop a powerful understanding of capitalism and socialism as social systems providing wholly different moral influences on conduct.[27]

In 1919 he was appointed lecturer at LSE, at a time when Harold Laski was developing his brand of English socialism, somewhat more radical than that of the New Liberals, and much more concerned with detailed constitutional arrangements. Laski used his influence with the *New Republic* to bring the final chapter of Tawney's *Religion and the Rise of Capitalism* to the attention of an American audience.[28] Made Professor in 1931, Tawney remained at 'the School' for the rest of his working life, in an atmosphere in which the idea that the state could act as a liberating force persisted across the disciplines. Bronislaw Malinowski, for example, was an LSE anthropologist who clearly expressed the belief in the possibility and desirability of 'positive' freedom:

The instrumentalities of freedom we find in the political constitution of a community, its laws, its moral norms . . . its religious or artistic gifts of culture. To scour the universe for possibilities of freedom other than those given by the organization of human groups for . . . the production of desirable results, is an idle philosophic pastime.[29]

The determining conditions of an individual's freedom are to be found in the way society is organized: 'in the way instrumentalities are made accessible; and in the guarantees which safeguard all the rewards of planned and purposeful action and secure their equitable distribution'. All other claims for freedom are 'idle and irrelevant'.[30]

THE FIRST WORLD WAR

Apart from his secure personal religious faith and his education with and from working people in the provinces, Tawney had one overwhelming experience—his service in the Great War. For years afterwards he was to be seen in the slowly disintegrating remnant of

[27] R. H. Tawney, *The Establishment of Minimum Rates in the Chain-Making Industry under the Trade Boards Act of 1909*, Studies in the Minimum Wage No. 1, The Ratan Tata Foundation (London, 1914).
[28] *New Republic*, 12 and 19 May 1926.
[29] B. Malinowski, *Freedom and Civilization* (1944) (Bloomington, 1960), 95. The book was produced from Malinowski's papers by his widow, Valetta, who specially thanks Gilbert Murray and Laski as other exponents of 'positive' freedom, p. vii.   [30] Ibid. 25–6.

his army sergeant's tunic. To Lenin, soon to become the leading Marxist of his time, wielding world-wide influence, the First World War had a 'predatory, imperialist, reactionary, slaveowner' character, which made the admissibility of defending the homeland 'nonsensical in theory and absurd in practice'. Instead of defending one's own country, advantage must be taken of the state of war to 'rouse the masses'.[31] Scandalously, from Lenin's standpoint, in England the Labour party was one of the strongholds of patriotism—'social-chauvinism'.[32]

In 1914 Tawney was not even as 'marxist' as the Labour party. He volunteered early in the war (November 1914) and served with the Manchester Regiment. This (and others, like the Durham Light Infantry) was a regiment based on intense regional solidarity and local patriotism, especially strong in the English provincial working class in the first half of the twentieth century. Heavy losses in battle united local communities at home in grief and, at any rate for a time, renewed loyalty to the national cause.

The Battle of the Somme during the summer and autumn of 1916 drew thousands of the most idealistic, courageous, and dutiful young men from Bradford, Sunderland, or Sheffield, from Bacup, Crook, or Leasingthorne to their death.[33] On the first day of the battle Sergeant Tawney led an assault on the German lines at Fricourt salient. Over half of his company were casualties. He was severely wounded in the abdomen by shell fragments, and remained alone in no man's land for a day and a half before dragging himself back to the British trenches. He was on the critical list for two weeks, and almost given up for dead, before being sent back to England. He recuperated in Oxford at the home of Bishop Charles Gore, and was discharged in September 1917 after an appeal to Beveridge had persuaded the War Office that Tawney was more important to the war effort as a civilian teacher than as a soldier.

His service with the Manchesters, and especially the part he took in the Battle of the Somme, fixed an attitude of moral commitment and utter lack of frivolity in his socialism. Referring to the Hundred Years War and to the fifteenth-century founder of All Souls

---

[31] V. I. Lenin, *Selected Works*, (Moscow, 1947), i. 621.   [32] Ibid. 623.

[33] By mid-1915 over 230,000 miners—approximately one quarter of the work-force—had voluntarily enlisted. Durham was one of the coalfields showing the highest rates. (Departmental Committee Appointed to Enquire into the Conditions Prevailing in the Coal Mining Industry due to the War, *Second Report* (London, 1916), 307.)

College, Oxford, he wrote that England stood, for a moment, where Chichele stood, 'because we stand upon a world of graves'.[34] After his experience in the trenches he had no more use for the opinions of those brittle intellectuals who cracked beneath a strain, or who 'chattered in the lobbies and lounged in the gentlemen's clubs'.[35]

In the war Tawney saw the best and worst of England. On the credit side his faith in the capacity of human beings for some degree of fraternal, socialist, as opposed to self-seeking, capitalist, co-operation, was reinforced by his own daily direct experience. Neither anti-war debunking from Bloomsbury, nor the anti-war poets' perfectly valid responses to their own experiences of the horror of battle, could ever convince him that he had been either the victim of jingoistic propaganda in the war or of his own romanticized nostalgia afterwards. On the civilian front, whatever had been true of governments, the spell that had bound 'the common people of England' was their feeling of a shared duty to defend the liberal and humane ideals which had been central to the development of English culture, and their faith in a fundamental notion of 'right'—which was only in part also a claim to individual and irresponsible 'rights'—as the basis of human association.[36] Capitalism was a temporary aberration in the development of English cultural values. It produced in both profiteer and worker 'a hell of embittered suspicion'. But his war experiences proved, in the face of all the evils of war and of military life, that selfishness was not necessarily the dominating trait of human nature; that when each worked for all, each was the gainer. Not of course 'the British soldier' but, for Tawney, an impressive number of the British soldiers he personally knew, faced hunger and thirst, cold, heat, and total fatigue, because the loss of one is not the gain of another. What he saw realized in war was the ideal of 'comradeship in service'.[37]

> The pallor of girls' brows shall be their pall:
> Their flowers the tenderness of patient minds.[38]

[34] Tawney, *The Attack*, 29.
[35] R. H. Tawney, *Democracy or Defeat* (London, 1917), 8.
[36] S. E. Chapman (ed.), *Labour and Capital After The War* (London, 1918), 96.
[37] Ibid. 110.
[38] W. Owen, 'Anthem for Doomed Youth', in *The Collected Poems of Wilfred Owen*, ed. C. D. Lewis (London, 1974), 44.

England would only deserve to win the war, Tawney concluded, if fellowship replaced acquisitiveness as the rationale of the social order. Tawney saw the war as national mobilization for the prosecution of a just cause. In an utterly un-marxian way he interpreted the *best* of wartime life at home and in Flanders as the prefiguration of a future democratic and socialist society in which men and women would work together, each for the benefit of all. It was the soldiers' task to remake society according to the soldiers' standards of 'fellowship in a moral purpose' and put an end to capitalistic individualism—'a game played by monkeys and organized by lunatics'.[39] In the opinion of Tawney's biographer, Ross Terrill, there is no better statement of what a People's War means, not by Mao or Lin Piao, than Tawney's *Democracy or Defeat*.[40]

At least for Kitchener's army—Tawney's army—it was a civilians' war, fought by soldiers who were incurable civilians, for civilian purposes.[41] He shared this conception (or misconception) with others, so that the Day of Remembrance for the men and women who died has not been in England an annual victory parade with goose-stepping troops and displays of armaments. As conspicuous as the soldiers is the organized column of men who, in an orderly walk, pass the Cenotaph not with the gun and the helmet, but with the bowler hat and rolled umbrella.

Tawney was a Christian. He therefore did not enter the war with a vision of a humanity perfectible on this earth, but with a belief in original sin and the ineradicable tendency of human beings to fall into wickedness. He was not shattered nor was his philosophy transformed by the war. On the contrary, the war revealed to him the depths of most men's propensity, including his own, to desecrate, destroy, and kill. He had discovered the internal beast that 'shouts to be given a chance of showing his joyful cunning in destruction', which, given that chance, turns a human being into 'a merry mischievous ape tearing at the image of God'. 'God forgive us all!', he wrote. 'But then it was as I say.'[42]

He reserved his particular disgust for the non-combatants, journalists and others, who, safely at home in England, bravely bore the tortured deaths of his friends on the Western Front, and

---

[39] Tawney, *The Attack*, 25.
[40] R. Terrill, *R. H. Tawney and His Times* (London, 1974), 49.
[41] R. H. Tawney, 'The Personnel of the New Armies', *Nation*, 27 (Feb. 1915).
[42] Tawney, *The Attack*, 16.

who interpreted their fate as 'the last word in Christian wisdom'.[43] Henceforth, Utopianism (in the pejorative sense of false hopes of heaven on earth for human beings assumed perfectible) was for Tawney as much an emotional as an intellectual impossibility.

Such was the worst of human nature. The worst of England was revealed to him by the conduct of some of the private soldiers and NCOs. After a year in the army he complained to Beveridge that the workman's philosophy was that of his masters, 'Get as much, and give as little as possible.'[44] The same attitudes led to labour unrest at home which, so commendable to Lenin, was to Tawney a disgrace, even though it was explicable in terms of the evils sown and ripened in 150 years of capitalist morality.[45]

Tawney's war experiences led him to the same conclusions about the officer class as those of that other private soldier and army sergeant, William Cobbett. Even before their most hideous blunders were made, the war revealed to Tawney the stupidity, conceit, and plain idleness of the staff officers. Their incompetence, he bitterly wrote just before Christmas 1915, was paid for with the lives of the common soldiers; yet they escaped 'Scot free, or with nothing worse than a peerage'.[46]

The war also brought to Tawney's attention the coal, food, and freight profiteers—the *Daily Herald* called them the War Hogs— who made money from the needs of the volunteers who were risking their lives in the trenches. Still in uniform and not yet recovered from his wounds, Tawney helped draft an official memorandum for the Prime Minister, Lloyd George, recommending that more rights should be given to those 'who sweat half-naked, in the mine and at the forge'; but even more that profiteers should lose theirs—that, in certain areas of activity, state control should be extended 'regardless of property rights'.[47] The restrictions placed upon property during the war confirmed for him, finally, that in England substantial economic changes could be rapidly but peacefully introduced. The common soldiers had been told by politicians, and politicians had been told by *laissez-faire* philosophers, that change could only be gradual. They had been told by the Marxists that morality was the pawn of economics. 'Now they

[43] Ibid. 26.
[44] J. M. Winter, *Socialism and the Challenge of War: Ideas and Politics in Britain 1912–18* (London, 1974), 159.   [45] Chapman, *Labour and Capital*, 95.
[46] Winter, *Socialism and the Challenge of War*, 158–9.
[47] T. Jones, *Whitehall Diary*, (London, 1969), i. 3.

discover that the economic mechanism . . . has been transformed in three years by a collective act of will, because there was a strong enough motive, *which was not an economic motive*, to transform it.'[48]

Thus Tawney's interpretation of the nature of capitalism and the basis for its overthrow in terms of minds and wills rather than material interests is made explicit. His view was rooted in pre-war experience. One influential episode was the so-called 'labour unrest' of the year immediately preceding the Great War. Though England was the first industrial nation, from a marxist standpoint it had been for years a backward country in the development of revolutionary working-class consciousness. In 1892 Engels rated the working classes of both France and the newly industrialized Germany as 'well ahead' of the peaceable, respectable, co-operative working class in England.[49] But in 1911 began a turbulent period of industrial disputes which ended only with the outbreak of war in August 1914. There was violence in the mining valleys of Wales, with syndicalists advocating the use of the General Strike as a weapon of violent revolution,[50] and there was a London transport workers' strike.[51]

Tawney derived from the strikes a message which reinforced his moral judgement upon industrial England. It seemed to him that the strikers were not protesting primarily against material deprivation. They were protesting against spiritual deprivation, about being treated with insufficient respect, having insufficient control over their own lives, and insufficient scope for self-fulfilment in the work they were compelled to do. The strikes were only superficially about wages. Discontent expressed consciousness of a moral wrong—the strikers had now recognized that their position in society was 'an outrage on what is sacred in man'. The strikes and disturbances were a demand for fraternal relationships, for a renewal in personal life of humane association: 'loyalties, affections, pious bonds between man and man which express his personality and become at once a sheltering nest for his spirit and a kind of

---

[48] Chapman, *Labour and Capital*, 96.

[49] K. Marx and F. Engels, *Selected Works*, (Moscow, 1951, 1958), ii. 105.

[50] *Colliery Strike Disturbances in South Wales*, Cd. 5568 (London, 1911); Reform Committee of the South Wales Miners, *The Miners' Next Step* (Tonypandy, 1912).

[51] B. Tillett, *History of the London Transport Workers' Strike, 1911* (London, 1912).

watch-tower from which he may see vision of a more spacious and bountiful land'.[52]

The labour unrest also confirmed his belief that ordinary people had a sound sense of justice. He drew a historical parallel in *The Agrarian Problem in the Sixteenth Century*. In the rebellious protest against the Tudor enclosures he found the last great literary expression of the appeal to 'the average conscience'. As discontent in the sixteenth century had travelled across the enclosing counties, so it did in 1911 in the Welsh mining valleys, 'precoursing oppression itself . . . like Elijah running before Ahab into Jezreel'. Such movements were proof of the accurate perception and the moral rectitude of a happy nation which had not forgotten how to rebel; they were the 'blood and sinew of a high and gallant spirit'.[53]

This labour unrest may have influenced him—temporarily and uncharacteristically—to see unauthorized violence as an efficacious and acceptable instrument of change under contemporary British conditions. He wrote that the Great Rebellion of the seventeenth century had been necessary, morally correct, and ultimately beneficial. 'When we cut off the heads of our industrial Lauds and Staffords, we shall probably for a century or so have to put up with ineptitude.' Would that be wise? He answers, 'Yes. This too is worthwhile.'[54] Whether he really meant 'cut off the heads' of British industrialists, however, is to be doubted. It is more likely that this was simply an Edwardian English gentleman, pleasantly curdling his own blood. What Orwell said of fishing and the solid, peaceful names of English coarse fish, could be said of Tawney's pre-war style: it doesn't belong to the modern world, but to a time 'before the war, before the radio, before aeroplanes, before Hitler', and before people spent their times in wondering how to keep out of the extermination camp.[55]

AFTER THE GREAT WAR

Post-war experiences in politics matured Tawney's understanding of social transformation. If progress towards socialism was to be

[52] R. H. Tawney, *R. H. Tawney's Commonplace Book (1912–14)*, ed. J. M. Winter and D. M. Joslin (Cambridge, 1972), 10 June 1912.
[53] Tawney, *Agrarian Problem in the Sixteenth Century*, 321, 340, 348.
[54] Tawney, *Commonplace Book*, 3 June 1912.
[55] G. Orwell, *The Orwell Reader* (New York, 1956), 230–1.

made, patience and courage would be needed as much as on the Western Front. He served on the 1919 Coal Industry Commission. As representative of the Miners' Federation of Great Britain he tried to demonstrate that the mining industry in private hands, quite apart from the immorality of providing unearned wealth to the royalty and equity owners, was not an effective producer of goods under the impulse of market forces. It was chaotic and hopelessly inefficient. His work on the Commission also heightened his interest in the forms of worker-participation that might be possible in mining, as compared with the very differently structured industry of house-building.[56] It was against the background of the Commission that 'The Sickness of the Acquisitive Society' was written, the article which he was later to expand into his best-known book of socialist argument, *The Acquisitive Society*.[57] The cure for the social malady of false capitalist values could only be taken by a brave patient convinced of the need for socialist therapy. Only socialism could provide social unity.

Visiting China in 1931–2 as educational adviser to the League of Nations,[58] Tawney saw at first hand what life was like in a country in which law and order had collapsed. China had experienced its revolution in 1911 only to find irrational conservatism replaced by an equally irrational 'but more ruinous' anarchy. Banditry was rife. In spite of his initial prejudice in favour of the Chinese, he was left with an irresistible impression 'of futility, of violence, of a meaningless welter of unending chaos'.[59]

Chinese experience reinforced his scepticism about schemes of social reform that depended for their success on too idealistic a conception of human nature. China, with its chaos of warring groups, needed a unitary state, authorized by the people to secure compliance with rules and orders. China required the equivalent of a nineteenth-century Piedmont or Prussia to serve as a basis of order, efficiency, control, public spirit, and good government. The desirability of the withering away of the state; the existing state as merely a body of armed men for the oppression of the exploited by

[56] Coal Industry Commission, *Reports and Minutes of Evidence*, Cmd. 359–61 (London, 1919).
[57] R. H. Tawney, 'The Sickness of the Acquisitive Society', *Hibbert Journal*, 17 (1919); R. H. Tawney, *The Acquisitive Society* (London, 1921).
[58] C. H. Becker, M. Falski, P. Langevin, and R. H. Tawney, *The Reorganization of Education in China* (Paris, 1932).
[59] R. H. Tawney, *The Condition of China* (Newcastle upon Tyne, 1933), 23.

their exploiters—these were ideas repugnant to Tawney. With his base in the England of the 1930s, and with the example of China before his eyes, he shifted his emphasis towards morally motivated political measures aimed at establishing an economy congruent with the moral conduct proper to socialists.[60]

China also reinforced Tawney's attitudes to war and pacifism. He became exceptionally aware of the brute power and indifference to civilized morality of Japan at that time. Japanese forces had invaded Manchuria. Japan had converted it into the puppet state of Manchukuo, and faced an armed rebellion among the native Chinese. In foreign affairs, therefore, Tawney was never a supporter of the pacifist movements of the 1930s. He could admire but not agree with the principled pacifist who was realistically prepared to accept all the consequences of his pacificism—not to use violence even if England were attacked, not to use violence even though loved ones were directly threatened with or subjected to humiliation, torture, or death, not to use violence even though pacifism did not lead to peace, but resulted in a country then torn by bloody internal civil strife. But he could not join those who based their pacifism on the, to him, erroneous belief that there was no significant risk that an aggressor would take advantage of a pacifist country, or the equally erroneous belief that foreign invasion was to be preferred to war, ignoring or under-estimating the possibility of a vicious circle of resistance to and reprisals from the occupying power. After his months in China, Tawney regarded such views as infantile wishful thinking and a refusal to take account of world history.

Yet some inter-war events were so dramatic, and put such a strain upon Tawney's beliefs about human nature and social life, that their influence can be discerned in a redefinition of the relationship between religion, morals, political action, and economic production and consumption. Outside Britain, Italy soon succumbed to Mussolini's (relatively mild) brand of Fascism. This was followed in 1933 by the National Socialist conquest of power of Germany, and during the following decade by an unparalleled period of Nazi repression, war, and systematic genocide. Tawney did not join the Communists, but his later work pays increasing attention to the elements he had become aware of in China—economic determinants of social stability and change.

[60] R. H. Tawney, *Land and Labour in China* (London, 1932).

But Tawney's attitudes had been largely set by the time of the Armistice. He was a party man, the sort of loyalist to be called for when an independent commission of experts is required to assist the government—as Tawney was called for by the Labour Prime Minister to serve on a committee MacDonald himself chaired in 1930.[61] He interpreted most subsequent events as confirming his factual and moral world-view. The 1930s saw both the consolidation of Stalinism in the USSR and a growing admiration of the USSR among those circles of the English intelligentsia so accurately depicted and so vehemently detested by George Orwell. Stalwart Labour figures such as John Strachey and Harold Laski joined the Webbs in its praises, and Bernard Shaw returned to announce that the nation he had just visited was a Fabian-type society already in existence.[62] To Tawney only 'uninstructed critics' could suggest a resemblance between 'Russian Police Collectivism' and the politics of the British Labour party.[63] To go further and suggest that the Labour party had something to learn from marxist collectivism in practice was either plain ignorance 'or credulity so extreme as to require, not argument, but a doctor'.[64] Inside Britain, the interwar years brought their own problems. Structural unemployment in formerly basic industries was added to severe cyclical unemployment. Nevertheless these, in Tawney's view, were adequately to be met by the policies put forward especially by Maynard Keynes and William Beveridge.[65]

During the Second World War Tawney saw the desirability of the intervention of the state, to provide social security for the unfortunate and to foster 'the good life of its citizens', increasingly accepted by public opinion across the social classes.[66] This opinion was crystallized in the Beveridge Report of 1942, which was designed not only to combat the evils of material want—'in some ways the easiest to attack'—but also as part of the wider plan to tackle the more intractable evils of 'ignorance', 'squalor', 'disease', and 'idleness'.[67] The method and performance of the Labour party

[61] R. Skidelsky, *Politicians and the Slump 1929–1931* (1967) (Harmondsworth, 1970), 156–8.   [62] W. Jones, *The Russia Complex* (Manchester, 1978).
[63] Tawney, *Radical Tradition*, 158.   [64] Ibid. 170.
[65] Ibid. 145.
[66] Rt. Hon. Lord Soulsbury, Chairman of the Assistance Board, National Council of Social Service Conference 1941, quoted in M. P. Hall, *The Social Services of Modern England* (1952), 3rd edn. (London, 1955).
[67] *Social Insurance and Allied Services* (The Beveridge Report), Cmd. 6404 (London, 1942), para. 8, 6.

in power 1945–51 appeared satisfactory to Tawney. 'People no longer contemptuously dismiss Parliament as a mere talking-shop',[68] and a social revolution, he believed, had been peacefully achieved.

[68] The quoted phrase is Herbert Morrison's. (A. H. Hanson, *Planning and the Politicians* (London, 1969), 45.)

8

ETHICAL-SOCIALIST MOVEMENTS

During Tawney's formative years ethical socialism was being developed in four social movements: the Workers' Educational Association, Christian Socialism, the New Liberalism, and the pre-1914 Labour party. All four attracted his enthusiasm. None responded to the obvious pressure in a capitalist society towards the formation of exclusively class-based organization.

THE WORKERS' EDUCATIONAL ASSOCIATION

Unlike the German 'Proletcult' and its British counterpart, the National Council of Labour Colleges, the WEA set its face against adult education in the service of class struggle and adopted an assimilationist view of educational need. Albert Mansbridge, William Temple, and Tawney (who was the President from 1928 to 1944) subscribed to the creed that there was a high culture which could and should be democratized. Such a movement, they believed, held out the promise of widespread equality of citizenship. Self-improvement brought men and women together in voluntary association in which no seeker after knowledge could claim to be another's superior if for no other reason than that before limitless knowledge, as before God, all men are equal—'because all are infinitely small'.[1] The development of a social apparatus of self-help and mutual betterment beyond the strong and salient working-class family offered hope that such aspirations might be realized. Chapels, Friendly Societies, trade unions, co-operative stores, choirs, working-men's clubs, and sports clubs of many kinds all demonstrated a capacity for fraternity, equality, and effective organizational self-management.

Within the movement was a corresponding disdain for the 'lower' values, including those which emphasized economic enrich-

[1] R. H. Tawney, *R. H. Tawney's Commonplace Book (1912–14)*, ed. J. M. Winter and D. M. Joslin, (Cambridge, 1972), 30 Nov. 1912.

ment beyond the level of material security necessary for a civilized existence. Even supposing that material plenitude were attained, a society which neglected the more refined for the more vulgar would consume them all and 'look up with an impatient grunt for more'.[2]

The WEA was committed to a threefold understanding of social advance. First, revolutionary violence was in itself an evil. Repeating Cobbett's dictum of a century before, Tawney wrote that 'one may not do evil that good should come'.[3] Second was the idea that no institution, however ingenious or perfect in conception, can work unless operated by people whose morality is adequate. Good institutions, said Tawney, merely 'make binding objectively conduct which most individuals already recognize to be binding subjectively'.[4] No machinery, 'whether of the state or minor corporations can apply ideas that do not already exist in society'. Third was the completely un-marxian idea that where a sound morality was lacking, it could be supplied. 'Our principal task is to create one', for effective programmes are built on ethical as well as factual definitions of situations that people accept as true, relevant, and valid.[5]

The dominant motif of the pre-1914 world, Tawney said, was not to be discovered in the material forces of production or in institutional forms, but in the revival among large masses of men of the idea of the sacredness of human personality. This was the lamp, newly rekindled, by which a host of old oppressions were being examined. Ultimately, it was not their material circumstances or social existence that determined the consciousness of men, but on the contrary their social consciousness that determined their material life and institutions. As J. M. Winter remarks, 'in the WEA Tawney's egalitarian Anglicanism found its most complete expression'.[6]

CHRISTIAN SOCIALISM

Within the peculiar blend of ecumenical and ethnocentric culture which was the Church of England, Tawney was a Christian. He accepted the doctrine of original sin and could therefore neither

---

[2] Ibid., 22 July 1913.   [3] Ibid., 6 Mar. 1913, 29 July 1913.
[4] Ibid., 29 July 1913.
[5] R. H. Tawney, 'The Theory of Pauperism', *Sociological Review* (Oct. 1909), 372.
[6] P. Barker (ed.), *Founders of the Welfare State* (London, 1984), 100.

envisage a faultless future society, nor accept the utopian visions of others. 'What goodness we have', he wrote, 'is a house built on piles driven into a black slime and always slipping down into it.'[7]

He believed in a permanent and God-given law which provided the 'unifying centre' for ethical precept. Great moral truths exist; their source is divine; they are knowable; and the means of knowledge is 'transcendental, religious, mythical', just as the means of knowledge of the immanent God is simply a fact of mystical and religious, not rational experience. He valued casuistry, not of the kind that Pascal condemned which is used to absolve those who have no intention of obeying God's commandments, but that which helps good people to resolve genuine difficulties in applying God's law in the particular cases of experience. Tawney's wife edited a book of seventeenth-century casuistry, on which Tawney's voice-print (unless Jeannette wrote all Tawney's other books) is conspicuously evident. (As Tawney would have said, the hand is the hand of Esau, but the voice is the voice of Jacob.)[8] Tawney studied Thomas Wilson's *Discourse upon Usury* (1569), because of Wilson's 'preoccupation with morality'. As a man of affairs (though he was later Dean of Durham) Wilson worked within the tradition of More and Latimer, who based their economics upon morality and their morality upon religion, rather than abandoning society to 'a welter of disorderly appetites'.[9]

Tawney believed in the possible efficacy (and possible failure) of religiously-based moralizing in determining how people would treat each other in producing and distributing goods and services.[10] One moral code will mean that people are efficient, prudent, and peaceful; another code will allow or not be capable of controlling idleness, prodigality, negligence, and hatred. The assumption that people always use available technical possibilities and physical amenities to the best effect, in the long or the short run, in small groups or in the mass, was foreign to Tawney's Christian thought.

---

[7] Tawney, *Commonplace Book*, 10 June 1912.

[8] R. Baxter, *Chapters from a Christian Directory* (1673), selected by Jeannette Tawney (London, 1925), p. viii. Tawney's friend, Bishop Gore, wrote the Introduction; in it he said that there was an urgent need for 'a casuistry of a like kind addressed to the Christian conscience of today'.

[9] T. Wilson, *Discourse upon Usury* (1569) (New York, 1925).

[10] In examining empirical situations, as distinct from formulating their generalizations, Marxists have frequently come to the same conclusion. Engels, for example, argued that from the time of the collapse of Chartism, the British

The natural choice is neglect, slovenliness, short-sightedness, disorder. That way is broad and easy; and it is for that reason chosen, though it leads to chaos.

The Christian Tawney was also a socialist. Nineteenth-century Christian Socialism as an English phenomenon grew out of the clash between Christian ideals and the philosophy of predatory business (rather than, as in Germany and elsewhere on the continent, out of a wish to challenge marxist trade unions and parties). In Britain the name Christian Socialism was chosen by a few clerical and lay members of the Church of England in the early 1850s. Inspired less by the German Marx than by the German-influenced Southey, Coleridge, and Carlyle,[11] the movement was instituted on the failure of Chartism by John Ludlow, Frederick Maurice, and the novelist Charles Kingsley.[12]

They were not operating in an entirely hostile environment. They had the example of the Roman Catholic Church. Especially among the immigrant Irish in the industrial towns and cities it was already 'biased to the poor' and was building the school and welfare institutions of an alternative society. H. E. Manning, a High Anglican who joined the Roman Catholic Church in 1851 (becoming Archbishop of Westminster in 1865 and Cardinal in 1875) was influential in arousing church concern with social and economic questions. Among the extreme Evangelicals in the Church of England, the Earl of Shaftesbury was also a constant

bourgeoisie, more than ever convinced of the value of 'maintaining the common people in a religious mood', succeeded in doing so and in postponing the revolution for at least half a century (until it was again imminent, in Engels's view, in 1892). The ideal type of working man—from the bourgeois point of view—*had* been produced, proving that the English respectable middle class was 'not as stupid as it looked to the intelligent foreigner'. K. Marx and F. Engels, *Selected Works* (Moscow, 1958), i. 94, 101.

[11] R. Southey, *Sir Thomas More: or Colloquies on the Progress and Prospects of Society* (London, 1829); S. T. Coleridge, *On the Constitution of the Church and State According to the Idea of Each* (1830) (London, 1972); T. Carlyle, *Past and Present* (1843) (London, 1899). Southey, Coleridge's brother-in-law, and Words-worth's friend, was interested in the settlement of a 'pantisocratic' colony on the Susquehanna.

[12] F. D. Maurice, *The Kingdom of Christ* (1837) (London, 1906); C. Kingsley, *Alton Locke, Tailor and Poet* (1850) (London, 1910); C. Kingsley, *Yeast: A Problem* (1851) (London, 1912). Thomas Hughes (*Tom Brown's Schooldays*), though at one time a Liberal MP, counted himself among the Christian Socialists (seeing the better England as a vast version of Rugby School). Six of the leading early Christian Socialists are dealt with in E. Norman, *The Victorian Christian Socialists* (Cambridge, 1987).

promoter of schemes for alleviating the conditions of the poor.[13] The first Christian Socialists experimented in producers' co-operatives; they were successful in securing the Industrial and Provident Act of 1852; and in 1854 they founded a Workingmen's College.

In 1877 S. D. Headlam set up the Guild of St Matthew in Bethnal Green, uniting the theology of Maurice with the theology and practices of Anglo-Catholicism.[14] Its successor, the first anglican society definitely committed to socialism, was the Church Socialist League, founded in 1906 by pupils of Headlam's including the Reverend W. E. Moll of Newcastle upon Tyne, who was the compiler of a book of Christian Socialist hymns,[15] and the Reverend Lewis Donaldson, who led the first hunger march of the twentieth century from Leicester to London. Tawney belonged to the League.[16] Side by side with the Guild of St Matthew grew up the more respectable, because not explicitly socialist, Christian Socialist Union, many of whose members gave great support to the groups from which the Labour party was to be constituted. The first president was Bishop Westcott. Prominent members were Henry Scott Holland and Tawney's friend Charles Gore.

The history of the movement when its outlook was to be more formed by, than a formative influence on, Tawney, is less relevant here. Briefly, the Catholic Crusade welcomed the Russian Revolution and split from the Church Socialist League in 1918. The Catholic Crusade then itself split on the Stalin versus Trotsky issue, the Trotskyists forming the Order of the Church Militant. A less socialist element in the Christian Socialist League formed the League of the Kingdom of God, with the intention of fostering a Christian sociology. A more socialist element formed, in 1924, the Society of Socialist Christians, which Tawney later joined. In 1930 a group of MPs led a Christian Socialist Crusade, which then merged with the Society of Socialist Christians, Tawney's group. George Lansbury, who was to become Leader of the Labour party in 1932, joined the new body. The Christian Socialist Movement was formed two years before Tawney's death, the first chairman

---

[13] R. Gray, *Cardinal Manning* (London, 1985); J. Pollock, *Shaftesbury: The Poor Man's Friend* (London, 1985).

[14] S. D. Headlam, *Christian Socialism* (London, 1892). The weekly paper of the Guild of St Matthew was *The Church Reformer*.

[15] W. E. Moll, *Songs for the City of God* (Newcastle upon Tyne, 1899).

[16] S. Mayor, *The Churches and the Labour Movement* (London, 1967), 225.

being the Methodist Donald (later Lord) Soper. Attlee's accession
to Downing Street in 1945, along with Temple's to Canterbury in
1942, marked the zenith of the anglican socialist movement.[17]

Christianity reinforced Tawney's belief in the high moral value of
fraternity. The Church was created in fellowship. Were not the
disciples together in brotherhood when the Spirit descended upon
them? Social unity, irrespective of all previous divisions of class or
colour, takes its strongest form in Christian fellowship based upon
sharing. Even at its weakest it still demands at least the moral use of
property: negatively in refraining from oppression, positively in
acting simply as the steward of God's common wealth.

Jeannette Tawney's selection from Baxter's *Christian Directory*
was intended to show, and implicitly approve and propagate, the
economic ethics of this Church of England clergyman and Puritan
chaplain. 'Oppression is the injuring of inferiours who are unable
to resist or right themselves: when men use power to bear them
down . . . But yet oppression is a very common and heynous sin.'[18]
Property, the right to dispose of a thing, is either absolute or
limited. Absolute property 'belongeth to none but God'. The
only property a human being can claim is 'respective and limited',
being subordinate always to its use in accordance with the God's
will.

Tawney's socialist conviction, that equality is a morally binding
value, was also derived from his socialist Christian background.
Scaled against the majesty of God all human beings were equally
insignificant. Against the goodness of God, all were equally sinful.
In taking the outward material form of bread and wine, all equally
received the life of God himself. Tawney regarded it as necessary to
believe in God in order to believe in human equality. Equality of
worth was a simple fact of the human condition; it was therefore
fraudulent for one person to claim that, because he was better or
more deserving than another, he was entitled to extraordinary
privileges.

Liberty, equality, and fraternity were all involved, finally, in
Tawney's disposition towards frugality in material life. Religion
and religiously-based morality showed that everyone's standard of
living should be adequate; but no more than adequate. (Thomas
Burt did not simply say that his parents were poor, or that they

---

[17] Ibid. 381.   [18] Baxter, *Chapters from A Christian Directory*, ch. 20.

suffered their poverty with fortitude. They had 'a horror of Mammon-worship'.)[19] What, after all, had to be promised for every person baptized and by every person confirmed in the Church of England? It was to renounce 'the pomps and vanities of this wicked world, and all the sinful lusts of the flesh'.

Of particular importance to Tawney was his friendship with the Christian Socialist William Temple, Archbishop of Canterbury (1942–4), the son of a former headmaster of Rugby School, Frederick Temple, himself Archbishop of Canterbury (1896–1902). Temple and Tawney were at Rugby and Balliol together, and Temple officiated at Tawney's wedding. They were closely associated in the WEA. Tawney dedicated *The Agrarian Problem* to him. In 1917 Tawney and Temple worked together in forming the Life and Liberty movement, which aimed at the Christian reconstruction of all aspects of social life.[20] Two years later they again collaborated to prepare a conference on the application of the social ethics of Christianity to contemporary problems. In 1924, by which time William Temple (who had been headmaster of Repton), was Bishop of Manchester, the Conference on Christian Politics, Economics, and Citizenship met. The style of its ninth report, *Industry and Property*, is clearly Tawney's. As a principal exponent of anglican socialism, he was invited to deliver the Scott Holland lectures on 'an aspect of the religion of the Incarnation in its bearing upon the social and economic life of man'. These lectures on 'a forgotten chapter of social history', delivered in 1922, became his *Religion and the Rise of Capitalism*, which he dedicated to Bishop Charles Gore.[21] Christian Socialism was for Tawney the basis for a permanently 'right order of life', materially ascetic and spiritually splendid.

THE NEW LIBERALISM

Belief in a standard of living which was not contaminated by waste also came to Tawney from such New Liberals as J. A. Hobson.

[19] T. Burt, *Pitman and Privy Councillor: An Autobiography* (London, 1924), 9.
[20] W. Temple, 'Life and Liberty for the Church', *Christian Commonwealth*, 18 July 1917; W. Temple, 'The Life and Liberty Movement', *Contemporary Review*, Feb. 1918; G. Lansbury, 'Life and Liberty', *Daily Herald*, 20 July 1918.
[21] R. H. Tawney, 'Religion and Business: A Forgotten Chapter of Social History', *Hibbert Journal*, 21 (1922); R. H. Tawney, *Religion and the Rise of Capitalism* (1926) (Harmondsworth, 1938).

Ruskin's distinction between those material goods and services which constituted wealth and those which were counted as wealth but really constituted 'illth', was strongly pursued by them. Ruskin had laid 'a true scientific foundation' for social economics, Hobson wrote, by insisting upon the replacement of commercial by human costs and benefits.[22] Were this standard to be applied—the standard of the value of economic activities to human life—then not all work would be a cost and not all goods and services would be a gain. Some productive activities—constructive labour and aristic activites—were interesting, pleasant, educative, or otherwise organically useful. Others—toil and malproduction—were uninteresting, painful, depressing, or otherwise organically costly. On the side of consumption, while some goods were conducive to a healthy, pleasant, and profitable life, others were patently wasteful or actually injurious to the life of the consumers themselves as well as their neighbours.[23] Individual character should be formed in the rejection of 'the cherished lure of pomp', and society should be so organized as to secure an organic unity between the related faculties of effort and enjoyment.[24] Otherwise the result is what Durkheim called 'the futility of endless pursuit'.[25] The New Liberals therefore took from Ruskin, and passed to Tawney, the notion of the establishment of a social standard of living corresponding to that which is consistent with and contributory to 'goodness or happiness as an ideal'.[26]

As we pointed out in our chapter on Hobhouse, Marxism was not formidable to the New Liberals. To them it was interesting but old-fashioned and exploded doctrine. They therefore did not bother to contest the marxist argument against moralizing—that the problem of greed was of no consequence because greed was inevitable in all class societies and would simply and spontaneously disappear in the classless community. Their opponent was *laissez-*

[22] J. A. Hobson, *John Ruskin: Social Reformer* (London, 1898), 309.
[23] J. A. Hobson, *Work and Wealth: A Human Valuation* (New York, 1916), 159. Hobson, a leading New Liberal, was also the mainstay of the London Ethical Society. (I. D. MacKillop, *The British Ethical Societies* (Cambridge, 1986).)
[24] Hobson, *Ruskin*, 309. 'The cherished lure of pomp' is Coleridge's phrase.
[25] Durkheim, in his *Division of Labour in Society*, deals centrally, and in his *Suicide* explicitly, with the results of people failing to control their infinitely expansive demands on nature and on other human beings, and the absence of effectively binding rules which do it for them. (See E. Durkheim, *The Division of Labour in Society* (1893) (Glencoe, 1947); *Suicide* (1897) (London, 1952).)
[26] Hobson, *Ruskin*, 309.

faire, a set of doctrines which also assumed economic moralizing to be redundant. According to *laissez-faire*, however, it was not even necessary to destroy the contemporary institutions in order to realize the moral social order; the 'Invisible Hand' ensured that out of the activities of self-seeking individuals, morally-elevated results emerged.

But to the New Liberals specific and continuously-made moral judgements were needed. They had to be successfully urged on others if commendable results were to be derived from economic activity. Thus Hobson had no more compunction than had Marx in dismissing as obnoxious and insupportable not only the parasitic upper class, but also the proletarian under-class. While most of the attention and indignation of the New Liberals was directed at the rich, poverty was no protection from their condemnation. Some were poor through innocent misfortune but others were 'parasites': they had never enlisted in the army of industry or had deserted in favour of a free life of dependence or plunder. There was a large and growing lower leisure class. It imitated, as far as its circumstances permitted, the values and habits of the upper leisure class: 'fighting, roving, generous, reckless, wasteful . . . the same unaffected contempt for the worker, the same class of camaraderie, often with a special code of honouf, the same sex license'. Their withdrawal from all useful activity, coupled with 'the debased mode of consumption' they practised, counted heavily in the aggregate of social waste.[27]

Morality and moralizing, 'to clarify the vision, to elevate the aim, to humanize and so to dignify, the ends of conduct', were, therefore, the New Liberals' persistent endeavour.[28] They felt it their duty, not merely to describe and publicly to praise or condemn, but to go beyond the realm of calculation into intuition and faith, so that whether or not it could be 'scientifically' shown, they were prepared to affirm that, for example, the Church was guilty of 'corrupt torpor'; the City of London of 'degrading selfishness'; the middle class of 'miserable and sordid vulgarity'; politicians of 'godless irresponsibility'; modern artists of an 'evil tyranny'; and industrial workers of spreading anarchy under the masquerade of individual liberty.

The moral judgements considered valid by the New Liberals were those which approved liberty, equality, and fraternity. Liberty

[27] Hobson, *Work and Wealth*, 155–6.   [28] Hobson, *Ruskin*, 302.

meant, for them, optimal opportunity for individuals, consistent with optimal opportunity for all others, to conduct their own lives so that they acted morally out of their own inner conviction and not under coercion. Exponents of *laissez-faire* still persistently claimed that capitalism delivered a viable economy without political tyranny. But John Stuart Mill had argued decades before that the market economy might fail to produce and sustain the conditions for the promotion of widespread freedom. The actual experience of capitalism confirmed to the New Liberals that state intervention was necessary to provide most citizens with the realistic possibility of exercising individual choice.

Laissez-faire economists at the end of the nineteenth and the beginning of the twentieth century—Alfred Marshall, Pigou, Cannan—also believed that equality was desirable, but that it was not obtainable by state intervention without too high a cost in other values sacrificed, at least until other necessary motives were strengthened. Otherwise the overall result would be that the supposed beneficiaries could be in practice the losers.[29] Equality meant for the 'liberal socialists' (as Morris Ginsberg called the New Liberals, bracketing Tawney with Hobhouse and Hobson) the feasible pooling by taxation of the Hobhousian 'surplus'—for the purpose of insuring to all the conditions of well-being which belong otherwise only to the rich.[30]

In 1919 Tawney acknowledged his debt to Ruskin and the New Liberals when in a newspaper article he directly approved Hobson's judgement on Ruskin. In language of penetrative force Ruskin had told 'the largest number of important truths upon the largest number of vital matters'. For that reason he would rank as 'the greatest social teacher of his age'.[31]

THE PRE-1914 LABOUR PARTY

Tawney was influenced in the development of his perceptions of fact and in his moral attitudes by the early Labour party both

[29] A. Marshall, *Principles of Economics* (London, 1890), i. 712–19; A. C. Pigou, *Economics of Welfare* (London, 1924), 76–81, 713–22; E. Cannan, *A History of Theories of Production and Distribution, 1776–1848* (London, 1924), final chapter.

[30] M. Ginsberg, *The Science of Society and the Unity of Mankind: A Memorial Volume for Morris Ginsberg*, ed. R. Fletcher (London, 1974), 96.

[31] R. H. Tawney, *The Radical Tradition: Twelve Essays on Politics, Education and Literature*, ed. R. Hinden, (London, 1964), pp. v–vi.

positively and negatively. He joined the Independent Labour party in 1909 and the Labour party in 1918, the year it adopted its new constitution. He remained a member for the rest of his life. He stood as ILP candidate for Rochdale in the General Election of 1918, and served on Labour party advisory committees on education and international affairs.

Tawney was repelled by the strand in the Labour movement before the First World War which, like H. M. Hyndman and his Social Democratic Federation, was influenced by Marx. To Tawney Marxism was 'a barbarous, inhuman, sordid doctrine', as amoral and materialistic as capitalism itself. In addition it was avowedly anti-religious. It scaled down human beings by denying that they were possessers of immortal souls—the soul being still for Tawney a known objective reality and a familiar concept which he felt no need to apologize for or explain away. Tawney's own view, that there were eternal, immutable rules of conduct to be advocated and inculcated at all times in all societies, was strengthened by his opposition to the marxian view that hitherto all so-called 'morality' had been in reality special pleading, expressing only the interest of the ruling or the indignation of the oppressed classes.

Tawney had joined the Fabian Society in 1906, but his own writings constitute a critique of, rather than support for the views of Sidney and Beatrice Webb. They paid too much attention to changes in institutional arrangements and too little attention to the facts of human nature in earthly and eternal life. Writers who only piled up statistics never reached the heart of the problem. 'That heart is not economic. It is a question of *moral relationships*.'[32] Here again we have the insistence that formal rules could be constructed and reconstructed, but without the inner moral commitment of those to whom the rules applied, each invention or readjustment merely provided new materials for manipulation. Tawney's pre-war aversion to 'Webbism' was later modified (he dedicated *Equality* to the Webbs with gratitude and affection); but it was resurrected when the Webbs produced a comprehensive vindication of Stalin's dictatorship at its most brutal in their report on the Soviet Union in the mid-1930s.[33]

The moral climate of the pre-1914 Labour party reinforced

[32] Tawney, *Commonplace Book*, 10 Sept. 1913.
[33] S. and B. Webb, *Soviet Communism: A New Civilization?* (London, 1935).

Tawney's ethical socialism in many ways. It is a cliché but true that the party 'owed more to Methodism than to Marx': and it was committed to peaceful change by means which are democratic in the precise sense of using the existing institutions of the British parliamentary system. In Tawney's England the views of Edouard Bernstein were not 'revisionism', but the more-or-less unquestioned orthodoxy of the Labour party. In his *The Socialist Movement* the dominant pre-war figure in the party, Ramsay MacDonald, lauded the House of Commons, contrasting it sharply with its deceptive equivalent in Germany, the *Reichstag*. The *Reichstag* was little more than a talking-shop in which polarized parties debated impossible futures, with the socialists occasionally frightening the real rulers into making concessions. By contrast, the House of Commons could make its will effective, and made a socialist party 'dwelling in a fairyland of economic justice' an impossibility. In Britain, what could not be achieved in Parliament could certainly not be achieved at the barricades.[34] Effective democracy was not a matter of more numbers 'participating'—that could be mob rule at one extreme or plebiscitary dictatorship at the other. Macdonald echoed Burke's view that, over the course of centuries, innumerable adjustments had been made to the entire complex system of British democracy, from the ballot box to the monarch's veto. Bold proposals for reform might be enticing and in isolation apparently just and reasonable. In their effect on the total system, however, they were more likely to be 'will-o'-the-wisps leading into bogs those who foolishly follow'.[35]

A third tendency which struggled for recognition within the pre-1914 Labour party also influenced Tawney. The writings and the varied practical work of William Morris glorified the small group of self-governing workmen engaged in fulfilling artistic labour for the public good, a point of view later to be called 'guild socialism'.[36] In the very name there is a hankering after a

---

[34] J. R. MacDonald, *The Socialist Movement* (London, n.d.), 110–11. MacDonald, like Hobson, was an atheist.

[35] J. R. MacDonald, *Socialism and Government* (London, n.d.), pp. xxiii–xxv.

[36] W. Morris, *News From Nowhere or an Epoch of Rest* (1890) (London, n.d.). Guild socialism's prolific advocate was A. J. Penty, whose *The Restoration of the Guild System* was published in 1906 (London) and *Old Worlds for New: A Study of the Post-industrial State* in 1917 (London). Guild socialist ideas were propagated by S. G. Hobson, and by A. R. Orage in his periodical *The New Age*. In 1915 the National Guilds League was formed, with the support of G. D. H. Cole and

supposedly lost medieval fellowship of masters and workers bound
in the honour and pride of co-operative endeavour to create the
finest products of their craft for the benefit of the consumer. Present
too is a tinge of primitive frugality in the guild's insistence on
adequate, but no more than adequate levels of consumption.

Conceived as a practical adaptation to the modern industrial and
urban England of the twentieth century, rather than a return to
medieval standards of workmanship and fraternity, a system was
envisaged in which the means of production would be owned by the
state, but leased out to workers' organizations. Geographically-
based parliamentary institutions would be reformed along functional (employment-group) lines, and certain features of parliamentary democracy would be extended into the organization of
industry. The conditions of working life would be brought more
under participatory control.

Tawney followed these developments of thought sympathetically.
He greeted with approval not only the appearance of guilds, but
also quasi-guild proposals such as those of the Building Trade
Committee of the Industrial Council for the Building Industry who,
as 'a body of practical men, caring nothing for socialist theories',
proposed in August 1918 that the building industry should be
organized as a public service, with workers at all levels devoting
themselves to their several tasks in accordance with the spirit of a
commonly agreed ethical code of practice.

Under the influences we have outlined Tawney became a
formidable champion of a great and ancient moral tradition which
he then applied with vigour and persistence to British public life in
the twentieth century from a personal life as the eccentric ascetic
gentleman of Mecklenburgh Square and the respected historian of
Houghton Street. His habits of dress and speech marked him as the
unconventional yet unmistakable product of the upbringing afforded
to boys of the upper-middle class in late Victorian England. His

Bertrand Russell. G. D. H. Cole was particularly active, and his *Guild Socialism
Restated* (London, 1920) was a comprehensive statement of guild socialist beliefs.
For an excellent retrospect of Cole see A. W. Wright, *G. D. H. Cole and Socialist
Democracy* (Oxford 1979). After the war a number of working guilds were formed,
including the National Building Guild (1920–2). With the practical failure of the
National Building Guild the movement waned. The National Guilds League was
dissolved in 1925. In the 1970s there was some revival of these ideals—one of the
survivors of a 1970s guild-socialist attempt, the building guild of 'Sunderlandia' in
Sunderland, managed to awaken some interest in his ideas in the Liberal party.

moral outlook reflected the spirit of Victorian evangelical high-mindedness: but he fused it with the tragic realism of his experience in the trenches, tempered it with an English devotion to the rights of the individual, and directed it towards the *koinonia* of his religious conviction. A man of his time and class and country, of course: but one whose integration of private gifts with public responsibilities lent him wisdom beyond the confines of his period and his party.

9

TAWNEY'S SOCIAL THEORY

Tawney the historian and Tawney the patriotic, egalitarian moralist commands widespread respect if his views do not enjoy universal assent. He was sceptical of social 'knowledge' that departed very far from common sense, and extremely wary of any morality that did not appeal to the conscience of the 'decent man'. We have traced the influences on his remarkable character. The next step is to examine his social theory—his view of the causes of things and the application of his sociology to the practical reform of his own country.

Tawney was not a sociologist with a systematic theory of social causation. He believed so passionately in the rightness of his religion and morality, which he also insisted could be a powerful source of economic and political change, that in all his work explanation and advocacy are intimately married. Nevertheless his principles of explanation can be deduced from his historical writing and disentangled from the moral crusading for which he so often took up his pen.

The broad outline of his sociology can be sketched in relation to the leading theorists of his time. Marx he studied carefully and rejected. He knew and admired Weber as a historian. Durkheim he ignored. Yet Durkheim's concern with the *conscience collective*, his emphasis on the causal power of the common moral sentiments as determinants of individual behaviour, his concepts of anomie and the cult of the individual, his sense of the gulf between the sacred and profane, and his astringent rebuttal of the utilitarian theories put forward by Herbert Spencer constituted an analysis of industrial society remarkably similar to Tawney's own interpretation of Britain—a similarity made all the more striking by the difference between their personal religious convictions.

Any analysis of social change depends on prior assumptions about free will and determinism. Tawney was familiar with this ancient religious and theological dispute. In German historiography as he knew it the battle was joined between *Geisteswissenschaft* and *Naturwissenschaft*, between the view that human beings were unique phenomena because they had the capacity to exercise choice in all circumstances, and the contrary view that they were part of the predictable universe studied by natural science. Tawney took the former position—but in no simplistic fashion. Certainly any denial that people are free to choose between alternatives of conduct would make nonsense of everything Tawney longed for and stood for. But the circumstances of choice and the degrees of freedom available were the object of elaborate attention in all his historical and political work. And in that respect he followed the principles of *Naturwissenschaft*: he approached social analysis with the methods of the natural sciences.

Such are the twists and turns of controversy that this methodological view, labelled positivism, came to be used (paradoxically, as we have argued in our Preface, by neo-Marxists) as an all-purpose term of abuse against any sociologist attempting the testing of theory by even the most elementary quantitative method. Yet Marxism leaned heavily towards a positivistic view of human behaviour. Marxism was a positivistic doctrine, moreover, which attributed high importance to motives of physical survival. Correspondingly high significance was attached to those aspects of the individual's environment which bore on these motives—especially the 'material forces of production'. Thus Marx and Engels quote Shakespeare on money with approval:

> Thus much of this will make black, white; foul, fair;
> Wrong, right; base, noble; old, young; coward, valiant.
>
> . . . .
>   this is it
> That makes the wappened widow wed again;
> She, whom the spital-house and ulcerous sores
> Would cast the gorge at, this embalms and spices
> To the April day again . . .
>
> . . . .
>   thou visible god,
> That solder'st close impossibilities.
> And mak'st them kiss![1]

---

[1] K. Marx and F. Engels, *The German Ideology* (1845–6) (London, 1970), 102. (*Timon of Athens*, IV. iii.)

From a marxist standpoint religion and religious struggles were only distorted reflections of material interests. They were not independent variables. Not as personal beliefs and motives; nor as cultural bodies of institutional doctrine; nor as forms of social organization; nor as physical structures of chapels, churches, and cathedrals, did they deserve notice in their own right.

Tawney did not completely distance himself from this view. He explicitly states that *Religion and the Rise of Capitalism* was intended to show (in relation to Weber's thesis that Protestantism had originally created attitudes which led to capitalism) that Protestantism was itself the creation of economic forces and (as Weber had also argued) was overcome by economic forces. J. M. Winter discerns here a structuralist phase in Tawney—an emphasis on the causative strength of the individual's environment rather than his or her personal way of handling it, and also a stress on the non-moral aspects of circumstances.[2] An example of strong structural analysis is his essay on the American labour movement where he argues that the weakness of American socialism must be sought in the social structure of American industrial capitalism—in the requirements of the material economy.

It would be wrong to suppose, therefore, that Tawney neglected material constraints (wealth and greed, as well as poverty) on human choices. But he modified their causal status. The essence of his theory, expressed characteristically in moral affirmation, is that adverse material circumstances and an adverse moral environment can prevent or destroy good conduct if the individual's ethical code is too weak to combat them. Tawney, like others in his radical tradition, was a Utopian to this extent, but only to this extent: he believed that, within limits, people could be sufficiently motivated by appropriate ideals to alter or transcend their environment. His style of thought is manifested in his extreme fondness for the double conjunction 'not only . . . but also'.

Nevertheless the attribution of structural determination had to fit the facts. He refused to regard the English Civil War as a bourgeois revolution—because the bourgeoisie fought on both sides. When the evidence warranted it he was ready to admit, given the individual's moral code, the economic determination of attitudes and events. Thus he sees Harrington as the first English thinker to

[2] R. H. Tawney, *History and Society: Essays by R. H. Tawney*, ed. J. M. Winter (London, 1978), 33.

find the cause of political upheaval in antecedent social change.[3] Harrington conceived society as a mechanism obeying laws (which it was the first duty of the writer 'not to praise or denounce but to explain'). A political structure could only be stable in a state if it rested upon the economic foundations appropriate to it. In his *Oceana*, a thinly disguised analysis of seventeenth-century England, Harrington argued that to retain power a state must be able to use subjugating military force, and that behind that force lies the economic system that supports it. Economic power—and therefore the resources to maintain troops—had passed out of the hands of the monarch. 'It was not the Civil War which destroyed the old regime, but the dissolution of the social foundations of the old regime which had caused the Civil War.'[4]

In 'The Rise of the Gentry 1558–1640', Tawney similarly endorses the views expressed by Sir Walter Raleigh in his *Dialogue* (1615). He was 'the man who saw deepest into the moral of it all' by attributing the decline in political stability to an imbalance between possession of property and possession of state power. The English gentry was rapidly accumulating wealth and economic influence through its superior capacity to adapt to tensions and opportunities as rising prices struck the dyke of customary obligations. And in *Business and Politics under James I* Tawney is again concerned with the limits placed on the moral intentions of any particular individual or group by the existing configuration of the economy.

Yet 'not only but also' was Tawney's crucial amendment. The question at the heart of *Religion and the Rise of Capitalism* is, how did it happen that a predominantly Christian nation, where commitment to the religious control of economic appetites and interests was no less strong than it had been in the middle ages, ended by breaking so decisively with the ethics of the medieval Church and adopting the doctrine of *laissez-faire*? The answer lies *partly* in the economic opportunities afforded to individuals by a new physical science, a new material technology, and the gold and markets of a New World. But the *decisive* determinants lay in the realm of ideas—in morals and religion. Within the bosom of religious theory itself a new system of ideas was being matured, which was destined to revolutionize all traditional values, and to

[3] Ibid. 67.   [4] Ibid. 75.

turn on the whole field of social obligations a new and penetrating light. So Tawney wrote:

On a world heaving with expanding energies, and on a Church uncertain of itself, rose, after two centuries of premonitory mutterings, the tremendous storm of the Puritan movement. The forest bent; the oaks snapped; the dry leaves were driven before a gale, neither all of winter nor all of spring, but violent and life-giving, pitiless and tender, sounding strange notes of yearning and contrition, as of voices wrung from a people dwelling in Meshech, which signifies Prolonging, in Kedar, which signifies Blackness; while amid the blare of trumpets, and the clash of arms, and the rending of the carved works of the Temple, humble to God and haughty to man, the soldier-saints swept over the battlefield and scaffold, their garments rolled in blood.[5]

Thus there can be no doubt that Tawney was overwhelmingly committed to the view that human choice was a crucially important factor in determining the course of individual and institutional life. Such choice was based on moral assessments of conduct under given environmental opportunities and obstacles. And these assessments themselves were heavily influenced by the cultural values and social controls at work in the milieu, independently of any given state of the means of production. Explanatory social science had to give full weight to personal perceptions and evaluations, and appreciate the force of 'definitions of the situation' and of ethical beliefs which contemporaries applied (or failed to apply) to each others' behaviour.

Accordingly, in 1918, Tawney stressed that post-war England would differ from the England of 1914 because 'not merely the facts, but the minds that appraise them, have been profoundly modified'.[6] Three years later he put the pure view of the exponents of *Geisteswissenschaft*: 'Mankind has at least this superiority over its philosophers, that great movements spring from the heart and embody a faith, not the nice adjustments of the hedonistic calculus'.[7] Social institutions and personal conduct are the visible expression of the scale of moral values which rules the minds of individuals. It was impossible to alter institutions or conduct without altering those values. Drawing the moral inference,

---

[5] R. H. Tawney, *Religion and the Rise of Capitalism* (1926) (Harmondsworth, 1938), 197.
[6] S. E. Chapman (ed.), *Labour and Capital After the War* (London, 1918), 93–4.
[7] R. H. Tawney, *The Acquisitive Society* (London, 1921), 17.

Tawney added that false perceptions were a burden no society can afford to carry. An environment constructed to reduce error and ignorance—an effective system of education—was therefore essential.

Continuing the tradition and repeating the language of Carlyle and Arnold, he argued that the attempt to do without morality in the explanation of human action robbed a doctrine of the capacity to offer an authentic critique of capitalism. Both *laissez-faire* and Marxism failed to see that dependence on 'no other end but the temporary appetite of individuals' had as its natural consequence 'oppression, the unreasoning and morbid pursuit of pecuniary gain of which the proper name is the sin of avarice, and civil war'.[8] Near the end of his life Tawney showed his continuing adherence to this tradition in associating himself with the work of the Hammonds. Their books, *The Village Labourer* (1911), *The Town Labourer* (1917), and *The Skilled Labourer* (1919), Tawney said, had properly depicted the workers as concerned not only with material well-being, but also with issues of 'profound and not yet exhausted moral significance'. They had interpreted Chartism not in the conventional manner as a struggle of classes contending over their material interests, but as a moral revolt against the weakening of their community life and the lessening of their share in the common culture.[9]

Tawney drew the theoretical implication that those who defined factual and moral situations, those whom C. Wright Mills calls the 'cultural workmen',[10] can be influential. This influence was of both moral and practical importance. Those who can speak for virtue must do so. Tawney adopted the words of Matthew Arnold as the motto for the 'Epilogue 1938–1950' to his book *Equality*:

> Charge once more, then, and be dumb,
> Let the victors, when they come,
> When the forts of folly fall,
> Find thy body by the wall.[11]

Tawney never failed to insist on the potency of human choice. He attacked the fatalism of the Marxists who saw only an inevitable clash of irreconcilable opponents—a clash that had indeed already

---

[8] Ibid. 234.   [9] Tawney, *History and Society*, 240, 245–6.
[10] C. W. Mills, *Power, Politics and People: The Collected Essays of C. Wright Mills*, ed. I. Horowitz (London, 1967), 408.
[11] M. Arnold, 'The Last Word' (1867), *Poems* (London, 1965), 231.

'destroyed the political civilization of Germany and Italy'. Equally he saw the potential force of false assumptions about social structure and so attacked the complacency of those who thought that Britain was for ever safe from violent revolution. The future was made by people articulating their public position on important issues. 'If, in this country, democracy falls, it will fall, not through the fortuitous combination of unfriendly circumstances, but from the insincerity of some of its professed friends and the timidity of the remainder. It will fall because, when there was still time to make it unassailable, public spirit was too weak, and class egotism was too strong.'[12]

Much of Tawney's interest in social theory was centred on the causal power of religious ideas, whether they took the form of conceptions of what was factually true or beliefs about what was morally imperative. Before the First World War there was widespread acceptance of the thesis that Puritanism had produced an intense spirit of persistence, enterprise, and frugality which had an independent and strong causative effect in the genesis of early capitalism. Alfred Marshall writes in these terms in the fifth edition of his *Principles of Economics*;[13] and H. G. Wood (a contributor with Tawney and Hobhouse to *Property: Its Duties and Rights* (1914)) states that the great contribution which the Puritan moralists had made to the industrial development of Great Britain, 'is now generally recognized'.[14]

In *The Acquisitive Society* Tawney noted that there were, of course, religions which made few demands on the secular life of their adherents; religions whose demands had become mere formalities; and individuals who were lukewarm in their faith. But the opinion that the religion of a society makes no practical difference to the conduct of its affairs 'is not only contrary to experience . . . it is of its very nature superficial'. Christianity at one time and another had been a cloak under which errors had been perpetrated. But as a matter of historical fact—said Tawney—it had also at one time or another successfully taken the whole world of human interests as its province, seeking to 'lead the lowest

---

[12] Tawney, *Equality*, 30–1.
[13] A. Marshall, *Principles of Economics* (1890), 5th edn. (London, 1907), 742–4.
[14] C. Gore (ed.), *Property: Its Duties and Rights* (1914) (London, 1915), 136–7.
The whole subject, he said, had already been handled in detail by Max Weber, by Weber's friend Ernst Troeltsch, and by Max Levy in his book *Economic Liberalism*.

through the intermediate to the highest things'.[15] What was distinctive about capitalist Britain was that the *attempt* to make religion influential had been abandoned and was being replaced by the assumption that everyday human affairs should be conducted without any reference to religious beliefs and values. In consequence the horrors which sixty years before [1861] were thought to be exorcised by the advance of civilization had one by one rolled back:

The rule of the sword and of the assassin hired by governments . . . a hardly veiled slavery . . . a contempt for international law by the Great Powers which would have filled an earlier generation with amazement, and in England the prostitution of humanity and personal honour and the decencies of public life to the pursuit of money.[16]

As Matthew Arnold had suggested, Christianity was being replaced by a secular creed, the repudiation of any authority but the individual's own interests, ambitions, or appetites untrammelled by common obligations or the demands of conscious altruism. The particular perversion of individualism was industrialism. Tawney defined industrialism as an inflated estimate of the importance of industry—the elevation of one minor department of life to the major department of life. 'So they destroy religion and art and morality . . . and having destroyed these, which are the end, for industry, which is a means, they make their industry itself what they make of their cities, a desert of unnatural dreariness, which only forgetfulness can make endurable, and which only excitement can enable them to forget.'[17]

In his 1925 Introduction to Wilson's *Discourse upon Usury*, Tawney again makes clear his conviction that religion can be a powerful independent influence in moulding personal conduct and social institutions. In the *Discourse* of 1569 the preacher converts the merchant to his version of Christian morality. The businessman is made responsible for the direct and indirect effects of his activities on other people. Tawney wished to bring Wilson's case to the attention of his own generation.

He was closely associated in 1925 with his wife's book on Richard Baxter, a real-life preacher a century after Wilson. Baxter assumed that religion could be, and that Christianity specifically ought to be, an important influence on conduct. The

[15] Tawney, *Acquisitive Society*, 235.
[16] Ibid. 234.   [17] Ibid. 49.

Tawneys presented him not as a unique figure but as a representative thinker of the Puritans and all the English Reformers:

That economic transactions are to be judged by a rule of right derived ultimately from religion, and that the exposition of the moral standards by which they are to be tried is as much the function of the Church as is teaching with regard to any other aspect of human conduct—these conceptions had been the foundation on which not only the medieval schoolmen, but every section of the Reformers had based their teaching.[18]

The essential difference between a secular view and Baxter's religious view was his belief that an all-seeing, immediately-present God kept all actions and thoughts under unceasing surveillance, and meted out—foreordained—rewards and punishments accordingly.

Remember always that God is present and none of your secrets can be hid from him. . . . . What blind Atheists are you who dare do in the presence of the most righteous God, which you durst not do if men behold you? . . . *Forget not how dear all that must cost you, which you gain unlawfully.* . . . . If *Achan* had foreseen the stones, and *Gehazi* the leprosy, and *Ahab* the mortal arrow, and *Jezebel* the licking of her blood by dogs, and *Judas* the hanging . . . or any of them the aftermisery, it might have kept them from pernicious gain.

Usually in this life a curse attended what was ill-gotten; in the eternity of the afterlife the flouting of God's law brought Hell-fire. Woe unto them who have gone in the way of Cain, or ran greedily after the error of Balaam for reward.

> Go to now, ye rich men,
> weep and howl for your miseries that shall come upon
> you.
> Your riches are corrupted,
> and your garments are motheaten,
> Your gold and silver are cankered. . . .
> Behold, the hire of the labourers
> who have reaped down your fields,
> which is of you kept back by fraud,
> crieth:
> and the cries of them which have reaped,
> are entered into the ears of the Lord of Sabaoth.[19]

[18] R. Baxter, *Chapters from a Christian Directory* (1673), selected by Jeannette Tawney (London, 1925), p. xvi.

[19] Ibid. 65–6; Jude, 11; and James 5: 1–4.

The attempt to control economic life according to a morality 'springing directly from Christian thought' had been abandoned to two hundred years of *laissez-faire* and to the doctrine that economics was one thing, religion and morality another. That did not prove that religion had always been powerless or that it could not become powerful again. Much of Jeannette Tawney's Introduction to Baxter's *Christian Directory* is scattered, without any substantial alteration throughout Tawney's next book, *Religion and the Rise of Capitalism.*

'Harrington's Interpretation of his Age' is an essay in which Tawney pays close attention to examples of the failure of religion to determine the manner in which individuals, and groups with their institutions, handled their environment. Yet he remains critical of those who depreciate its importance; including Harrington, who 'habitually underestimates', Tawney writes, 'the dynamic power of religious conviction'.[20]

Political as well as religious ideas and the actions of politicians as well as preachers, Tawney thought, could also exert an independent influence on belief and conduct and create or alter economic conditions as well as reflect them. He shared these views with those critics who believed that the spread of industrialization could (and should) be restricted—the nineteenth-century French socialists, Fourier, Proudhon, and Louis Blanc (and earlier Saint-Simon, who emphasized before Durkheim the value of religion as a mechanism of restraint as well as cohesion).[21]

When Tawney did his research for *The Agrarian Problem in the Sixteenth Century* the subject of the ownership of the land had already been extensively dealt with in publications from many parts of Europe by writers who hoped to learn from English history the scope and limits of political action in rural change. This was the precise question posed from Moscow by Paul Vinogradoff: 'how far legislation can and should act upon the social development of the agrarian world.'[22] The cautious answer given by Tawney on the attempts to control the sixteenth-century enclosure movement was that 'the slack and biased routines of rural administration' did not provide an effective machine for carrying policies into effect, and

[20] Tawney, *History and Society*, 80–1.
[21] Leslie Sklair deals with the 'reactionary' progressivism of Fourier, Proudhon, and Blanc, and Saint-Simon's 'strains of primitivism' in *The Sociology of Progress* (London, 1970), 49.
[22] P. Vinogradoff, *Villeinage in England* (Oxford, 1892), p. vi.

that the statesmen of the Tudor period failed to alter significantly the course of economic development. He was certain, however, that the intervention of the government had mitigated the hardships of the movement for the rural classes. 'It retarded, though it could not check altogether, economic changes. It imposed a brake that somewhat eased the shock of sudden movements.'[23] The Tudor monarchs themselves had attempted to preserve by political means the economic base of their power—the royal demesne and the peasant cultivator—and had been partially successful.

In Tawney's sociology, political organization rests on economic foundations; when the latter crumble, it crumbles with them. But this did not at all mean that Tawney embraced economic determinism or moral and political passivity. It meant that politicians must always be alert to attend to the economy to ensure that it provided a firm and suitable base for other desirable social institutions. Tawney's historical generalization was that political ideas and values normally *did* dominate economic organization.

Apropos the wage regulation provisions of the Trade Boards Act of 1909 and the miners' Minimum Wage Act of 1912, he argued that the determination of wages by the market was exceptional. Free enterprise was a brief interval of the primacy of economic forces, erected into a supposed universal theory by the classical economists and applied to all pre-communist societies by the Marxists. Collective control, and in complex societies that meant political control, Tawney believed, was normal and would reinstate itself.[24] Similarly the problems associated with structural and cyclical unemployment were susceptible to political solution or mitigation. Pre-1914 Germany rightly defined such unemployment as the result of politically correctable industrial disorder; pre-1914 England erroneously defined all unemployment as the result of uncontrollable market forces and irremediable personal deficiencies.[25]

Politics were also potent in other areas of social life. One of the most important of these was education. Carlyle had labelled education 'The One Institution', and had argued that a state

[23] R. H. Tawney, *The Agrarian Problem in the Sixteenth Century* (London, 1912), 289–91.

[24] W. E. Minchinton (ed.), *Wage Regulation in Pre-industrial England* (Newton Abbot, 1972).

[25] Tawney's evidence to the Royal Commission on the Poor Law, *Report*, Cd. 5068 (London, 1910), App. 49.

teaching service, headed by 'some Education Secretary, Captain-General of Teachers' was essential. For Tawney, too, education could (and must) be provided by the community, acting politically through the state. The resulting quality of teachers would largely determine the cultural quality of the next generation. 'Millionaires may endow education with buildings, libraries, and laboratories as opulent as they please; but serious people will measure the education of the nation by the degree to which it enlists the best intelligence in educational work.' The teachers the state recruits, trains, and employs must be people of intelligence, knowledge, and professional skill. Ultimately, however, the influence of teachers depends above all on their character, on what they are, not only on what they formally teach. 'They must, in short, be men and women . . . of culture.' Political action, therefore, by selecting and forming educators, plays a central role in shaping personal and social life.[26]

Tawney gave no less weight to the causal power of the morality and the commonsense view of the world of ordinary people—the force of traditional culture. His evidence that public opinion could be influential was that in the Tudor period it *had* been. In the sixteenth century, though many old economic ideas were going by the board, the common man still clung to the conception 'that there is a standard of fairness in economic dealings which exists independently of the impersonal movements of the market, which honest men can discover if they please, and which it is a matter of conscience for public authorities to enforce'.[27]

Tawney's historical research was designed to reveal the responses of people whose voices has been only feebly heard—the partly successful resistance of communities to the imposition on them on alien modes of capitalist perception, morality, and conduct. The substitution of sheep for the plough produced an outcry, Tawney argues, because the manorial authorities had to deal with villagers who were members of a fraternal society, not individuals to be picked off one by one. They were 'trade unionists to a man'.[28] They had considerable control over their affairs collectively, and the individual had a considerable say in the affairs of the collectivity. The ordinary villagers of Southern England and the Midlands,

---

[26] R. H. Tawney, *Education: The Socialist Policy* (London, 1924), 37, 42.
[27] Tawney, *Agrarian Problem in the Sixteenth Century*, 307.
[28] Ibid. 131.

typically of from ten to one hundred households, formed 'small democracies' of property-holders. Capitalism worked its damage in such communities by breaking down complex, almost sacramental, relationships in order to turn agriculture into a business. In the villages the Tudor opponents of enclosure acted with terrible tenacity because they were not demoralized individuals, as would be the wretched rural labourers of Cobbett's later generation. They were well-fed yeomen with their distinctive world-view, sharing a living body of assumptions as to the right conduct of human affairs. There was no resemblance, either in men or methods, in Tawney's view, 'between the agrarian disturbances of our period and the riots of starving agricultural labourers who burned ricks under Captain Swing'.[29]

An adequate explanation of social change had to take account of opinion and outlook as well as of circumstance and social structure. A critical case for Tawney was that of the English gentry in the sixteenth century. How did this class, under non-cultural circumstances objectively similar, obtain and keep wealth and power much more successfully than otherwise comparable strata elsewhere in Europe? It was because their *values* did not bar them from supplementing their incomes from industry, commercial farming, and trade. They kept their family wealth intact by primogeniture, pouring 'the martyrs of their prudent egoism', their younger sons, into the learned professions and every branch of business enterprise, into exploration, war, and colonization. They never severed their rural roots, and were able in due course to restore the popular and local attachments essential for a representative role. Their culture, finally, was one which demanded a hard-headed recognition of the means by which and the conditions within which their ends were pursued; 'they played each card in turn with tactful but remorseless realism'.[30]

Thus, while the economic difficulties caused by the sixteenth-century influx of gold from the New World were not confined to one country, the English response to it had a character of its own. In East Prussia the Junker estate became the dominant institution, 'half farm, half fortress'. In France the aristocrat adopted the tactic of a more rigorous exaction of his feudal dues. In England the country gentleman met the situation of falling fixed incomes and

[29] Ibid. 325.   [30] Tawney, *History and Society*, 86.

rising profits by shifting his role from that of landlord to that of entrepreneur. The durability—and in that sense the success—of the culture in holding on to power as well as wealth through changing circumstances is indicated by the fact that one-eighth of the members sitting for English and Welsh seats just before the Reform Act of 1832 belonged to families which two centuries before had given representatives to the House of Commons in the Long Parliament.[31]

Tawney argued, too, that within the stratum of the nobility different ways of perceiving and evaluating the same external situation, differences in world-view, determined the fate of particular families. In the difficult century of currency inflation between the accession of Elizabeth and the Civil War, some nobles adopted the culture of the gentry and prospered. Others, while their incomes declined, added to their traditional liabilities of hospitality an acquired taste for the new luxury and fashion.[32] The worst placed, ironically, were those nobles who, in addition, continued to undertake public duties in the old grand manner: under Elizabeth, James I, and Charles I more than one bearer of a famous name was brought near to ruin by 'the crowning catastrophe of a useful career'.[33]

The difference in social organization and cultural values between different groups facing approximately the same material restrictions and opportunities was a well-worn topic before the First World War. Troeltsch's discussion of the salient points made by Weber and Sombart and by their critics had been published in Britain in 1912.[34] But Tawney wanted to explain an even more heterogeneous set of responses to the same set of material circumstances. It was obvious to him—which is not to say that it was true—that what each and every person *believed* made a great difference to his or her own peculiar conduct, even among, say, Victorian evangelical Christians. Like Lord Shaftesbury (the evangelical philanthropist intent on directly improving the lot of the wretched through legislation) one could believe in a God who in a personal way constantly intervened to correct Nature, and in a divine Christ whose Second Coming was imminent as Governor of the world. Or one could believe, like others of the evangelical party, that God

[31] Ibid. 85.　　　　[32] Ibid. 78.　　　　[33] Ibid. 91.
[34] E. Troeltsch, *Protestantism and Progress: A Historical Study of the Relation of Protestantism to the Modern World* (London, 1912).

operated through an orderly universe as described by Newton in physics, and Ricardo and Malthus in economics, in which case correct conduct was to leave problems to be settled by *laissez-faire* and the operation of natural restraints on population.[35]

Unlike marxist writers, therefore, whose tendency is to look for salvation in the remorseless sweep of supra-personal history, Tawney asserted the theory that for beneficial change to take place individuals had to hold or adopt the appropriate attitudes. Changes in structure without changes in perception and evaluation were futile. Hence, in the tradition of Robert Owen and F. D. Maurice, he looked to the educated person, poor or rich, as the motor of social change, and to what Marxists dismiss scornfully as 'the individual pirouetter of solitary repentance'.[36]

---

[35] For a detailed discussion of these differences within the Evangelical Movement see D. Beales and G. Best (eds.), *History, Society and the Churches: Essays in Honour of Owen Chadwick* (Cambridge, 1985).

[36] D. Cooper (ed.), *The Dialectics of Liberation* (Harmondsworth, 1968), 16.

10

CHARACTER AND SOCIETY

A SOCIALIST CHARACTER

A tradition, and the personal life led by Tawney, have bequeathed an exacting definition of the character appropriate to a socialist. This is virtually and paradoxically to say that socialism is what socialists are. Tawney's socialism was centred on people. It is a collective culture carried or lost by the strength or weakness of individual character. Simplistic arguments distinguish sharply between the individual and society and postulate crudely that one is cause and the other consequence. Tawney took a more difficult view. On the one hand socialism as a mode of social organization produced good people: on the other hand only good people could sustain socialist relationships. The relation between character and society was a continuously complex interaction. The resulting society could be judged by what type of character it cultivated and esteemed: the resulting person would find it easier to emulate the virtues which we have found manifested in Tawney himself. To describe the socialist character is also to describe Tawney.

His first premiss was that, although joyful and fulfilling, life is not frivolous. Carlyle had adopted Schiller's *Ernst ist das Leben* as the motto of *Past and Present*. The idea that people must take their own lives seriously if they are to live them fully was expressed in Schiller's model of a life of restless striving, of perseverance, of total commitment, of pushing always to the limits of experience for clarity in self-knowledge. Life is not to be frittered away. '*Live not in idleness or sloth, but be labourious in your Callings* . . . Idleness is a crime which is not to be tolerated in Christian Societies.'[1] Tawney supported this view as expressed in Richard Baxter's

---

[1] R. Baxter, *Chapters from a Christian Directory* (1673), selected by Jeannette Tawney (London, 1925), p. xviii, Direction 6. The reference given (2 Thess. 2) does not appear to be correct, and must be 2 Thess. 3—'Withdraw yourself from every brother that walks disorderly . . .'

Christian Directory. And reward for effort was not to be sought in personal material gain.

Tawney's dedicated asceticism is not to be dismissed as the unrealistic recommendation of one born to professional security. It was also commonly found among the working people in his time—in the respectable, often Methodist, English and Welsh working class. Their daily lives hinged on personal pride in managing well on little; confidence that with what they had, or with not much more, all worthwhile things in life could be accomplished; and contempt, not admiration, for the materialistic bourgeoisie and the parastic rich whom the bourgeoisie aped.

In elaborating this moral outlook Tawney repeatedly advanced his own aversions and preferences behind Baxter's prose. '*Overvalue not the accommodation and pleasure of the flesh, and live not in the sins of gluttony, drunkeness, pride, gambling or ryotous courses . . .* As a philosopher said to *Diogenes*, If thou couldst flatter *Dionysius*, thou need not eat herbs: But, saith *Diogenes*, If thou couldst eat herbs, thou needest not flatter Dionysius.' A humble and temperate man could look on a rich man's possessions 'and bless himself as *Socrates* did in a Fair, with *Quam multa sunt quibus ipse non egeo*: How many things be there which I have no need of'.[2] And Tawney re-echoed these sentiments on another occasion by borrowing from the eighteenth-century Chinese emperor Ch'ien Lung who, after he had received a commercial mission from England, replied to George III: 'I set no value on objects strange and ingenious, and have no use for your country's manufactures.'[3]

There are many stories that show that Tawney held riches in light esteem. The former secretary of his local ward, Cliff Tucker, recalled that Tawney was one of the last people in the district to have a slot meter for the gas. When he made his monthly collection of Tawney's sixpenny Labour party subscription, he would make sure to take some change for it, which Tawney always lacked. The former head of the TUC education department, Jack Wray, recalled the occasion when Tawney entertained Archbishop William Temple to supper and removed volumes from the bookshelf to reveal two cold chops on a plate.[4] Tawney himself wrote of the state of

[2] Ibid. 13.
[3] R. H. Tawney, *The Condition of China* (Newcastle upon Tyne, 1933), 10.
[4] *The Times*, 1 Dec. 1980, 2.

'superblessedness' in which it would be 'contemptible to be rich and honourable to be poor'.[5]

No one has a right to be paid in work what he or she is 'worth'. What a person is worth is a matter between his own soul and God. 'What he has a right to demand, and what it concerns his fellowmen to see that he gets, is enough to enable him to perform his work.' If a person has important work and enough leisure and income to enable him to do it properly, 'he is in possession of as much happiness as is good for any of the children of Adam'—the happiness of toil unsevered from tranquillity. In a socialist society that is what he would enjoy.[6]

This message may be unfashionable now: but it is no denial of *joi de vivre*. Rather is it a clear pointer to the sure sources of happiness. Of course people should want to have enough material resources. 'Ordinarily the common sort of tenants of England', Baxter had written, 'should have so much . . . that they may comfortably live upon it and follow their labours with cheerfulness of mind and liberty to serve God in their families, and to mind the matters of salvation, and not to be necessitated by such care and toil and pinching want as shall make them more like slaves than free men.'[7] It is sometimes forgotten that 'L'Allegro' was written by a Puritan; and Weber, writing of the *schutterijen*, the Dutch champions of Calvinism, remarks that they do not look the least ascetic (*sich recht wenig ‚asketisch‘ gebärden*) in the pictures of Frans Hals.[8]

Tawney, like those Puritans whose ideal of life he so closely studied, never meant to remove durable and mutually reinforcing pleasures, but to cut off dissipating and ultimately destructive or restricting habits.

Tawney accepted as a fact that there were ill consequences from certain ways of life. He looked for the character that sought the maximum development and use of aesthetic, intellectual, and athletic capacities, each with its due place in a well-balanced whole—the real condition of a joyous life. People who are set on the path of harmonious development of their personal potentialities

[5] R. H. Tawney, *The Radical Tradition: Twelve Essays on Politics, Education and Literature*, ed. R. Hinden (London, 1964).

[6] R. H. Tawney, *The Acquisitive Society* (London, 1921), 221; M. Arnold, 'Quiet Work' (1849), *Poems* (London, 1965), 1.

[7] Baxter, *Chapters from a Christian Directory*, p. xv.

[8] M. Weber, *Die protestantische Ethik* (1904–5) (Hamburg, 1984), 264.

become progressively freer and more fulfilled. With each step forward new possibilities, new choices—the enlarged freedom to select the elements of well-being—are the reward. People who are not set on this path find with each step that the diminution of their powers of knowledge, physique, foresight, or courage has still further narrowed the range within which choices are available to them.

The ideal character, the individual grown to full stature, seen by Tawney as the product of socialism, was founded on good fellowship. It was not the outcome of a competitive struggle for individual self-advancement at the expense of others. Among the traits of a fully-developed personality is a capacity to enjoy sociable relationships. One may therefore lead a good life 'in all senses of the term' whether one climbs the economic ladder or not. The ideal character can pursue the intellectual interests and culture which human nature demands while deriving a sense of personal dignity from, and retaining the social contacts of, a familiar community of kinsfolk, neighbours, and workmates.[9]

The Aristotelian ideal of the fully-developed person in a community which values and sustains cultivated persons is thus Tawney's vision, as it was Hobhouse's. Such persons would be sensitive to, and care about, the impact of their actions on others. Self-regarding, we ideally perfect our nature; other-regarding, as Newman said, we ideally direct ourselves towards aims higher than our own.[10] Tawney commended Baxter's rejection of 'the convenient dualism which exonerates the individual by representing his actions as the result of uncontrollable forces'. Whatever the laxity of the law, the ideal individual is internally committed to consider first the Golden Rule and the public good.[11] 'See that your hearts have the two great principles of Justice deeply and habitually innaturalized or radicalized in them: viz. The true Love of your neighbour, and the Denyal of yourself.' Tawney similarly praised the Hammonds. Their politics were based, he wrote, on moral premises, not on economic expediency, and their first question was always not what would pay but 'what was true, what was right,

[9] Tawney, *Radical Tradition*, 178.

[10] J. H. Newman, *The Scope and Nature of University Education* (1859) (London, 1903), 115.

[11] Baxter, *Chapters from A Christian Directory*, pp. xiii–xiv; R. H. Tawney, *Religion and the Rise of Capitalism* (1926) (Harmondsworth, 1938), 220–1.

what was human'.[12] If his socialist society was to work, there must be commitment by individuals to altruistic values; there must be 'a spirit working within', not merely a body of rules externally imposed. The foundations of British socialism, the character and social existence that he preferred, were ethical.

Internalized commitment to serve others was, in Tawney's perception, the mark of the 'gentlemanly' character. In schools for the inculcation of professional *mores* students would come to feel that to snatch special advantages for themselves 'like any common business man' would be 'an odious offence against good manners'.[13] He recommended the substitution of fixed payments for variable payments throughout industry in the belief that this arrangement was then preferred and in future would be accepted by 'any man of honour'. The fixed salary would never be large, for such large salaries are 'ungentlemanly'.[14]

The ideal character is spontaneously generous. Adam Smith had sensibly and unexceptionally observed that it was not from the benevolence of the butcher, the brewer, or the baker that we expect our dinner, and that we never talk to them of our own necessities but always of their advantages.[15] But that did not make egoism a moral rule for all times and circumstances. Ethical socialists were repelled by the modern apotheosis of personal comfort and private interest—by utilitarian individualism's cult of the self-regarding ego.

Tawney validated his ideal of generosity by appealing to religious standards, and expended some of his most vivid and inaccurate biblical references on the subject. Cash payment was not the only nexus between man and man. The buyer, 'pondering on the dealings of Ephron the son of Zoher with Ormon the Jebusite', would then not always drive down the seller to the lowest price he would take.[16] Tawney again uses Richard Baxter as the proxy for his

---

[12] R. H. Tawney, *History and Society: Essays by R. H. Tawney*, ed. J. M. Winter (London, 1978), 251–2.

[13] Tawney, *Acquisitive Society*, 196.   [14] Ibid. 219–20.

[15] A. Smith, *An Inquiry into the Nature and Causes of the Wealth of Nations* (1776) (London, 1950), i. 16.

[16] Baxter, *Chapters from A Christian Directory*, p. xii. Tawney somewhat improves this in *Religion and the Rise of Capitalism*, 224. 'The dealings of Ephron the son of Zohar, and of David with Ormon the Jebusite.' The dealings were in fact between Abraham and Ephron the son of Zohar and between David and Ornan, and actually concern Abraham and David both paying the market price *as* the fair price. (Genesis 23: 1–4, 14–16; 1 Chronicles 21: 22–5.)

own view. Asked about the repair of the damage done by the Fire of London, Baxter replied that whatever might be the legal obligation or lack of it, costs must be borne out of 'humanity and charity'. Motives must be based on the acceptance of the three rules: 'Love your neighbours as yourselves; Do as you would be done by; and Oppress not your poor brethren'.[17]

Socialism, a doctrine of concern for others, could only be realized by human beings who were personally willing to make altruistic sacrifices, and not by 'socialists' who were simply those loudest in their demands that others sacrifice for others (or worse, the loudest in demands that others make sacrifices for them). Personal generosity as a character trait was not unique to socialism, it was not by itself socialism, but it was essential to socialism. Tawney laboured what might seem an obvious point, that kindliness was commendable, because he was familiar with what was to him a common and curious perversion: a marked tendency among people calling themselves socialists to denounce and repudiate it. To such socialists 'Lady Bountiful' was a term of abuse. They felt it their bounden duty to be among the most tolerant towards their neighbours' lapses, except when some misguided creature appeared in order to pick up commonly offensive rubbish or mow the common green. Then they would feel even more obliged hotly to insist that that was the council's job, and that it was an offence against the first principles of socialism for anyone to engage privately in furthering the public good.

There was, to be sure, an understandable basis for abhorrence in the experience of being always the suppliant, never the benefactor. Where (to use Malinowski's phrase) the 'principle of reciprocity' in human relationships is permanently in abeyance because of structured social inequalities, where generosity can flow in only one direction and gratitude in only the other, then pride, complacency, and censoriousness are set against humiliation, dependence, and resentment.

Concern for the common good or commonwealth, the totality of persons and their artifacts that constitute the good society, was for Tawney a distinguishing mark of the socialist. He agreed with John Stuart Mill, who looked forward to a time when people would think good citizenship paramount—'when it will no longer either be, or be thought to be, impossible for human beings to exert

[17] Baxter, *Chapters from a Christian Directory*, 113.

themselves strenuously in procuring benefits which are not exclusively their own, but to be shared with the society they belong to'.[18] Durkheim similarly saw socialism as based on the individual who is motivated by concern for the common good, and objected to the moral poverty of those who—sometimes deliberately—confused individualism with the 'utilitarian egoism of Spencer and the economists'.[19]

Baxter, Tawney's stalking-horse, laid great emphasis on personal commitment to improving what is *shared by all* in society. Everyone who is able must be regularly employed in activity that is 'serviceable to God and the common good'. The good person prefers the good of many to his own good or to the good of few, and prefers a durable good that will extend to posterity before a short-lived and transitory good. In an essay which first appeared in a book entitled *The Christian Demand for Social Justice* (1949) Tawney argued that the democratic socialist stood for 'the establishment for all of the conditions of a vigorous and self-respecting existence', personally and actively committed to promoting the welfare of others through the provision of common goods and the promotion of the common good.

Tawney himself required that his ideal of character include the components of common sense, prudence, and intelligent realism. The common sense of ordinary people—what Tawney more grandly terms 'the instinct of mankind'—warns against accepting spiritual demands which cannot justify themselves by practical achievements.[20] In 1942, by which time he was Archbishop of Canterbury, William Temple published his *Christianity and Social Order*, ending with six objectives which Christians should call upon the government to pursue, dealing with family life, education, income, leisure, liberty, and labour's share in management. He was uncertain whether to include the Appendix, 'A Suggested Programme'. He consulted Tawney. He should include it, Tawney advised, for it contributed the indispensable element of 'realism'.[21]

Very few fanatics pursued evil objectives. In most cases the damage they did stemmed from inability to assess the cost of

[18] J. S. Mill, *Autobiography* (1873) (London, 1924), 196.

[19] E. Durkheim, *Durkheim on Religion: A Selection of Readings*, ed. W. S. F. Pickering (London, 1975), 63.

[20] Tawney, *Acquisitive Society*, 201.

[21] F. A. Iremonger, *William Temple, Archbishop of Canterbury: His Life and Letters* (London, 1948), 439.

achieving their obsession in terms of other good things sacrificed. The anti-fanatic aspect of Tawney's ideal of character appealed to the prejudices of many of the still religiously-minded labour and co-operative rank-and-file of the first half of the twentieth century. Had not Wesley instructed his followers to use their 'common sense' and all the understanding God has given them?[22] Once again Baxter is allowed through Tawney to address a 1920s audience. Though the correct course is always to go the morally safer way, and to keep a peaceful conscience, one-sidedness is itself a sin and a corruption of religion: 'Causeless perplexing, melancholy scruples, which would stop a man in the course of his duty, are not to be indulged.'[23] Baxter's teaching, says Tawney, is above all 'realistic'. He appeals to 'the enlightened common sense of the Christian reader'. The ideal character, that is, never lets a person lose sight of the fact that socialism has to be realized in 'Rome or London, not Fools' Paradise'.[24]

A SOCIETY OF SOCIALISTS

If the socialist was a free person brought up in material equality with his or her fellows to value the activities of the spirit, the socialist society was a democracy for the promotion of these values, enabling its members to grow to their full stature, to make the most of their powers, to do what they conceive to be their duty and—since liberty should not be too austere—have their fling when they feel like it.[25] It was a society that offered liberty, equality, fraternity, and circumstances of material sufficiency for all.

Liberty was for Tawney a primary objective. 'Words', Hobbes says, 'are wise mens counters, they do but reckon with them: but they are the mony of fooles.'[26] If so, the only sensible question is not 'what is liberty?', but 'what does this person mean when he or

---

[22] J. Wesley, *Standard Sermons*, ed. E. H. Sugden (London, 1921), Sermon 50.

[23] Baxter, *Chapters from A Christian Directory*, 111, 131.

[24] Tawney, *Religion and the Rise of Capitalism*, 220. Robert Browning uses the same phrase in 'Bishop Blougram's Apology': No abstract intellectual plan of life | Quite irrespective of life's plainest laws | Best one, a man, who is a man and nothing more, | May lead within a world which (by your leave) | Is Rome or London, not Fool's-Paradise.

[25] Tawney, *Radical Tradition*, 160. Tawney repeats this passage, including the light-hearted reference to having one's fling (by which it is unlikely he meant the equivalent in his day of, say, hiring pornographic videos), in his *Equality* (1931), 4th edn. (London, 1952), 235.

[26] T. Hobbes, *Leviathan* (1651) (London, 1914), 16.

she uses the word liberty?' On the one side are those who argue, as has Isaiah Berlin, that the term should be used to signify the absence of restraints (the so-called 'negative' concept of liberty).[27] On the other side, there are those like E. H. Carr who define liberty positively as 'the opportunity for creative activity'.[28] This was Tawney's usage. 'The meaning of freedom', he writes, 'is not obscure': people are free if and in so far as they have the opportunity, in fact and not merely in theory, 'to lead a life worthy of human beings'.[29] There is no such things as liberty in the abstract: 'liberty is composed of liberties.' It exists only when there is an exercisable choice between alternatives. If socialists condemned capitalist society for its poverty and physical squalor, they did so in protest against a restriction on freedom and not merely a deficiency of physical resources. It was for that reason that hostility to capitalism was most acute among those sections of the working class whose material misery was least.[30]

As a means to freedom Tawney wanted a society of equals. In his emphasis on the removal of socially imposed inequalities of environment he was thus a Rawlsian long before Rawls. His socialism was a struggle against privilege. He was one of the many of his class who migrated in the late Victorian and Edwardian period to the New Liberalism, to Fabianism, and then to the new Labour party. They knew that the accident of birth had enabled them to become intelligent, competent, and cultivated men and women who were able in turn to provide the same advantages for their own children. England was a rich and stable society. Why, then, should working-class children, also by accident of birth, be poorly fed, poorly housed, inadequately educated, and then thrown into dead-end jobs in squalid towns? The first task in a socialist reconstruction of the institutions of society was 'the resolute elimination' of all forms of privileged environment. Tawney was undismayed by the charge that socialism meant 'levelling down'. His answer was, if that was the cost of levelling up, and as it affected some of those who were unjustly advantaged, of course it did.

Tawney's *Equality* had originated as the Halley Stewart Lectures

[27] I. Berlin, *Four Essays on Liberty* (London, 1969).
[28] E. H. Carr, *The New Society* (1951) (Boston, 1957), 118.
[29] Tawney, *Radical Tradition*, 160.
[30] Tawney, *Acquisitive Society*, 8.

for 1929. The following year the Hammonds published *The Age of the Chartists 1832–1854*.[31] Tawney approved the levelling up towards equality of environment which it describes—a movement of 'doctrineless collectivism'. On the one hand there had been progress towards equalizing conditions of employment through the Factory Acts; of schooling through the Education Acts; and of culture and leisure through the extension from the 1840s onwards of public libraries, museums, swimming baths, art galleries, and public gardens and parks. On the other hand there was increasing control of those who damaged or ruined common goods because it suited their private interests, especially those who did so in the disposal of industrial waste. The ordinary householder was stopped from 'committing a nuisance': but a greater problem was the entrepreneur who, while able himself to escape upstream and upwind, could pollute the air or turn the lower stretches of rivers into open sewers. Partial abatement of nuisance, at least as much as rising household income in a period of economic prosperity, explained the transition from working-class unrest in the first half of the nineteenth century to working-class tranquillity in the second.

An egalitarian culture of citizenship was also essential to a socialist society as Tawney conceived it. He was a parliamentary and committee democrat. He believed in universally equal access to rules which themselves equalized opportunities for effective participation in matters to be decided collectively: in the nation Parliament, in the towns democratic councils, and in the localities committees of working-men's clubs and trade unions. He was not by any stretch of the imagination either an anarchist who rejected the necessity for authority, or a populist who believed that delegates must speak for the 'demands of the masses'. A socialist society would offer to all the same conditions of civil liberty—freedom of speech and publication, of meeting, of combination, of choice of occupations, of worship. Citizens would also enjoy the constitutional arrangements for the operation of representative and responsible government. Democratic procedures would control access to power on the same terms for everyone, irrespective of class, sex, race, religion, or region. Equality under the rules of decision-taking would extend to all areas of public life. In particular, socialism would convert 'economic power, now often an

[31] J. L. and B. Hammond, *The Age of the Chartists 1832–1854: A Study of Discontent* (London, 1930). (*The Bleak Age* (Harmondsworth, 1947).)

irresponsible tyrant, into the servant of society, working within clearly defined limits, and accountable for its action to a public authority'.[32]

Tawney was keenly interested in equality of 'common' goods. He wanted a society which defined certain stocks as common, and distributed them on the basis of egalitarian principles. Equality in this connection meant everyone's equal right to a certain minimum from the common stock below which collective decision would ensure that no one could fall.[33]

Tawney drew his argument for a guaranteed minimum from both Christian and secular sources. Hugh Latimer, the great English Reformer, had maintained that prosperity depended upon prayer. 'Then it appeareth that you have your riches not through your own prayers only, but other men help you to pray for them: for they say as well, "Our Father, give us this day our daily bread", as you do.'[34] This assumption of inalienable right to subsistence could also be found in the tradition of English liberalism—through one of its principal philosophers, John Locke. Religion—'revelation', which Locke puts into inverted commas—gives us an account of those grants made of the world to Adam. It is therefore 'very clear that God, as King David says "has given the earth to the children of men", given it to mankind in common'.[35] As an Anglican Tawney was not indifferent to such arguments, although the general feeling for the poor's claim on religious grounds, if it was ever strong, was obviously weaker in the mid-twentieth century than when Tawney was a young man. He also used, however, the principal marxian argument, without referring to Marx. As a historian Tawney knew that a crude version of the theory of surplus value, familiar to him through Hobhouse, was available within English culture long before it was elaborated in *Das Kapital*. 'All rich men live at ease, feeding and clothing themselves by the labours of other men, which is their shame and not their nobility.'[36]

Equality did not, of course, mean sameness of either ability or character. Tawney knew well that people are not equally clever or equally virtuous any more than they are equally tall or equally fat.

[32] Tawney, *Equality*, 30.   [33] Ibid. 29.
[34] C. Gore (ed.), *Property: Its Duties and Rights* (1914) (London, 1915), 161–3.
[35] J. Locke, *Two Treatises of Civil Government* (1690) (London, 1924), 129; and Psalm 115: 16.
[36] L. B. Berens, *The Digger Movement in the Days of the Commonwealth* (London, 1906), 173.

Nor did equality mean identity of provision for the strong and the weak, the sane and the insane, the capable and the incompetent. 'It means that equal pains must be taken by society—i.e. their fellow-men—to make for all the provision appropriate to their needs.' It is true that some of these needs were identical, but others differed widely. The basic point was that diversity of provision must be based, not on the accident of the class or income of one's parents, on sex, religion, colour, or nationality—not on status criteria at all, but on functional criteria. This, for Tawney, was 'the essence of equality'.[37]

This conception echoes Aristotle's ancient and familiar argument, fundamental to the teaching of T. H. Green and Tawney's Oxford: there is 'numerical' equality but there is also 'proportional' equality. 'To lay down that equality shall be exclusively of one kind or another', Aristotle wrote, 'is a bad thing, as is shown by what happens in practice; no constitution lasts long that is constructed on such a basis.' In the well-constituted society use must be made of both.[38]

Tawney's ideal society of equality was organized more for a certain kind of similarity of taste and conduct than for sameness of income. Social organization would aim to raise the taste and conduct of all. As we have seen, in More's Utopia the day's work took only six hours, and eight hours were spent in sleep. But the society was organized in such a way that the other ten hours were used somewhat uniformly by the population. There was no waste of time. The inhabitants were up at 4 a.m. and their activities were constrained within a range of wholesome pursuits—educational lectures, gardening, music. 'Foolish and pernicious games they do not know', though there were two pastimes not unlike chess. Tawney may not have accepted More's medieval discipline but he agreed with Ruskin that to overcome enervating self-indulgence required a sense of duty and even some social compulsion. The ideal society would foster a culture of industriousness, obligation, and endurance. As much work as possible should be made immediately fulfilling and interesting, but for worthwhile activities there was a residue of toil and self-sacrifice which was not to be negatively evaluated. High achievement in art and aesthetics was

---

[37] R. H. Tawney, *The Attack and Other Papers* (1953) (Nottingham, 1981), 183.
[38] Aristotle, *The Politics* (Harmondsworth, 1962), 191–2.

necessarily based on the effort and monotony of preparation. The ultimate aim was joy, but through activity which was always fine and serious. Schiller had said 'Life is grave'; but he added, 'art, serene'. A high culture was taken for granted, a visit to a Hallé concert was better use of time than a visit to a public house, Clara Butt preferable to George Formby. There were, of course, occasions when people would want to let their hair down in the public house or music hall. But the ideal society would be organized to encourage people to choose the more elevated pursuits. To the extent they did not, the environment provided by social arrangements would have proved itself defective.

Tawney contrasted the world he deplored, which was one 'organized for enjoyment'—in the sense of frivolous and stunting self-indulgence—with the society 'organized for the encouragement of creative activity'—a society of sober and strenuous Tawneys. Whatever the differences of pecuniary rewards, there would exist the equality of 'a high standard of civilization'.[39] As an academic Tawney tended to think that, among permanently joyful activities, 'scholarship' was one of the most obvious and uncontroversial. The American Thorstein Veblen, an older academic and socialist, put this old-fashioned earnest view in an extreme form. For good or ill, Veblen wrote, civilized men had come to hold that matter-of-fact knowledge of things was 'the only end in life that indubitably justifies itself'.[40]

In a country without socialist values, material standards of living, however high, would be associated with the 'futilities' of self-indulgence, irregular habits, and gambling, and a wider dissemination of the capitalist leisure and work cult of 'betting-coupons, comforts and careers' rather than the expansion of individual human capacities or, as Wordsworth said, 'joy in widest commonalty spread'. Such failings were no more edifying in millions of wage-earners, than in a handful of monopolists, speculators, or urban landlords. If these, and not a higher level of general culture, were to result from full employment and improved material conditions, then the diseases socialism was to have cured would have simply 'altered their incidence without diminishing

---

[39] Tawney, *Radical Tradition*, 178, 207.
[40] T. Veblen, *The Higher Learning in America: A Memorandum on the Conduct of Universities by Businessmen* (New York, 1918). Francis Bacon in his essay on 'Truth' describes it as 'the sovereign good of human nature'.

their virulence'. So dark a future, Tawney wrote in 1937, need not at present be foreseen. But were these choices to be made within the structure of a future welfare state, though in total there might be some gain, 'it would hardly be worth the century of sweat which, together with some tears, has been needed to produce it'.[41]

A contrast in the cultural outlook of two men is relevant here. Tawney was the Labour party's main philosopher. Hugh Dalton was the main architect of its practical policies. Both were born in the 1880s; both died in 1962. Both were from the professional upper-middle class. (Dalton's father was tutor to the future King George V.) They were close colleagues at the London School of Economics. Dalton was MP for the County Durham mining constituency of Bishop Auckland and Tawney's ethical socialism found a strong echo in the Primitive Methodist and Temperance communities of the coalfield. But while Tawney, the old Rugbeian, followed a familiar Oxford path of taking the culture of the gentleman to the workers, Dalton, the old Etonian, adopted the deviant Cambridge style of the rebel-élitest and delighted in infuriating gentlemen by his vulgarity. Dalton was consciously a traitor to his class; Tawney was consciously a missionary for his class.

In the three decades from 1930 to 1960, these representatives of two aspects of the Labour party's persona complemented one another. The Tawney Dr Jekyll, scholarly and subdued, attracted the respectable, respectful, earnest, religious working class. Dalton, the bullying and raucous Mr Hyde, arrogant and adept at publicly insulting his opponents, appealed broadly to the bohemians and iconoclasts of all classes, and more narrowly to young Labour academics and politicians (many, though not all, from upper-middle-class families) whose eyes were on the higher reaches of influence and government power.[42]

Dalton was mainly interested in equalizing income and wealth. His biographer considers that among the seven Labour Chancellors of the Exchequer he was unique in the consistent emphasis he placed upon redistribution, and the determination with which he fought to preserve it as the Government's main purpose.[43] In 1920

[41] Tawney, *The Attack*, 190–1.
[42] Ben Pimlott lists twelve members of Wilson's second (1966) Cabinet as 'Dalton poodles'. B. Pimlott, *Hugh Dalton* (London, 1985), 642.
[43] Ibid. 452, 455.

Dalton had published his doctoral thesis on inequality.[44] His argument was technical, and based on the economics of Alfred Marshall and A. C. Pigou: inequality was economically inefficient. On the side of investment, inheritance put wealth in the hands of incompetents. On the side of consumption, the less urgent needs of the rich were met, while the more urgent needs of the poor were left unsatisfied.[45] Tawney, by contrast, argued that inequality was primarily to be condemned for 'violating human fellowship'.[46] He took a passage from William Morris's *The Dream of John Ball* as the motto of a collection of his essays—'fellowship is heaven, and lack of fellowship is hell'. This expressed, Tawney wrote, 'the noblest aspect of the popular movements of this country'.[47]

Even so he discussed the problem of fraternal relationships in only a few areas of life. He has almost nothing to say about relationships within the family. He could not have been unaware of the progressive views on sex, reproduction, and child-rearing, hostile to the family as an institution, represented in Fabian circles (especially in pre-1914 Cambridge) by, for example, Edward Carpenter.[48] But Tawney himself took little or no part in the movement intended to extend fraternity by freeing sex from the obligations accompanying marriage, and freeing procreation from lifelong monogamy. He accepted the conventional view of his day that the loyalty and self-sacrifice demanded from a spouse, parent, child, or sibling were not destructive of wider obligations of fraternity, but provided formative experiences which could then be imitated outside the family.

'A well-conducted family does not, when in low water, encourage some of its members to grab all they can, while leaving others to go short. On the contrary, it endeavours to ensure that its diminishing resources shall be used to the best advantage in the interests of all.'[49] The inescapable obligation of kinsfolk to live together, through bad times as well as good times, in 'godly love and honesty, that they may see their children christianly and virtuously brought

---

[44] H. Dalton, *Some Aspects of Inequality in Modern Communities* (1920) (London, 1925). See also his *Principles of Public Finance* (1922) (London, 1954); *The Capital Levy Explained* (London, 1923); *Practical Socialism for Britain* (London, 1935); 'Our Financial Plan' in Fabian Society, *Forward to Victory! Labour's Plan* (London, 1946).

[45] Dalton, *Aspects of Inequality*, 242, 284–5.

[46] Tawney, *The Attack*, 175.   [47] Ibid. 191.

[48] E. Carpenter, *Love's Coming-of-Age: A Series of Papers on the Relations of the Sexes* (1896) (London, 1948).   [49] Tawney, *The Attack*, 184–5.

up', and, whatever the state of personal feelings, to provide companionship, help, and comfort, was not a competitor to, but the pattern for, all relationships in a socialist society. Nothing was further from Tawney's thinking than that the family should be assimilated to the free, self-regarding, contractual relationships of the capitalist economy. The hedonistic individualism of capitalist society was to be superseded by a socialism modelled on the responsibilities kinsfolk owed to one another. His socialism was based on a conception of society as being composed of members of the same family.[50]

He took its benignity for granted and its permanence as essential. 'Like religion, the family is an aspect of life whose deceitful quiescence in tranquil times cajoles successive generations of bright intellectuals into paeans ... on its supposed demise, but which revives, when hit, like a watered flower. If blows are sufficiently violent, it displays, to the confusion of the prophets, an almost bloodthirsty vitality.'[51] In relation to the family, as elsewhere, the common sense of Henry Dubb, good-hearted, patient, and courageous, was worth 'nine-tenths of the gentilities, notabilities, intellectual, cultural, and ethical eminences put together', and the divisions of the future, for which Tawney had only hope not confidence, would be between the different estimates put upon Dubb's muddled soul.[52]

In discussing fraternity Tawney was mainly concerned with the capitalist economy itself. Here again, he appealed comfortably and without elaboration to the standards of the decent man. There is room for a proper concern for one's personal interests, but when important issues are at stake everyone realizes that decent people do not stand out for their price. 'A sentry who gives the alarm to the sleeping battalion does not spend the next day collecting the capital value of the lives he has saved; he is paid one shilling a day and is lucky if he gets it. The commander of a ship does not cram himself and his belongings into the boats and leave the crew to scramble out of the wreck as best they can; by the tradition of the service he is the last man to leave.' There was no reason to insult manufacturers and men of business by treating them as if they were of necessity inclined to be any less decent, that is to say, any less fraternal.[53]

---

[50] Ibid. 183.   [51] Ibid. 150–1.   [52] Ibid. 163.
[53] Tawney, *Acquisitive Society*, 220–1.

Tawney accordingly condemned a social system that applauded the self-regarding success of the economically strong, whether the success was linked to service or not. He looked back to a religious tradition of fair dealing in pre-industrial times and to philosophical protest against nineteenth-century *laissez-faire*. John Wycliffe had claimed that the validity of ownership depended upon a man's standing in grace. As soon as he fell into sin, his ownership was transformed into usurpation. In the late eighteenth century Woolman's *Word of Remembrance to the Rich* reproduced Wycliffe's position from the Quaker standpoint. To increase possessions contrary to the principle of universal love, or to dispose of lands in such a way as to knowingly oppress some in order to exalt others, meant that he who had been an owner had become a tyrant. Excessive interest (under Cromwell, the Act of 1651 set the maximum at 6 per cent a year) was regarded by the Puritans as a civil offence and as a cause for exclusion from the sacraments. A fair price for labour, as Jeremy Taylor put it, is 'that which is established in the fame and common accounts of the wisest and most merciful men, skilled in that manufacture or community'.[54]

In his 1919 essay on John Ruskin, Tawney set out his views on industrial activity in a fraternal society. 'The userer's trade will be abolished utterly; the employer will be paid justly for his superintendence, but not for his capital; and the landlord paid for his superintendence of the cultivation of land when he is able to direct it wisely.' Among those capable of doing so, only people who performed worthwhile services for others would be rewarded.[55] In *The Acquisitive Society* he repeats the point that the first principle of organization should be 'that those who render service faithfully should be honourably paid, and that those who render no service should not be paid at all'.[56]

In his inaugural address as Director of the Ratan Tata Foundation he highlighted an exploitative social structure as the cause of unacceptable poverty. Since 1834, when the new Poor Law was introduced, attention had shifted from the pauper to poverty, and then to the pattern of the distribution of wealth. But in the Minority Report of the Poor Law Commission (1909) even Beatrice Webb

[54] Gore, *Property*, 142, 154, 163–5. The Taylor passage is from his *Holy Living and Holy Dying*, ch. 3, sect. 3, para. 4.
[55] Tawney, *Radical Tradition*, 41, 44.
[56] Tawney, *Acquisitive Society*, 7.

(greatly praised by Tawney after *My Apprenticeship* led him to a reassessment of her[57]) had still dealt only with the symptoms, not the causes of poverty. Poverty was the result of the private ownership and oligarchic control of the means of production.

Tawney's main target was the functionless yet wealthy owner. He had no more right to negotiate his share with the workers than had the German invaders to negotiate with Belgium from Brussels in 1914. The Germans had no right to be in Brussels in the first place, and the owners contributed nothing to production, so neither of them were entitled to put forward proposals at all. The channels through which resources leaked away to people who served no purpose would be closed. Tawney mentions three in particular: mineral royalties, urban ground-rents, and inherited wealth. The community as a whole would resume the ownership of minerals and urban land. Taxes on inheritance would be increased so that the heir would receive no more than personal possessions, and be stripped of 'the right to a tribute from industry which, though qualified by death duties, is what the son of the rich man inherits today'.[58]

Tawney believed that fraternity expressed itself most effectively when society was so organized that all those capable of doing so worked conscientiously for one another in their ordinary full-time occupations. This view, too, was strongly represented in the tradition within which Tawney placed himself, and to which he constantly appealed. As we have noted, Locke had based his theory of private property on the premiss that God has given the world to men in common. He had given it, however, so that all could benefit from its resources. It could not be supposed, therefore, that He meant it always to remain uncultivated, still less that He had endowed the earth to a hereditary class of rich men. 'He gave it to the use of the industrious and rational (and labour was to be his title to it); not to the fancy or covetousness of the quarrelsome and contentious.'[59] Carlyle's hero was Noble Labour 'the truest emblem there is of God' (for all true work was religion and all true work was sacred) who would in due course overthrow the idle dilettante and 'sit on the highest throne'.[60] John Stuart Mill saw

[57] Tawney, *The Attack*, 126, 130.
[58] Tawney, *Acquisitive Society*, 114–5, 103–4.
[59] Locke, *Two Treatises*, 132–3.
[60] Carlyle, *Past and Present*, 170, 173, 202–3, 207.

himself as a socialist because he deplored the division of society into the idle and the industrious. He wanted the rule that they who do not work shall not eat applied not to paupers only, but impartially to all. He expressed this opinion least clearly and fully in the first edition of his *Principles of Political Economy*, rather more so in the second, and quite unequivocally in the third.[61]

Mineral royalties and urban ground-rents were for Tawney the essence of parasitism. People who had never seen a coal-mine distilled the contents of that place of gloom into elegant chambers in London. The ownership of urban land had been refined until none of the work and all of the luxury was left to the landlord. He uses Mill's view in support of his own: that in no sound theory of private property was it ever contemplated that the proprietor should be a mere sinecurist. Every economic right was properly embedded in a system of fraternal give-and-take: 'a commission of service' not 'a property'.[62]

Liberty, equality, and fraternity were only possible in a community in which all members were adequately fed, clothed, and sheltered. 'The work of the community must be done, and it ought to be done with the aid of the ever-changing improvements made possible by science and invention.' If one group in the community vetoes the solution to industrial problems propounded by another, it must play its part in discovering better solutions.[63] Security in claims to an adequate standard of living was fundamental. Characteristically, Tawney frames the discussion around the assumption, not of members of the community who are permanently dependent upon state assistance, but of the normally self-sufficient person in paid employment. He therefore looked with particular favour upon insurance as a means of maintaining family income in the event of sickness, in old age, and on the death of a breadwinner.[64] State insurance was already a feature of the 1911 contributory sickness and unemployment schemes introduced by Lloyd George and state insurance was central to the Beveridge Report's conception of the post-1945 welfare state.

But what standard of living was 'adequate'? Sidney Webb's views do not seem strange today. He advocated 'the highest Standard of

[61] Mill, *Autobiography*, 196, 198.
[62] Tawney, *Acquisitive Society*, 102, 234.
[63] S. E. Chapman (ed.), *Labour and Capital after the War* (London, 1918), 109.
[64] Tawney, *Acquisitive Society*, 85–6.

Life, rising with every advance in our power over Nature, that the economic circumstances of the community can afford'.[65] By contrast, Tawney did not calculate any 'poverty line' in either absolute or relative terms. His discussion is always general and his stress is always upon the importance of *curbing* the desire for material wealth at the standard necessary for a full life. 'Give me neither wealth nor poverty, but enough for my sustenance.' Experience shows that an unceasing struggle against destitution is a sure barrier to civilized conduct; but this dictum reminds us also, Tawney writes, that neither does 'a privileged immunity from the trials of the common lot' offer an environment conducive to spiritual health.[66] Certainly cold and hunger can drive people to vice, but if their desires remain or become excessive, wealth does not drive them away from it. As Aristotle on one occasion laconically enquired, 'Who ever heard of a man making himself a tyrant in order to keep warm?'[67]

According to Tawney, once the threshold of the minimum standard of civilized life had been crossed by all, the basic defect of capitalist societies (and of totalitarian regimes which in this respect perpetuated the worst features of capitalism) was not the continued existence of relative poverty, but an over-estimation of the importance of material wealth. Both capitalists and communists substituted the ideal of progress for that of righteousness and regarded an increase in comfort as convincing evidence of moral superiority. These virtues of capitalism and Communism are vices for Tawney's Christian Socialism: they are 'more ruinous to the soul than most of the conventional forms of immorality'.[68] Above a modest standard of material living those who valued further possessions more than the enjoyment of the highest achievements of human culture were to be pitied, not emulated. The thrust of Tawney's *Equality* is much less that the English working class is wretchedly poor than that the English bourgeoisie is ridiculously rich.

It is basic to Tawney's socialism that material circumstances, traditional culture, individual abilities, character traits, and other practical and personal constraints set boundaries to human choice.

[65] S. Webb, *The Story of the Durham Miners 1662–1921* (London, 1921), 132–3.

[66] E. Brontë, 'The Old Stoic', *The Complete Poems of Emily Jane Brontë*, ed. C. W. Hatfield (New York, 1941), 163; Tawney, *The Attack*, 190.

[67] Aristotle, *Politics*, 75.   [68] Tawney, *The Attack*, 170, 174.

In some societies, and for some people in all societies, those boundaries are narrow. But in a rich and non-totalitarian country such as England, there is for most people room for crucial choices. 'The effect of conditions depends upon the response to them.'

The English peasantry and working class, ever faced by the temptation to snatch and hoard advantages instead of sharing them under remorseless conditions of meagre material resources, had responded with 'a great tradition' of an 'unbreakable spirit of comradeship'. Prosperity was no guarantee that greed and jealousy would diminish in intensity and extent; an ever-rising standard of living would not itself lead to socialist values. Moral choices were required. 'The name of the materialist devil is legion. In the war against him no final victories are won.'[69]

The grand heretical doctrine of capitalism was the idolatry of selfish riches and the neglect of fraternal duty. Its reign had been long. Full employment and greater power and responsibilities for trade unions might lead to abuse of the former and rejection of the latter. Capitalism may place material riches too high in the scale of human values but so may trade unions.[70]

The task of the democratic socialist was to domesticate the serviceable but indisciplined monster, modern urban industrialism, to force a bit and bridle between its reluctant jaws in the shape of Factory and Mines Acts, Public Health and Social Security Acts, but not to set it on a madder gallop along the path of indiscriminate economic growth.[71] Putting the Bank of England into public hands and such measures as the establishment of a National Investment Council were means, for Tawney, of managing the economy 'with a single eye to the public interest'. The public interest meant neither coercing nor pandering to consumers of frivolous goods and services. He wanted to prevent the 'recurrent imbecility' of pouring resources into investments which chanced to hit the public fancy (among which he singles out cinemas) as long as, in human terms, resources could be more appropriately employed elsewhere.[72]

Tawney fought persistently for high-minded austerity against a false evaluation of material welfare. The appearance in 1956 of *The Future of Socialism*, the work of Hugh Dalton's 'adopted son', Anthony Crosland, marked his final defeat on this issue, and in the

---

[69] Ibid. 191.   [70] Ibid. 190.
[71] Tawney, *History and Society*, 240.
[72] Tawney, *Radical Tradition*, 150.

Labour party his arguments came to appear quaint where they were not simply unknown. Henry Dubb, with his deplorably undeveloped desire to discover a formula for fermenting permanent discontent, had mocked a preoccupation with what others possessed as 'keeping up with the Joneses'. After Tawney's death von Wiese's concept of 'subjective poverty' or later of 'relative deprivation', by which an insufficiency of material resources was defined in terms of current 'expectations', were comprehensively victorious and became impregnably part of the conventional wisdom. Indeed when they re-emerged in the Continental Green movement Tawney's old and nearly forgotten assumptions carried the shock of novelty, and aroused feelings of condescending incredulity. Yet the underlying economic strategy of fair distribution as against growth and the basic social preference for quality of *koinonia*, as against plenitude of material possessions, remain the fundamental principles and practice of a socialist society.

II

THE CASE FOR A SOCIALIST BRITAIN

Tawney made his case for a socialist Britain out of the moral and sociological theory we have outlined. He was the unflagging theoretical exponent in the British Labour party of Weber's type of politics as a vocation, which combines an unwavering clarity of vision as to the ultimate ends to be achieved with determination to work towards them in the world 'as it really is in its everyday routine'. To be passionately realistic about the means as well as to be passionate about the ends is the most difficult political task of all. It requires a kind of hero—a hero in a very sober sense of the word. In politics, Weber affirmed, 'even those who are neither leaders nor heroes must arm themselves with that steadfastness of heart which can brave even the crumbling of all hopes'. Only he who is sure that he will not despair when the world seems too stupid or too base for what he wants to offer has the calling for politics. Only he who can say that his efforts were worthwhile 'in spite of all' is worthy of political trust.[1]

Tawney met Weber's criterion in full. He was a steadfast political realist, even though he barely noticed two issues that became critical in political debate. He had little awareness that the legally and socially approved relationships between men and women in civilized England should or would be fundamentally disturbed. His people are almost always men. He had no familiarity with gender, equality, and sexual liberation as it is now understood. And he disregarded race, assuming as he did a Britain of ethnic homogeneity.

WHAT WAS WRONG WITH BRITAIN

To identify what was wrong with his country he looked primarily to the economic base of wholesome life—food, clothing, shelter, pure air, and, in Hobson's phrase, 'free communication with the

---

[1] 'Politics as a Vocation' (1918), in M. Weber, *From Max Weber*, ed. H. H. Gerth, and C. W. Mills (London, 1948), 127–8.

powers of the uncontaminated earth'.[2] Workmen consented to degrade themselves by producing shoddy goods for the poor, 'boots that are partly brown paper, and furniture that is not fit to use'.[3] Goods were produced on the principle that all economic activity was equally justifiable, when much that was called wealth was strictly speaking waste. When what was required were six-roomed cottages to house families living three persons to a room, building fashionable houses was squandering both materials and human energy. The permanent physical manifestation of this indiscriminate production were Britain's towns and cities: the illth of the 'hideous, desolate and parsimonious' manufacturing and mining areas, and the illth of the pointlessly magnificent and luxurious districts where most of what was produced was consumed.[4]

Egoistic co-operation, based on individual calculation of advantage, had produced the thoroughly unfraternal state of affairs in which some enjoyed the results of other people's work while doing nothing in return. Fraternity would require that all the fruits of co-operation should be distributed fairly among the producers—managers, technicians, and workers—and that none sought to secure advantages for themselves at the expense of others. In capitalist Britain workers and managers were hired at the cheapest price the market allowed, and the surplus, somewhat diminished by taxation, went to functionless property owners.

The inheritance of property was not in itself inconsistent with a fraternal society. Property in England had once been widely distributed, and the greater part of it had consisted of land, equipment, and tools employed by their owners. In such a society inheritance was a convenient arrangement for allowing the work of the world to be carried on without interruption. But in inter-war England, where nearly two-thirds of the aggregate wealth was owned by one-hundredth of the population, inheritance had become a 'strong poison'. It meant that rich men bequeathed to their worse than useless heirs 'a right to free quarters at the expense of their fellow-countrymen'.[5] The unfraternal affirmation of the absolute rights of property was met by the counter-affirmation of the absolute rights of labour, a creed which was 'almost as

[2] J. A. Hobson, *John Ruskin: Social Reformer* (London, 1898).
[3] R. H. Tawney, *The Acquisitive Society* (London, 1921), 190.
[4] Ibid. 88.
[5] R. H. Tawney, *Equality* (1931), 4th edn. (London, 1952), 28.

dogmatic, almost as intolerant and thoughtless'.[6] Far from working conscientiously for one another's benefit, employees were deliberately withholding their capacity for efficiency. Capitalism, in devaluing fraternity, had 'shot the bird that caused the wind to blow' and now had to go about its business with the albatross round its neck. In comparision, the purely technical difficulties of British industry were minor. Capitalism had been able to work with fear, ignorance, passivity, and credulity. It could not work with permanent and widespread resentment and distrust.

Within industry a change had taken place as destructive of co-operation as that which had earlier separated entrepreneurship from labour. The financial and technical departments had drawn apart, and the former had found various devices to secure adroit profits without the tedium of having to increase efficiency to justify them. Selfish financial considerations maintained the wasteful system under which railway companies operated separately. Pits were flooded because colliery companies would not share the costs of common drainage systems. Egoistic co-operation and competition made it advantageous to incur expenses to absorb part of a rival's trade from a fixed number of customers. To the customer, who had eventually to meet these expenses, it was pure loss. Fraternity was lacking between groups of workers. Different sections exercised their group egoism against the interests of other sections, for they had no guarantee that if they showed restraint in wage demands the benefit would go to the weaker groups within the working class and not to the undeserving rich.

The age of easy capitalist affluence, Tawney said, had ended in 1914. It might turn out that no effort would be sufficient to prolong the episode of the nineteenth century's amazing outburst of riches. The old system based on rights divorced from obligations was visibly breaking down. In the best case fraternity would now be required merely to maintain existing standards. At worst fraternity would be the only way to cope with a once-more niggardly world in which people would be obliged to sweat, like a platoon of soldiers, for their daily rations.

Thus the main domestic forms of inequality lay in economic, not ethnic or gender relations:

The *rentier* and his ways, how familiar they were in England before the war! A public school and then club life in Oxford and Cambridge, and then

---

[6] Tawney, *Acquisitive Society*, 31.

another club in town; London in June, when London is pleasant, the moors in August, and pheasants in October, Cannes in December and hunting in February and March; and the whole world of rising bourgeoisie ... sedulous to make their expensive watches keep time with this preposterous calendar![7]

Two per cent of the population took one-quarter of the nation's output. Some people might approve of this distribution of income, and no logic could contradict them. But Tawney's sensibilities were outraged. They had done nothing to deserve their share, and they wasted it when they received it. Like Cobbett, he was the friend of the industrious, frugal, and exploited poor; he shared Cobbett's mighty contempt for the idle and spendthrift rich.

Within the productive economy, moreover, there were marked and undesirable inequalities of power. Inequality of power *per se* was not an evil for Tawney, any more than it was for the Engels of 'On Authority'.[8] In urban communities with dense populations, and in great productive undertakings employing armies of workers, someone had to make policies and have the authority to see that they were carried out. If power-holders carried no public account-ability, the effect was private dictatorship, albeit exercised less brutally in Britain—where the general culture was milder and where trade unions and legislation had 'long done their civilizing work'—than in other countries of the world.[9]

Non-functional and unjust inequalities of power were closely related to undesirable restrictions on liberty. An absolute deficiency of material resources was always a hardship. But it was much more easily to be borne if it originated in endemic natural shortages or natural disasters than if it was the result of the actions of other people. 'Hunger and cold cause misery, but men do not revolt against winter or agitate against the desert. The fundamental grievance is that the government of industry and the utilization of both land and capital is autocratic.'[10]

The idle rich use property for functionless gain. The active rich use it for irresponsible power. The many may or may not possess constitutional rights, and may or may not believe that life, liberty, and the pursuit of happiness are their heritage. But they do not enjoy liberty. They have to accept the beating down of salaries and

[7] Ibid. 37–8.
[8] F. Engels, 'On Authority', K. Marx and F. Engels, *Selected Works*, (Moscow, 1951, 1958), vol. i. [9] Tawney, *Equality*, 229–30.
[10] S. E. Chapman (ed.), *Labour and Capital After the War* (London, 1918), 101.

wages, threats of arbitrary dismissal, involuntary unemployment without payment, nepotism, jobbery, and the hauteur of rich men and their servants. 'They live, in effect, at the will of a lord.'[11]

In Tawney's opinion about £1,000 a year at 1921 prices was sufficient money for the purposes of such liberty as was connected with its possession. He suggested that people should transfer anything in excess of that to the public purse. Not only had private property become the means of arbitrary private domination in the economy—property-owners were becoming increasingly hostile to English parliamentary democracy because it embodied political liberty and provided the threatening means of economic change. 'It may well be the case', Tawney wrote, 'that democracy and capitalism, which at moments in their youth were allies, cannot live together, once both have come of age.' When that contingency arises, it is necessary to choose between them.[12]

The problems of modern Britain revealed themselves in physical squalor and in social relationships which offended against the canons of fraternity, equality, and freedom. They were at bottom problems of belief. For Tawney, as for Weber, facts are important, but so are—in a phrase Tawney often used—'the minds that appraise them'. The British people 'cannot remove the defects they deplore unless they are willing to forgo the success they esteem, because both failure and success spring from the same false evaluations'.[13]

During a great part of history men had found the significance of their social order in its relation to the purposes given to them by their religion. Even if they personally failed to conform, they believed that society was and ought to be maintained by a common body of religiously sanctioned social ethics.

In the eighteenth century both State and Church gradually abdicated these claims. The idea of social purpose, of function rather than personal gratification, and of the discharge of detailed duties required by an all-seeing higher moral authority, was increasingly replaced by the idea of a social mechanism. This was true of the philosophy of *laissez-faire*; but it was no less true of 'the

[11] Tawney, *Acquisitive Society*, 92–3, 197.
[12] Tawney, *Equality*, 30.
[13] R. H. Tawney, 'John Ruskin' (1919), in R. H. Tawney, *The Radical Tradition: Twelve Essays on Politics, Education and Literature*, ed. R. Hinden (London, 1964), 40.

truculent hyper-intellectualism' of Marx.[14] During the greater part
of the nineteenth century a commitment to self advancement could
still be reconciled with a general commitment to public duty,
through the doctrine of the inevitable harmony of private interests
and the common good. 'Few now would profess adherence to that
compound of economic optimism and moral bankruptcy.'[15]

The false philosophy which overshadows the life of the wealthy
also haunts the poor. For they, too, come to make materialism the
guide of their lives; they continue to believe, *beyond the point at
which it is no longer true*, that the major solution to their problems
is an improvement in material conditions, and higher income and
expenditure. But if people recognize no laws superior to their own
desires, then discontent must be permanent, for desires are more
easily created in the imagination than the means of their fulfilment
can be created in hard struggles with intractable nature. 'Hence the
idea, which is popular among rich men, that industrial disputes will
disappear if only the output of wealth were doubled . . . is in its
very nature founded upon an illusion.' On the basis of materialism,
with its infinite capacity to create and re-create relative deprivation,
people are never satisfied; nor can they ever be satisfied, for
'nothing short of infinity could bring them satisfaction'.[16]

Here for Tawney was the key to the understanding and the
solution of the social problems of urban-industrial societies. In
these societies so-called wealth is an indiscriminate amalgam of
wealth and illth. He calls such societies acquisitive societies because
their whole tendency, interest, and preoccupation is to promote the
multiplication of commodities. The pursuit of things that money
can buy had laid the whole of the modern world under its spell.
Before the eyes of both rich and poor was suspended a golden prize,
the enchanting vision of endless expansion. It assured people that
there were no ends other than their ends, no law other than their
desires, no limit other than that which they thought advisable. It
relieved them of the necessity of discriminating between enterprise
and avarice, energy and unscrupulous greed, property which was
legitimate and property which was theft. It treated all economic
activities as standing on the same level, and suggested that excess or
deficiency, waste or superfluity, required no conscious effort of the

---

[14] R. H. Tawney, *History and Society: Essays by R. H. Tawney*, ed. J. M. Winter
(London, 1978), 251.
[15] Tawney, *Acquisitive Society*, 30.   [16] Ibid. 45–6.

social will to avert them, but were corrected by the mechanical play of economic forces. People in an acquisitive society did not become religious, wise, or artistic; for the acquisition of these characteristics required submission to rules whose existence was independent of and frequently opposed to the individual's private and momentary desires. Some people did become rich in an acquisitive society; but the single-minded pursuit of wealth makes at length even riches meaningless.

In the England that emerged after the Civil War and the Glorious Revolution there remained little trace, Tawney argued, of the conception of men as united to each other, and of all mankind as united to God, by mutual obligations arising from devotion to a common end. What remained in the eighteenth century were private rights, the most obvious and fundamental being the absolute and unconditional rights of private property. The state was essential as the guarantor of these rights. Otherwise it was to be treated with all the circumspection due to an entity that combined 'the manners of a Japanese customs official with the morals of a human tiger'. Marxists had no higher a conception of the state. For them it was merely the executive committee in charge of a body of armed men who could be called upon to use physical force to suppress any dangerous elements within the exploited proletariat. Marxists had been joined in the 1930s by Bloomsbury intellectuals who, fresh from discovering the class struggle, had with 'blood-curdling bleats' announced that parliamentary democracy was futile.[17]

WHAT WAS RIGHT IN BRITAIN

Tawney, however, saw strengths as well as these weaknesses in both his country and his compatriots. That people are capable of evil and tend to fall into evil ways, that this is a fact of the human condition for which there is no miraculous remedy, were beliefs basic to his outlook. No less strong was his belief that, with the aid of a moral code which their environment does not make too difficult to follow, people are capable of distancing themselves from evil. To that extent his was a radical image of man. If there was not an 'instinct of workmanship' human beings nevertheless could and should value work for its own sake, as well as for its results. In

[17] Tawney, *Radical Tradition*, 141, 164.

taking this factual and moral view, Tawney was associating himself
with the teaching of men as widely different as Emerson, Carlyle,
Zola, Ibsen, William Morris, Tolstoy, and Ruskin. While economists emphasized the separation of work and enjoyment, a revolt
from the ranks of literature and art enunciated distinctively a gospel
of work. 'Nature demands work', says Tawney. Given the chance
most people want to see work properly done, their own and
others'.[18] Economic science suggested a simplicity, uniqueness, and
permanence of motive, namely, personal pecuniary gain, derived
from the crude and dogmatic eighteenth-century rationalism that
presided at its birth. This was the economist's lazy substitute for
observation and was 'quite foreign to the facts'. Similarly, if there
was not an 'instinct of fellowship' there was a human capacity for
toil and self-sacrifice on behalf of others. It could be either
suppressed where selfishness was inculcated or elicited where
fellowship was nurtured.[19]

In addition to these beliefs about human nature in general,
Tawney shared in a tradition that attributed to the English a
particular and favourable national character. He began *The
Acquisitive Society* with the comment that, although they are not
good theorists, 'it is a commonplace that the characteristic virtue of
Englishmen is their power of sustained practical activity'.[20] This
fact or illusion was referred to by Carlyle in very similar terms.[21]
Ruskin shared Carlyle's views. Hobson in turn contrasts the West
European and Russian unfavourably with the English working
class. The continental working class, he said, had accepted Marx's

[18] Tawney, *Acquisitive Society*, 77, 213; Hobson, *Ruskin*, 305.
[19] Carlyle tells the story of Mungo Park who, though a horrible white object to
the African villagers among whom he had fallen ill, was nursed and fed by a woman
('and her daughter who stood aghast of him') whose earthly wealth consisted of one
small calabash of rice. 'She was a true Lady.' At all times and places, Carlyle wrote,
people had experienced injustice, suffering, heavy burdens; they had died of
weariness and hunger. What made capitalism uniquely unbearable was that the
individual was now also 'isolated, unrelated, girt-in with a cold universal Laissez-
faire'. Lack of fellowship, not only material deprivation, was at the root of such
movements of revolt as Chartism. (T. Carlyle, *Past and Present* (1843) (London,
1899), 201–11.)   [20] Tawney, *Acquisitive Society*, 178–9.
[21] 'Of all the Nations in the world at present the English are the stupidest in
speech and the wisest in action.' The English are a dumb people, conservative, thick-
skinned and patient, who are able to do great acts but not describe them. Their epic,
unsung in words, was written in huge characters across the face of the planet—sea-
defences, immense fleets, railways, cities: industrialization, and the organization of
foreign trade; the conquest of India and the settlement of North America. (Carlyle,
Past and Present, 160.)

doctrine that the idea of God was the keystone of a perverted civilization and must be destroyed. The English working class, in contrast, had remained Christian, partly due to what he calls a 'congenital' distrust of reason as an all-sufficient guide to conduct. In intellectual life English workmen rejected 'the falsehood of extremes' and in practical life 'their reason, their humour and their humanity' protected them against any wish to hate or to destroy their bourgeoisie.[22]

'Henry Dubb', the typical English working man, towards whom Tawney was patronizing rather than respectful, nevertheless had this virtue—an unfailing good-heartedness. Tawney believed that with this human material a more fraternal society could be created. There was already through the human nature of Englishmen the potentialities of equality built into English society.[23] There was great scope for further advances towards equality, because most English people, he believed, were capable of greatly benefiting from education. It was certain, Tawney said, that the overwhelming majority of children in the elementary schools, who at present left school at the age of fourteen, 'would repay a hundredfold the cost of their further education'.[24]

The tradition which Tawney shared—this time also with Marx—took the view that overall material plenty was already a fact in England. 'With unabated bounty the land of England blooms and grows', Carlyle had written in the early 1840s, 'waving with yellow harvests; thick studded with workshops.'[25] The Reverend Vernon Bartlet, who originated the idea of the volume on the rights and duties of property to which both Hobhouse and Tawney contributed, expressed this view, common to his circle, that the current wealth of Britain was 'adequate in gross for all the members of the social commonwealth'.[26]

Tawney assumed that the previous hundred years had seen the

[22] J. A. Hobson, *God and Mammon: The Relations of Religion and Economics* (London, 1931), 49.
[23] Again, this idea is strongly expressed by Carlyle. English workmen were 'the strongest, the cunningest and the willingest our Earth ever had'. (Carlyle, *Past and Present*, 1.)
[24] R. H. Tawney, *Education: The Socialist Policy* (London, 1924), 33. The Preface is by Charles Trevelyan, MP, President of the Board of Education. Trevelyan wrote in his Preface that generosity for three years, involving only some millions of pounds, would mean 'a new generation armed with knowledge and opportunity'.
[25] Carlyle, *Past and Present*, 1.
[26] C. Gore (ed.), *Property: Its Duties and Rights* (1914) (London, 1915), 116.

conquest of material nature. 'No instructed socialist disputes it.'[27] He recorded with bated breath that the national output a head was £40 in 1914 and that, speaking in 1921, it was not an impossibility that it might have doubled by the year 2000.[28] Thirty years later he emphasized not just the overall prosperity of the country, but the material richness of the average wage-earner, whose real income had increased by one-third between 1914 and 1937, and in the normal course of current progress might actually double between 1950 and 1978.[29] Resources were therefore already adequate for a society of free, equal, and fraternal citizens. 'There is no economic reason', he wrote, 'why the nation should be alarmed at the cost of introducing the educational reforms which are necessary if it is to cultivate to the full its human resources', and thus produce individuals capable of making intelligent and informed choices. Half the resources distributed in dividends to functionless share-holders in the early 1920s could have secured every child a good education up to the age of eighteen (and much else besides).[30] The people who spent £400 million a year on alcoholic drinks, and the royalty owners and urban landlords who received £26 million annually for doing nothing, might prefer not to spend money on the development of the powers of the nation's children; but they could not say they could not afford to do so.[31]

In the universities religious tests had vanished by the mid-1920s and (except in Cambridge) a handful of women shared university life, as Tawney believed, on the same terms as men. But able and diligent people were kept out of the universities by poverty. Stupid or idle people, for whom Oxford and Cambridge in particular were a species of Boys' Club designed to keep the children of the rich out of mischief, were admitted by wealth.[32] Tawney predicted that attendance at a university, the privilege of 30,000 young people (nearly all men) in England in 1921–2, would one day be free, as was elementary schooling. In the meantime a socialist policy must extend schemes for overcoming economic disabilities by mainten-ance allowances and remission of fees—and by making the standard of living in the colleges more austere.

Higher material standards without more liberty and equality, however, would undermine fraternity. Resentment against those

[27] Tawney, *Radical Tradition*, 142.
[28] Tawney, *Acquisitive Society*, 32–5.
[29] Tawney, *Equality*, 224.
[30] Tawney, *Acquisitive Society*, 90–1.
[31] Tawney, *Education*, 57–8.
[32] Ibid. 49–50.

who enjoyed felt by those who lacked liberty, equality, and fraternity grew as contrasts were perceived to be unnecessary. Resolve to end them had its root only partly in material misery; it was maintained also by demands for egalitarian fraternity which actually mounted with the alleviation of the grosser forms of poverty. In the face of equality and fraternity, conceived of as absolute values in a more human way of life, the argument that their demands could be appeased merely by additional increments of material income was, said Tawney, the clearest possible example of arguing the wrong point.[33]

Tawney was encouraged by the fact that Britian had already experienced great changes which, though not always desirable in themselves, pointed the way to his better society. Large corporate enterprises had been made legal by the 1844 Companies Act and the Acts establishing limited liability (the first being that of 1855), but it was only in the twentieth century that what Tawney calls their revolutionary effects began to show themselves. Between 1891 and 1918 the number of private banks fell from thirty-seven to six, and the number of English joint stock banks from 106 to thirty-four. With few exceptions the country's 1500 mines had become limited companies. In engineering, Vickers alone had 60,000 shareholders. Separate businesses in manufacturing industry were being absorbed into combines. The owner with the single retail shop he had established and continued to manage was being replaced by the new multiple store. All this made the existence of two groups of people, those engaged in constructive work, and those with rights to an income based only on property, more obvious to everybody.

Legal forms which anaesthetized the functionless owner were being quietly introduced. 'The elements of a new body of relationships have already been prepared, and find piecemeal application through policies devised, not by socialists, but by men who repeat the formulae of individualism at the very moment when they are undermining it.' In England the categories of private property were being bent until they were no longer recognizable and would in time be made harmless. Private property divorced from function as a claim to income and power was being refuted, Tawney said, 'not by the doctrines of rival philosophers, but by the prosaic course of economic development'.[34] Not all capitalists

---

[33] Tawney, *Equality*, 224–5.   [34] Tawney, *Acquisitive Society*, 82.

could now pay what wages they liked—there were Trade Boards and minimum-wage legislation. Factory Acts and Shop Acts controlled the hours of work of employees. During the First World War (and in some cases after it) there had been state control of prices, profits, and house rents. Private ownership was being whittled away by the necessities of protecting the consumer, eliminating waste, and meeting the claims of the workers. The system called 'capitalism' in the twentieth century resembled the so-called 'open field' system of the eighteenth century: behind a name and a traditional façade, it had 'crumbled from within before being dismembered by the parliamentary hatchet from without'.[35]

The state was becoming a welfare state. It was intervening to fill the gaps in private education and had made at least elementary education universal, compulsory, and free. The Education Act of 1918 had provided scholarships for children who could not pay fees (even though, in Tawney's opinion, the niggardliness of the Board of Education amounted to defiance of the spirit, if not the letter of the Act). In 1921 he looked forward to a time when the state would provide financial support to all who were involuntarily unemployed, and thus remove the power of employers to exploit their workers by the threat of starvation.

This was, so far as it went, the view held by the Fabians of the role of the democratic state, though Tawney himself was always sceptical of the state as manager of industrial enterprises. He looked only for the initial appropriation of certain private property rights by government, with the form of 'common ownership' and 'best obtainable system of popular administration' varying from industry to industry or public service to public service.[36] Sidney Webb had argued in *Fabian Essays*—reissued in 1920—that it was no less an empirical fact that large-scale private organizations had proceeded rapidly to state (and especially municipal) organization, than it was a theoretical truth that society was a social organism (not a haphazard collection of co-operating and competing individuals) the controlling centre of which was the state.[37]

Institutions other than the state were already successfully challenging *laissez-faire* capitalism. In some industries powerful

[35] Tawney, *History and Society*, 237.
[36] The constitution of the Labour party requires 'common ownership' and 'the best obtainable system of popular administration', not state control or nationalization.
[37] G. B. Shaw (ed.), *Fabian Essays in Socialism* (1889) (London, 1920), 46.

trade unions were shaking the foundations of the capitalist's authority, his right to hire and fire at will. The retailing co-operative movement, which aimed at service, was in those days strikingly more efficient from the consumer's viewpoint than profit-making enterprises (distributing coal, for instance, at 2s. to 4s. less a ton than private retailers).

There was thus, for Tawney, a basis for optimism in the historical development of the state and of organized society. But the case for a socialist Britain could also be grounded in English culture. Parts of the cultural system are incorporated in the personalities of individuals—in the 'human nature' of a given person or group. But they continue to exist even when they have fallen out of personal consciousness. Thus Shakespeare's plays could be forgotten, but regain their influence were they to be discovered anew, as Winston Smith in *Nineteen Eighty-Four* discovered the wonders of the old literature in the dusty bookshop of the Prole quarter.

Very striking to the modern reader is Tawney's belief that English culture has been outstandingly benign and provides the intellectual and moral materials out of which a better world, not just a better England, can be constructed. Milton, in his *Second Defence of the English People*, had said that when God wished to make his intentions known to mankind, he conveyed them first 'as his manner is' to his Englishmen.[38] Tawney and his circle frequently struck the same note. Thus Russell Wakefield, Bishop of Birmingham, wrote that God intended England to be an example to the world of high intellectual and moral qualities. 'Unrest will pass away; and under a free and enlightened government it will be considered a delight to spend oneself for the well-being of the country, and to show England as a model of true life, so that other countries who have wondered at her at war shall copy her in peace.'[39] Tawney was sympathetic to James Harrington, whose seventeenth-century Utopia was 'the blessed and fortunate' island of Oceana—England—and to Charles James Fox, who applied to England his general political faith, 'the right of a nation to choose and develop its own civilization'.[40]

England had, in the first place, a tradition of liberty. Literature on

---

[38] J. Milton, *The Portable Milton* (Harmondsworth, 1976), 193.
[39] Chapman, *Labour and Capital*, 12, 15.
[40] Tawney, *History and Society*, 231.

the continent as well as in England itself had long celebrated the sixteenth-century rise and subsequent consolidation of the free English gentry.[41] As we have noted, among the common people the disappearance of serfdom and the emergence of independence dated in England from the middle of the fourteenth century. The subsequent commutation of bondman's service for rent 'brought the mass of English cultivators to the most favourable position they have ever enjoyed'. This view, expressed in these terms by Hobhouse,[42] was repeated by Tawney, who makes the tradition still older. 'It is alien to the political tradition of Englishmen that the livelihood of the many should depend on the arbitrary decision of a few, or that they should be governed in their daily lives by regulations in the making of which they had no voice. In this matter the revolutionaries are the true conservatives. *Nolumus leges Angliae mutari.*'[43]

The idea that Englishmen were free-born, and that restrictions on liberty were an aberration, is constantly repeated. It is the message, for example, of Shelley's 'Masque of Anarchy'. Under capitalism he might be poor, but what was worse for an Englishman was to be 'a slave in soul'. Just as Marx saw the common Englishman being cast without any transition from his Golden Age into his Age of Iron,[44] so Tawney saw him losing under capitalism the independence most strongly realized among the artisans and yeomen farmers of the period immediately preceding the Industrial Revolution. 'Whatever the future may hold', Tawney wrote, 'the past has shown no more excellent social order than that in which the mass of the people were masters of the holdings which they ploughed and of the tools with which they worked, and could boast, with the English freeholder, that "it is a quietness to a man's mind to live upon his own and to know his heir certain".'[45]

The early exponents of *laissez-faire* were themselves, in Tawney's view, honoured exponents of English liberty. In the modern revulsion against economic tyranny, he wrote, there was a disposition to represent the writers who stood at the threshold of the age of capitalist industry as the prophets of a vulgar selfish

---

[41] Ibid. 87.
[42] L. T. Hobhouse, *Morals in Evolution: A Study in Comparative Ethics* (London, 1915), 331, 349.   [43] Chapman, *Labour and Capital*, 101.
[44] K. Marx, *Capital: A Critical Analysis of Capitalist Production* (1867), (Moscow, 1958), i. 719.   [45] Tawney, *Acquisitive Society*, 64.

materialism. 'No interpretation could be more misleading.' Adam Smith had shot his arrows at the abuses of his day, not ours. His ideal was a society in which all people had free access to the economic opportunities they could use and in which they enjoyed the fruits of their own efforts; he desired that 'men should be free to become themselves'.[46]

Part of the English tradition of liberty was the state's subordination to the citizen, not vice versa. Looking back to the English Civil War, Tawney wrote that 'if the English Social Democratic movement had any single source, that source is to be found in the New Model Army'.[47] Much later, in answering Hayek's eventually influential anti-socialist book *The Road to Serfdom*, Tawney pointed firmly to an English tradition of successful control of the state. In countries not so fortunate as England, where the agents of the state had not yet been taught the lesson that they were the citizen's servants, thoroughgoing hostility to the state was justified. 'We, in England, have repeatedly remade the state. Why, in heaven's name, should we be afraid of it?'

> It is really too much to expect us, at this time of day, to relapse into hysterics because some nervous professor has decided, on grounds of high theory, that the harmless and obedient creature, whom we have cursed, kicked, and fondled all our lives, is, in reality, not a dog at all, but a ferocious species of Siberian wolf.[48]

In Tawney's opinion his countrymen had also a notable tradition of fraternity, in the sense that they had been unusually successful in devising institutions through which co-operation could proceed with amity and with a strong sense of national community. The British nation was skilled in government and administration, he wrote in 1938. 'To suggest that it is unable to mobilize the intelligence to conduct in the general interest services necessary to its welfare ... is to bring against it a charge which its history, whatever the shadows upon it, does little to justify.'[49] He was reiterating a point he had often made. 'The subordination of strength and intelligence to the public service, and the organization of civil association in accordance with justice and freedom', he had written in 1918, 'are tasks in which the larger England of history

[46] Ibid. 19–20.
[47] R. H. Tawney, *Religion and the Rise of Capitalism* (1926) (Harmondsworth, 1938), 218–19.
[48] Tawney, *Radical Tradition*, 164–5.   [49] Tawney, *Equality*, 29.

may not unreasonably claim to have achieved such success as falls to the lot of political humanity.' She could solve her problems 'by her ancient methods worked out in her ancient spirit'.[50]

Paradoxically, private property itself had once been an institution not only of liberty but also of fraternity. In the sixteenth and seventeenth centuries it had ensured that each contributed to the common life and that each secured a fair share in its benefits. 'Property reposed, in short, not merely upon convenience, or upon the appetite for gain, but on moral principle. Property was protected for the sake of those who worked and of those for whom the work provided.' It was not a burden on society, but 'a condition of its health and efficiency'.[51] The rationale of private property traditional in old England was that it ensured that all who could work did work and that all were secure in the fruits of their labour. The meaning of private property had lain in the *public* purpose to which it contributed, whether the production of food by the farmers or the management of the state and local affairs by the gentry. If private property met these obligations it was maintained; if not it was withdrawn. Paley expressed the idea in religious terms, that it was 'the intention of God that the produce of the earth be applied to the use of man, and this intention cannot be fulfilled without establishing property'; Adam Smith expressed it in secular terms, that property was a technically effective device for offering protection to productive effort. However expressed, this was the view of private property common to Fortesque at the end of the fourteenth century, Bacon and the Cecils in the Tudor period, Harrington in the middle and Locke at the end of the seventeenth, Hume in the eighteenth, and Bentham into the nineteenth century.[52]

Tawney saw English history as the repository, too, of traditions of equality. The English had shaken themselves free from the functionless inequalities of income arising from the burdens of feudalism and the abuses of offices of the state before other European societies had done so. If they had escaped from the feudal dues of *quintaines* and *lods et ventes*, why should they be expected to suffer under the dues paid in royalties? If the monopoly profits of the owner of *banalités* proved an intolerable source of inequality, what sanctity could protect the monopoly profits of the capitalist?

[50] Chapman, *Labour and Capital*, 98.
[51] Tawney, *Acquisitive Society*, 60–4.
[52] Ibid. 58, 62–3.

How did the inequality stemming from the system of urban ground rents differ from the inequality stemming from payments to the sinecurists who were eventually dispossessed, as Cobbett had so earnestly desired, following the Reform Act of 1832?[53]

The English tradition was strong in political equality because of experience gained within a parliamentary system of democracy. Parliamentarianism was denounced by Marxists and others as a sham. But the rank and file of the English Labour movement had always been, and still were, Tawney asserted, unmoved by the antics of such people. The ordinary Briton knew the weaknesses of democracy and the abuses to which it was prone 'a good deal better than the melodious intellectuals who harrow refined audiences with cries of stinking fish'. But they also knew what they had gained from parliamentary institutions.

The equalization of power in the economy was an issue that would confront all nations. As a challenge it should appeal above all to Englishmen. 'It is perhaps not mere national vanity to hold', he wrote, 'that England is specially qualified by its political experience for solving that part of the problem of the modern world which is concerned with the organization of industry.'[54]

He believed that the temporary eclipse of the values of traditional English culture was coming to an end during his lifetime. The whole 'repulsive body of assumptions' which had made it seem natural for capitalism to use the mass of workers as instruments was weakening. There was growing acceptance of the principle that the payment of regular wages, instead of hiring and firing workers in response to fluctuation of the market, was part of the normal costs of the industry. 'In proportion as that result is achieved, capitalism will be unable to appeal to the terror of unemployment . . . and its prestige will vanish with its power.'[55] There was the emerging uniformity of opinion of what was required in such fields as health and education. There was no question here, Tawney said in 1938 (presaging Butskellism) of good intentions being paralysed by uncertainties about the nature of the measures required. 'There is sufficient agreement on the major issue of policy to keep administrators busy, were their hands untied, for the next fifteen years.'[56]

[53] Tawney, *Acquisitive Society*, 78–80.
[54] Chapman, *Labour and Capital*, 97.
[55] Tawney, *Acquisitive Society*, 176–8.
[56] Tawney, *Equality*, 28.

In Eastern Europe outside the Soviet Union, and before that in the Russian Empire, capitalism had struck recent and shallow roots, and had been extirpated by internal revolution or foreign armed force. But in Western Europe, and particularly in England, where capitalism had a history of three centuries of development and change, revolution 'even were that desired, would be out of the question'. In the first place, the complex mass of social institutions and individual psychologies was unamenable to predictable improvement by means of violent change.[57] In the second place, a reversal of attitudes towards capitalism had occurred in the first half of the twentieth century. In Britain and Western Europe its capacity for political leadership and its moral authority had been eroded, and new ways of thinking about human life and social organization had gathered to themselves loyalties which the old regime had lost the power to inspire.[58] Collective control—for some industries, indeed, plain nationalization—in place of private enterprise, Tawney said, was now demanded across the political spectrum. 'Just over thirty years ago', he wrote, recalling his work with the Sankey Commission of 1919, 'the recommendation that the mines should be nationalized . . . aroused a storm of opposition. When, in 1946, the proposal became at last an Act of Parliament, not a dog barked.'[59] There was an agenda of a peaceful transition to a society which embraced socialist values. 'We can certainly, if we please, wind up for good and all the whole odious business of class advantages and class disabilities, which are the characteristic and ruinous vices of our existing social system.'[60]

Class privilege based on functionless income had held for only as long as the absence of function had remained unrecognized. But rights without functions were like the shades in Homer, 'which drank blood but scattered trembling at the voice of a man'. To extinguish by violent revolution such things as royalties and urban ground rents was both dangerous and unnecessary; all that was required was to explode a superstition. 'It needs as little—and as much—resolution as to put one's hand through a ghost.'[61]

[57] Tawney, *Radical Tradition*, 169.
[58] Ibid. 138–9.
[59] Tawney, *Radical Tradition*, 152–3.
[60] Tawney, *Equality*, 29.
[61] Tawney, *Acquisitive Society*, 105.

12

GROUND GAINED

Tawney believed that ethical socialism had gained ground in twentieth-century Britain. He eschewed any claim for his own personal influence. Yet he must have known that his life's work had, at the level of general ideas, won signal victories against the theoreticians of both capitalism and Communism. He had worked with the grain of English popular culture to undermine the moral position of capitalist individualism and to establish the claim of socialism to provide individual freedom in a framework of national unity—a collective individualism, a community of equality.

The crucial argument which has appeared time and again throughout this book is that Tawney's conception of fellowship is the basis of both moral and economic rejection of the conception of society held by economic liberals. The rational pursuit by marginal calculation of the interests of individuals does not maximize the common good. The assumption that it does results in a fallacy of composition. Free market competition may serve the common weal adequately as an engine of economic growth alleviating shortage of material goods: it can no longer claim exclusive economic dominion in a society where, to use Fred Hirsch's term, scarcity increasingly involves not necessities but positional goods.[1] Positional goods are those which are socially rather than economically limited. By their nature they cannot be made available to all by economic growth. A viable theory of liberty cannot be derived from unsociological individualistic assumptions any more than a credible theory of equality can be advanced by positing a social structure which makes people into social puppets. Fraternity or solidarity has to be given a prior place and this is what Tawney's version of ethical socialism provides.

The theory that social structures interact with rather than determine individual character is fundamental to ethical socialism. It distinguishes the tradition of thought we have traced down the

---

[1] F. Hirsch, *Social Limits to Growth* (Harvard, 1976).

centuries from Thomas More. The socialism of character, as
formulated by Hobhouse, made it possible to define an active role
for the state beyond the confines of liberal individualism. The same
basic view of persons and institutions enabled Cobbett simultaneously to assert *both* the independence of the free-born
Englishman *and* the virtually sacred value of traditional English law
and custom. It enabled Orwell to see the character-forming
capacity of plain English, Donald McGill's comic postcards, or the
decencies of a working-class living-room. For T. H. Marshall it was
the starting-point for understanding the practice of citizenship, its
incorporation into the social personality of responsible democrats,
and its warfare with class in the twentieth century. In Tawney it
became a fully-developed world-view connecting contemporary life
to age-old values and conflicts, providing a clear definition of
private and civic virtue, and pointing forward soberly to an eternal
struggle for the preservation of the good society for and through
good people. Socialism is no inevitable transformation to a
mechanical Utopia. Revolution is no cleansing of vice from human
hearts. Ethical socialism is at once a demanding code of personal
conduct and of social organization, appealing to the same
principles of fellowship. Every day and every night, every family
and every factory, every committee and every congregation is an
event and a place to be won for the socialist principles of life.

Tawney's argument was as disconcerting to the Left as to the
Right. Raphael Samuel goes to the centre of the issue:

Tawney's Christianity makes his socialism different from a marxist-derived
socialism, and his idealized workman, Henry Dubb, was very different
from the marxian Prometheus—a captive giant—or that latter-day figure
of socialist rhetoric 'the militant'. But his Christianity gave him a sense of
the totality of social relations—including their psychic roots—which a
Marxist might well envy; and it saved him from triumphalism.[2]

Above all, Tawney had rescued socialism from the theory of
inexorable history propounded by Marx and Engels in their
polemics against the ruling philosophy of 'the dreamy and muddled
German nation', which had attributed prime importance to ideas
and morals.[3] The Communists, Marx and Engels wrote, were not
interested in mere talk about immorality and morality, about

[2] R. Samuel, 'The SDP's Escape from the Christian Heritage of Socialism', *The Guardian*, 29 Mar. 1982.
[3] K. Marx and F. Engels, Preface to *The German Ideology* (London, 1970), 37.

egoism and self-sacrifice. There is a higher moral form to which present society is irresistibly tending by its own 'economical agencies'. The working class have, therefore, 'no ideals to realize'. They have only to display their heroic resolve in setting free the elements in the new society with which the old collapsing bourgeois society is pregnant. This is their historic mission. Above all, the working class can dispose of the 'didactic patronage of well-wishing bourgeois doctrinaires, pouring forth their ignorant plati-tudes and sectarian crotchets'.[4] The Marxist does not preach morality. Egoism, just as much as altruism, is a necessary form of conduct in the particular circumstances in which it is found, and moral advance takes place by 'the materially determined destruction of the preceding materially determined mode of life'.[5]

It is alleged that when anyone began to talk to Marx about morality he would roar with laughter.[6] For him moralizing—other than his own—was both futile and pernicious. Thus the so-called True Socialists of Germany had lost all revolutionary enthusiasm by proclaiming, instead of the plain empirical fact of class enmity, the morality of the universal love of mankind.[7] Communism would transcend the 'speculative cobwebs, embroidered with flowers of rhetoric, steeped in the dew of sickly sentiment', in which the Germans 'wrapped their sorry "eternal truths", all skin and bone'.[8] To Marx's disgust it spread like an epidemic among working people. If the working class was to triumph it must first and foremost insist that all phrases were dropped which tended to dull the realization of the sharpness of the opposition between the bourgeoisie and the proletariat, and which might even give the capitalist class a chance to appeal to the philanthropic enthusiasms of their class enemies.[9]

But Tawney's work convinced many twentieth-century British socialists that moral definitions, not mechanical laws of motion, rule history. Tawney demonstrated that faith, albeit constrained

[4] In this characteristic feat of rhetoric Marx nevertheless passionately defends the morality of the communards of 1871 and remorselessly condemns the morality of their opponents. 'The Civil War in France 1871', K. Marx and F. Engels, *Selected Works* (Moscow, 1951, 1958), i. 523.

[5] Marx and Engels, *German Ideology*, 104–5.

[6] See S. Lukes, *Marxism and Morality* (Oxford, 1985), 27.

[7] Marx and Engels, *German Ideology*, 120.

[8] Marx and Engels, 'The Manifesto of the Communist Party' (1848), *Selected Works*, i. 59.

[9] Marx and Engels, 'The German Ideology', Ibid. ii. 312.

and conditioned by material circumstance, had in case after case crucially altered the course of history. That sociological lesson is needed now in yet another age of economic transformation. It is a lesson which not only guides analysis but also lays upon us, especially intellectuals, a moral obligation. It is a lesson made more difficult by the decline of Christian beliefs. To act wisely in the interests of civilized life for others as well as ourselves is no easy challenge even among people schooled in a clear moral tradition.

His books, though uneven in style and quality, have been extolled as contributions to English literature, to historical research, and to socialist political thought.[10] *The Acquisitive Society* was the only book by a living author to be included in the University of Chicago's list of seventy-two 'Great Books of Western Civiliz- ation'.[11] Geoffrey Elton did not doubt that any intellectual history of the twentieth century would have to include a consideration of Tawney.[12] Standing on the shoulders of such nineteenth-century critics of capitalism as Matthew Arnold and John Ruskin, he has carried their condemnation of capitalism as the destroyer of fellowship into the most widely influential modern statement of democratic socialism.

He was held in high esteem in the two areas of national life where he wanted most to make his presence felt, the Church of England and the Labour party. Bishop Gore, visiting Tawney in hospital in 1916, told the matron that she had one of the most valuable lives in England under her care. (The story is that the matron then scolded Tawney for not having let her know he was a gentleman and not just any wounded NCO.) Someone once remarked to Archbishop Temple that the Church needed more men like Tawney. Temple is said to have replied, 'There are no men like Tawney.' Tawney's ideas continue to attract Christians to democratic socialism and democratic socialists to the Church of England. His insistence on the social responsibilities of the Church still found expression into the 1980s, for example, in the Archbishop of Canterbury's report on the problems facing British towns and cities, in the politics and theology of yet another Christian Socialist Bishop of Durham,

---

[10] J. M. Winter describes him as writing like an angel, his style as Miltonic and so forth—see his 'R. H. Tawney', as well as David Donnison's 'Drawing Conclusions', both in P. Barker (ed.), *Founders of the Welfare State* (London, 1984), 100, 124.

[11] Cover of Harcourt, Brace (Harvest edn.), 1948, of *The Acquisitive Society*.

[12] G. R. Elton, *The Future of the Past: An Inaugural Lecture* (Cambridge, 1968), 16.

David Jenkins (formerly Director of the William Temple Foundation), and in the *cri de cœur* of one clergyman, 'Tawney! thou shouldst be living at this hour. England hath need of thee.'[13]

When Arthur Henderson decided to reform the Labour party into a distinctive parliamentary force he turned primarily to Sidney Webb. But Tawney was also there at this beginning. In October 1917 he was one of a group of Labour intellectuals who joined Henderson and Webb to discuss the new programme.[14] An Education Advisory Committee was set up in March 1918, on which Tawney was the leading light. Sidney Webb, G. D. H. Cole, and Tawney were the most influential members of the other eight advisory groups which were established at the same time.[15]

There was a period of disenchantment. Tawney and his friends repudiated MacDonald when he took the rump of the Labour party into his National government; Sir Charles Trevelyan resigned as Minister of Education in March 1931 and launched a general attack on Macdonald's administration.[16] Tawney detailed his criticism in an article entitled 'The Choice Before the Labour Party' (1934). But he showed his satisfaction that Labour had been restored to health, as a party pursuing socialist goals by ethical means, when he republished the article in 1953 with a note that 'it should be needless to remark that many of the defects ascribed in this paper to the Labour party no longer exist'.[17]

From within the Labour party Richard Crossman described *The Acquisitive Society* as his Bible. Tony Benn appealed to the Labour movement to follow the tradition of socialist writing represented, as he said, by no one more effectively than Tawney.[18] In short a wide spectrum of socialist and democratic reformers have found it appropriate or at least expedient to claim his authority.

How did he himself measure his success? He was well satisfied with the start that had been made on the Labour programme by the 1945–51 Parliaments. There is a certain poignancy in the fact that

[13] Archbishop of Canterbury's Commission on Urban Priority Areas, *Faith in the City: A Call for Action by Church and State* (London, 1985); Residential Canon of St Albans, *The Times*, 2 Dec. 1980.
[14] T. Jones, *Whitehall Diary* (London, 1969), 38 (entry for 30 Oct. 1917).
[15] J. M. Winter, *Socialism and the Challenge of War: Ideas and Politics in Britain 1912–1918* (London, 1974), 175–6, 272.
[16] R. Skidelsky, *Politicians and the Slump: The Labour Government 1929–1931* (1967) (Harmondsworth, 1970), 358.
[17] R. H. Tawney, *The Attack and Other Papers* (1953) (Nottingham, 1981), 52.
[18] T. Benn, Foreword to the 1981 edn., Tawney, *The Attack*, 10.

many of the social developments we note in Chapter 13 began to emerge after, and some of them immediately after his death. But in the early 1950s, when his own final assessments were largely completed, he felt that much of what he had worked for was being achieved.

While his particular brand of English patriotism now appears a relic of a bygone age, democratic socialism in this country can still be recognized as something peculiarly English. Certainly Tawney as an old man derived satisfaction from believing that this was so. The force behind democratic socialism was not merely a political party but the set of British life. It was a movement that, like earlier movements in British history, had wound its way amid shoals and sand-banks but which was producing a nationally distinctive social order. Parliamentary government and personal liberty, in particular, would continue unimpaired in a fully democratic-socialist Britain.[19] The Labour party, based as it was on broad popular foundations, distinguished Britain, Tawney believed, from the capitalist pluto-cracies and the communist one-party states, and enabled it to create a society in its own image unhampered by the dogmatic sterility of Marxism.[20]

Social arrangements for income security, education, health, and housing, providing not bread and circuses but the 'enrichment of the concrete substance of civilized life'—Tawney used T. H. Marshall's phrase—seemed to him to have been established. The essentials of civilization had increasingly become the nation's common possession. Cultural advance was definitely under way through the civilizing measures of the welfare state.[21]

In addition to organizational reform and the growth of prosperity he believed that there was a general acceptance of the democratic-socialist ethos in post-war Britain. The view that explicit moralizing had no place in economic life, the worm of the vicious principle at the root of society, was beginning to lose its power to warp and distort human relationships.[22] As far as the rank-and-file of the Labour movement was concerned the impulse had been and remained obstinately and unashamedly ethical. The judgement of the rank-and-file was his, that forms of organization ought not and need not be left to either the laws of capitalism or the laws of

[19] Tawney, *Radical Tradition*, 155. [20] Ibid. 169.
[21] R. H. Tawney, *Equality* (1931), 4th edn. (London, 1952), 218, 222; Tawney, *Radical Tradition*, 155. [22] Tawney, *Equality*, 220.

historical materialism. Economic interests were enormously power-ful, but so were moral sentiments. In the period following the Second World War British democratic socialism had proved, in Tawney's eyes, the power of appeals to human dignity, justice, and equality to check and channel market forces.[23]

British socialism was ethical, individualistic, parliamentary, and pragmatic. It was and remained so because it was based on the common-sense ethics of what Bevan called 'the solid artisan classes', the finest generation of workers Britain had ever produced and whose attitude corresponded most closely with that of democratic socialism.[24] 'All this, I am of course well aware, will be dismissed as deplorable Philistinism', Tawney wrote. 'But I remain unrepentant. I think that political as well as other truths concealed from the wise and the learned are apt to be revealed to babes.' Bludgeoned by his enlightened friends, his attitude to sophisticated amoralism remained the same as the attitude of one wise little girl to pins, who described them as most useful and admirable things, for they have saved many a person's life 'by not a-swollerin' of them'.[25]

Half-a-century and more of pressure from above by the state and from below by trade-unionism, he noted in 1937, had restricted the power of the capitalist employer—to Tawney an obvious point upon which he expected to be challenged only by someone who knew no history or whose eye was fixed on so remote a goal of perfection that all mundane measures of mitigation could be dismissed as nugatory.[26] He agreed with T. H. Marshall, too, that the post-war Attlee government had brought about qualitative, not just quantitative improvements in the social services by making them more equally available to all citizens and not just to the poor. 'To suggest that the old miasma of inequality had been wholly dispelled would be oversanguine', he wrote, 'but it is busy evaporating.'[27]

Although he believed that the distribution of wealth remained as unequal as ever, incomes—accepting the findings of Dudley Seers—had become substantially more equal after the redistributive

[23] Tawney, *Radical Tradition*, 168–9.
[24] A. Bevan, *In Place of Fear* (New York, 1952), 25, 179.
[25] Tawney, *Radical Tradition*, 169. Tawney constantly returns to the idea that institutional arrangements have to be justified in the 'consciences of decent men'. (R. H. Tawney, *Acquisitive Society* (London, 1921), 7.)
[26] Tawney, *The Attack*, 169.   [27] Tawney, *Equality*, 218.

measures of 1945–50.[28] Indeed, although there was a long way to travel, Tawney thought it was not practicable to proceed much further in the circumstances of the time.[29] By 1948 incomes were more equal than in pre-war England (or than existed in the Soviet Union, where in 1940 a professional man was left after tax with an income about fifty times the average).[30] The average income of the highest group was thirteen times that of the lowest group after tax, as compared with twenty-eight times in 1938.[31] As compared with 1938 the purchasing power of wages after the deduction of direct taxes was up by 25 per cent, that of distributed profits down by 37 per cent. The preponderance which formerly belonged to owner-ship, in the balance between functionless ownership and labour, now lay with creative work.[32] It is understandable that the experience of the Labour governments of 1945–51, including the experience of austerity that others found so distressful, should have aroused in Tawney a degree of optimism, even though his optimism was under test by the time of his death.[33]

Social surveys of the time show even among the poorest a level of satisfaction with income from state benefits remarkably high by later standards, and Tawney referred to 'the prevalent impression' in the early 1950s that a somewhat more egalitarian social order was emerging and that it was legitimate to feel a modest pride that a course in the right direction had been held in this country.[34]

Up to the time of his death he was able to detect, too, wide and strengthening approval of the institutions of the welfare state. At mid-century the conventional wisdom of Western Europe and the United States was that all advanced societies, whether their starting-point had been in capitalism or Communism, would be moved by the relentless 'logic of industrialism' toward the model of the welfare state. Urban-industrial societies would be composed of business firms; voluntary associations; and the state in overall control of the economy, providing essential common services, and

---

[28] D. Seers, *The Levelling of Income Since 1938* (Oxford, 1951), 5; 'Personal Incomes 1938–50', *The Economist*, Feb. 1950.

[29] Tawney, *Radical Tradition*, 173; *Equality*, 215.

[30] Tawney, *Radical Tradition*, 155.   [31] Tawney, *Equality*, 215.

[32] Ibid.

[33] Bevan, too, took some pride in Britain's austerity. Like Tawney he picked out cinemas as a particularly wasteful use of resources and as an example of the failure to 'attend to the needs of the common people as against the greed of a few'. (*In Place of Fear*, 213.)   [34] Tawney, *Equality*, 222.

guaranteeing social security for all. There would be a state-educated citizenry whose knowledge and wisdom would make them bargaining but also approving participants in the system. Such developments would mark the end of dogmatic fanaticism of all kinds. Conflicts of value would be replaced by technical issues of efficient management.[35] Within this consensus 'Left' and 'Right' signified a continuum stretching from those who argued that the welfare state was as yet imperfectly formed in Western Europe and the United States to those who believed that it was already admirably in existence. Such interpretations virtually constituted American (and therefore British) sociology by 1960.[36] The same view was reproduced in other liberal-democratic countries—that the aims and importance of social policy were no longer fundamentally in question, only the means of their execution.[37]

Tawney in the 1950s was on the right of this consensus, for he felt that Britain itself was a society with one of the strongest traditions of parliamentary-democratic government, voluntary association, civic virtue, and individual liberty. While being by no means triumphant, Britain had been among the most successful in expressing a spirit of social solidarity, in large part through the institutions of the welfare state. After Tawney's death T. H.

[35] The idea that the administration of things will replace the government of man goes back in marxist thought to the 'Communist Manifesto'. (Marx and Engels, *Selected Works*, i. 54.) Karl Mannheim characterizes the world-view of the conservative bureaucrat as one which regards politics as identical with the science of administration. (K. Mannheim, *Ideology and Utopia* (1929–31) (London, 1936), 105–6.)

[36] A leftist pluralistic liberal, famous in his generation, was C. Wright Mills (see, e.g., his *The Power Elite* (New York, 1956)). Somewhat less radical, but even more widely celebrated, was J. K. Galbraith (see, e.g., his *The Affluent Society* (London, 1958)). W. W. Rostow was a type of rightist pluralistic liberal (see, e.g., his *The Stages of Economic Growth: A Non-Communist Manifesto* (1960), 2nd edn. (Cambridge, 1971)). 1960 saw the definitive presentation of a right-wing pluralistic-liberal world-view: C. Kerr, J. T. Dunlop, F. H. Harbison, and C. A. Myers, *Industrialism and Industrial Man: The Problems of Management and Labour in Economic Growth* (1960) (Harmondsworth, 1973). Significantly the authors' 'Postscript 1971' is much less optimistic than the contents of the original edition. See also H. U. Wehler, *Geschichte als historische Sozialwissenschaft* (Frankfurt, 1973). This view was marked, too, in the 1950s and early 1960s in political science in, e.g. E. C. Banfield, *Political Influence: A New Theory of Urban Politics* (New York, 1961) and R. A. Dahl, *Who Governs? Democracy and Power in an American City* (New Haven, 1961).

[37] J. Reynaud, 'La Securité sociale en France', *Europ. Journ. of Sociol.*, 2 (1961), 270–2; E. Boettcher, *Entwicklungstheorie und Entwicklungspolitik* (Tübingen, 1964).

Marshall continued to express this view into the last quarter of the century,[38] and in his study of the blood-transfusion service R. M. Titmuss pointed to the strength of British fraternity and the superiority of at least this British institution in channelling it into humane purposes.[39] The state of affairs reported by Joanna Mack and Stewart Lansley in 1985 would have been regarded by Tawney as a continuing vindication of his views about the strength of fraternal feelings in Britain as embodied in the welfare state. Asked if they would be willing to pay an extra penny in the pound in income tax to provide everyone with 'all items you have said are necessities', 74 per cent of the sample said yes. (Only 34 per cent said yes to an extra 5p in the pound, but even so 30 per cent of these were Conservative voters.)[40]

On the question of measures to provide for an adequate standard of living Tawney expressed qualified satisfaction. Real expenditure by the state on education, health, housing, cash benefits, food subsidies, and grants for similar purposes made to local authorities in 1949–50 showed an increase on 1936 of 132 per cent. These measures, he wrote, formed a framework of provisions which, though varying in quality, left few sides of life outside their scope.[41] He learned from Rowntree's survey of York that people living in poverty (31 per cent at the time of the second survey in 1936) had fallen to under 3 per cent in 1950,[42] and attributed this directly and entirely to the social legislation of the intervening period.[43]

Opposition to an ever-rising money-based standard of living became for a time a small-sect eccentricity. But later it re-emerged with some force, especially among university students politicized by the Vietnam War, by the renewed struggle for black civil rights in

[38] T. H. Marshall, *Social Policy in the Twentieth Century* (1965), 2nd edn. (London, 1967).

[39] R. M. Titmuss, *The Gift Relationship: From Human Blood to Social Policy* (London, 1970).

[40] J. Mack and S. Lansley, *Poor Britain* (London, 1985). Mack and Lansley discovered by survey what items of expenditure a majority of the British population wished to be included in a list of minimum requirements. They arrived at a list of twenty-six (e.g. a bed for everyone, three meals a day for children, a washing-machine, a week's annual holiday) and defined the poor (five million adults and two and a half million children) as those who were in households which could not afford three or more of the items.

[41] Tawney, *Equality*, 217.

[42] B. S. Rowntree and G. R. Lavers, *Poverty and the Welfare State* (London, 1951).

[43] Tawney, *Radical Tradition*, 171.

the USA, and by Marcuse's doctrine of 'repressive' or 'false' needs. False needs had degraded the role of the proletarian from that of being the ferment of revolutionary social change to that of being the cement of the conservative social order.[44] They had impoverished all classes by sacrificing authentic human needs to meet them.

Tawney's positive evaluation of the adequate but no more than adequate standard of living appeared in the 'consumer' movement represented by Ralph Nader;[45] in Galbraith's argument that each increment to the standard of living contributed diminishing marginal utility;[46] in Ivan Illich's attacks on what he argued were dysfunctional services, consumer products and modes of producing them;[47] and in the policies pursued by adherents of the ecological movement and Green political parties.[48] In the later 1980s distaste for the overestimation of what money can buy began to be expressed more openly and generally. In terms reminiscent of Tawney the Director-General of the World Health Organization, addressing health ministers from thirty countries, spoke of the shallow and materialistic society where the norm was to demand more of everything, where 'more wealth, more food, more drink, more cars, more tobacco, more sex, more TV, and more videos sell more food, more cars, more tobacco, more sex, and so on *ad infinitum*'.[49]

In the sphere of parliamentary government and the basic procedural values of respect for truth, reasoning, tolerance, fairness, and freedom Tawney's mood was one not just of satisfaction but of jubilation that Parliament and political freedom

[44] H. Marcuse, *One-dimensional Man: Studies in the Ideology of Advanced Industrial Society* (Boston, 1964), 256.
[45] R. Nader, *Unsafe at Any Speed* (New York, 1955); *Taming the Giant Corporation* (New York, 1976); *The Menace of Atomic Energy* (New York, 1977).
[46] Galbraith, *Affluent Society*, 116–7.
[47] I. Illich, *Deschooling Society* (New York, 1971); *Medical Nemesis: The Expropriation of Health* (London, 1975); *The Right to Useful Unemployment and Its Professional Enemies* (London, 1978).
[48] E. F. Schumacher, *Small Is Beautiful: A Study of Economics as if People Mattered* (London, 1973); the Green point of view was represented fiercely in the mid-1980s by the newspaper *Die Tageszeitung*.
[49] *The Times*, 19 Mar. 1986. The subject of the conference was the increase in drug consumption, including alcohol, and the correspondingly 'enormous increase in health risks'. See also the report of *An Agenda for Action on Alcohol* (AAA). Daily expenditure on alcoholic drinks in Britain in the mid-80s was £35 million; AAA estimated the cost in terms of sickness absence, hospital treatment, unemployment, and premature death at £1.7 billion a year. (*The Times*, 25 Mar. 1986.)

had proved effective as means for creating his kind of socialist society. The question for him was not merely whether the state controlled the means of production, but also who controlled the state. Parliamentary democracy could establish the socialist commonwealth; it was an essential condition for maintaining a socialism congruent with British radical tradition; and as a system of government it was superior in itself to any alternative in view.[50]

He felt able to scoff at the inter-war *bien pensants* who had upbraided him for his naïvety in ignoring the fact that the capitalist class would inevitably wreck attempts to introduce socialism in Parliament, and for his cowardice in declining to proclaim 'the glad, emancipating truth that the sole and sufficient recipe for Co-operative Commonwealths was the liberal use of blood and iron'. Reply was now superfluous, he said, because events had proved him right and them wrong. Indubitable advances towards the conversion of a class-ridden society into a socialist community had taken place 'with almost melodramatic sedateness . . . by the unspectacular processes of democratic government'.[51]

He celebrated, too, the success of the pragmatism of the Labour party. It had discarded the doctrinal moulds prepared by men of letters when the Industrial Revolution was still young and avoided the deadly disease of dogmatic petrifaction that had afflicted the German Marxists, the Social Democrats, before 1914. Rather it had developed as a fusion of a thoroughly experienced trade-unionism and organizations like the Fabian Society whose forte was empirical investigation. Labour members in Parliament strengthened its empiricism. Of course the Labour party had a lunatic fringe as did any set of people aspiring to be representative. The bulk of its MPs, however, had governed great cities, administered great trade unions, practised medicine or the law. These sober and experienced people had not been the kind to succumb to either apocalyptic illusions or the worship of power politics.[52] The experience of 1945–50, with Labour in government fostering socialism of the Tawney type, proved to him that pragmatism paid. Contrary to what he called the suggestions of simpletons, the capitalist economy was not a monolith to be endured as a whole or overthrown as a whole. A socialist government, with the public behind it, had

---

[50] Tawney, *Radical Tradition*, 170–1.
[51] Tawney, *Equality*, 222–3.
[52] Tawney, *Radical Tradition*, 142.

changed the relations of power and directed resources to raising the quality of life of the whole population.[53]

Tawney's personal virtue, the grandeur of his private example, his generosity towards ordinary men, and his uncompromising contempt for the pretentious and the greedy remain as signal inspiration to the idealism of individual socialists. It is parodied in the subtle evasions and sophisticated hypocrisies of a modern establishment which has been forced into ideological lip-service to equality and social justice. Tawney has an assured place in authentic British socialism. He was as rational as any Fabian, as radical as any Marxist, and as devoted as either. Though he never wholly subscribed to any of the competing orthodoxies which have struggled for dominance in the British socialist tradition, he is perhaps the only man who can be saluted by Fabians, Marxists, Guild Socialists, trade-unionists, co-operators and Christian Socialists alike. As a great Englishman he bears comparison with Sir Thomas More; in appropriate recognition Ross Terrill ends his biography with a salute to Tawney as 'a socialist for all seasons'.

Appraisal of his achievement can never be final: and he would have shown little interest in such personal evaluations. His interest was above all in the fate of the movement towards ethical socialism to which he devoted his life. If other brands of socialism paid him the respect of claiming his mantle they could do so only with the discomforting knowledge that his position remained a threat to theirs. Nothing short of a fully developed ethical socialism was his goal. His Britain was in the foothills of assault on that high mountain.

[53] Ibid. 171–2.

13

GROUND LOST

In the middle of the nineteenth century, as he stood on his honeymoon at the window of a hotel on Dover sea-front, Matthew Arnold had a premonition of religious decline, the ebbing of the tide of faith, hearing

> Its melancholy, long, withdrawing roar,
>> Retreating to the breath
> Of the night-wind down the vast edges drear
> And naked shingles of the world.

A century later the then Archbishop of Canterbury, Michael Ramsey, delivered the twelfth annual Holland lecture in which he conceded that the replacement of a sacred by a profane world-view was all but complete. He looked back forty years to the time when Tawney had delivered the first of the Holland lectures. In the 1920s, however weakened and diluted, Christian ethical and social assumptions could be found even among many who had abandoned Christian belief. Trotsky, writing in 1925, had deplored the fact that Britain suffered from a tradition of 'Protestant piety' which still mystified the working class, and that the 'success of atheism' had been less noticeable in Anglo-Saxon countries than elsewhere. Commenting on an article written by Ramsay MacDonald when he was at the height of his influence and popularity, and Prime Minister of the first Labour government, Trotsky dismissed with contempt any socialism based on Christianity. MacDonald's views were nothing more than 'a prosaic rehash of the Sermon on the Mount'.[1] Trotsky acknowledged, too, that the influence of these views on the British working class (which as he describes them are point for point Tawney's) was, unfortunately, 'very great'. 'Those days seem far away', Archbishop Ramsey said in his 1964 lecture. 'Assumptions far different from Christianity are held in such wise

---

[1] L. Trotsky, 'The Fabian Theory of Socialism', in L. Trotsky, *Where is Britain Going?* (1925) (London, 1978), 45.

that we find ourselves reckoning not only with secular ideas but also with secular*ism*, a total complex of thinking and speaking to which Christian ideas convey nothing.'[2] By the time he died in 1962 Tawney also knew that the Christianity he embraced had substantially lost whatever grip it had had on the English, and that there were no signs of a religious revival. He might well have said with Hannah Arendt: 'The pillars of the best-known truths today lie shattered; we need neither criticism nor wise men to shake them any more.'[3]

In his last years Tawney, like Arendt, became pessimistic about the trend of political morality. Already in the 1950s, the further decline of traditional Christian culture made his prose, however powerful in itself, less and less accessible to generations without biblical knowledge, without memory and even without forgetfulness of the Catechism or the Book of Common Prayer, steeped and schooled in a culture of politics without religion. The world was in retreat, he wrote in 1960, not only from particular principles but from the very idea that political principles exist. That morality transcended economic expediency and that the ends do not justify the means were convictions that seemed now part of 'a remote and worn-out creed'.[4] These references to capitalism, Marxism, and Fascism were timely. New and strong currents of secular thought were re-entering the backwater of British Butskellism from the Left and the Right.

In the 1960s, when the Robbins proposals for the expansion of higher education were spectacularly executed, there emerged a powerful New Left reaction against Tawney's type of socialism. Social-science departments in the rapidly growing universities, where Tawney's world-view had been held in respect, were put on the defensive against a surge of marxist and quasi-marxist ideas. Among them the most conspicuous were those versions of Marxism most hostile to Tawneyite socialism—the 'critical sociology' of the

[2] A. M. Ramsey, *Sacred and Secular: A Study of the Otherworldly and This-worldly Aspects of Christianity* (London, 1965), 72. By 1987 the Archbishop of Canterbury, Robert Runcie, was revealing that even he had moved too far: 'but now I think we ought to be extending the area of the sacred rather than restricting it'. (*The Times*, 30 Mar. 1987.)
[3] H. Arendt, 'On Humanity in Dark Times: Thoughts About Lessing' (1960), in H. Arendt, *Men in Dark Times* (Harmondsworth, 1973), 18.
[4] R. H. Tawney, *History and Society: Essays by R. H. Tawney*, ed. J. M. Winter (London, 1978), 251–2.

Frankfurt School[5] and, later, one form or another of Trotskyism. What had been thought to be the strengths of British social research, its empiricism, its positivism, and its individualism, were redefined as its 'three outstanding limitations'.[6] Descriptive studies were shunned, for their purpose was control by the ruling class and the state, and the research relevant to the concerns of Tawney's welfare state was redefined as 'bourgeois reformism'.[7]

Tawney's vision of democratic socialism was neglected or scorned for a generation after his death: and not only by Marxists or Marxisants who dismissed his 'high-minded clichés'. Even Richard Titmuss, whose junior associates claimed for him the Tawney mantle, momentarily succumbed to the tide of fashion in his inaugural lecture as the head of the department at LSE in which Tawney had pursued his work on the sources of poverty as director of the Ratan Tata Foundation. He evoked applauding hilarity on that occasion by deriding old views that carried the absurd implication that character and choice affected conduct or that anyone who was poor had anything to learn from anyone else.

The appeal of Tawney's political ideals and practical proposals was weakened, too, by the posthumous decline in his academic reputation, beginning with G. R. Elton's severe criticism of *The Agrarian Problem*.[8] Eric Kerridge also pointed to serious faults in his work,[9] while J. H. Hexter argued that Tawney's attempt to show a historical connection between religion and economics was both ill-conceived and poorly executed.[10]

Meanwhile the Tawney outlook was obscured by the infiltration of Marxism. There were bitter battles for the control of the Labour party, locally and centrally, reducing it to exhaustion by 1981. Perhaps the greatest destructive achievement of the Marxists at that time was to drive out thousands of Labour activists who had thought of themselves as belonging to the party of ethical socialism.

No doubt other motives were at work among those party leaders (David Owen, Shirley Williams, and William Rodgers) who

[5] See, e.g. M. Horkheimer and T. W. Adorno, *Dialectic of Englightenment* (London, 1947).
[6] J. Rex, *Discovering Sociology* (London, 1973), 58.
[7] M. Shaw, *Marxism and Social Science: The Roots of Social Knowledge* (London, 1975), 37.
[8] G. R. Elton, *The Future of the Past: An Inaugural Lecture* (Cambridge, 1968).
[9] E. Kerridge, *Agrarian Problems in the Sixteenth Century and After* (London, 1969).
[10] *Times Literary Supplement*, 24 Oct. 1975.

responded to Roy Jenkins's call for the formation of a new Social Democratic party liberated from the old class politics in which the Labour party had been formed under the conditions of classical industrialism. Ironically the original SDP defectors created a Tawney Society as part of the hastily assembled apparatus of political organization—an unhistorical and implausible attempt to steal the mantle of a man so much more remarkable for his differences than for his similarities of political outlook compared with theirs. Tawney's Mecklenburgh Square was a long way from the Madison Avenue image of youth and glamour which was projected by the SDP.

A more serious ideological as distinct from electoral challenge to the Labour party came from the economic liberals of the Conservative party. By the end of the 1970s this was the most damaging thrust against Tawney's socialism. The view was that an economy is best left to market forces. Other aspects of social life, in so far as they tended to interfere with the free market, would then be subject to control by a strong capitalist state. A principal theoretician of this movement was the adversary Tawney had so lightly and confidently dismissed many years before, F. A. Hayek. The Institute of Economic Affairs, founded in 1957, propagated Hayekian ideas with an élan and confidence reminiscent of the early Fabian Society. Revived economic liberalism began to be put into practice with the election of the first Thatcher government of 1979.[11] Tawney was in passing condemned as one who had shaped a generation but whose promises had been falsified.[12] When Tawney's *Religion and the Rise of Capitalism* was issued as a paperback in 1938, the publisher's list for the series had included authors who were solidly in his tradition. But in the fiftieth anniversary year of the foundation of Penguin publications the noticed book was neither Fabian nor Marxist, but another attack on public service and state action, Martin Wiener's *English Culture and the Decline of the Industrial Spirit 1850–1980.*

[11] A. Seldon (ed.), *The Coming Confrontation: Will the Open Society Survive to 1989?* (London, 1978); D. G. Green, *The New Right: The Counter-Revolution in Political, Economic and Social Thought* (Brighton, 1987).
[12] J. Vaizey, *In Breach of Promise: Gaitskell, Macleod, Titmuss, Crosland, Boyle: Five Men who Shaped a Generation* (London, 1983); for an account in which Tawney is singled out for particular criticism, see A. Shenfield, *Daily Telegraph*, 16 Mar. 1982. Barnett's blast against 'New Jerusalemism' is particularly directed against Temple. (Barnett, C., *The Audit of War* (London, 1986), 15–17, 23.)

Tawney was in the last years of his long life when T. H. Marshall noted with disquiet that the 'realistic appraisal of welfare in terms of a civilized way of life' was being replaced by its natural antithesis, a euphoric enthusiasm for anything that money could buy.[13] It appeared to many observers that the acquisitive and individualistic society was now expanding its frontiers, and colonizing the territory of its natural antagonists, the Labour voters in the respectable working class.[14] In *The Future of Socialism* (1956), Crosland's vision was not of adequacy, but of mass abundance within ten years. When twenty years later such abundance as was available had failed to satisfy aspirations to the predicted degree, he turned for inspiration to the social arrangements which accounted for the impressive growth rates of West Germany and Japan.[15]

In the 1980s the tide of government policy flowed still more strongly against Tawney's ideas. Alterations in the provisions governing gifts made in the lifetime of the donor, for example, went a long way towards destroying the principle—avoidance had long been the practice—of limiting the inheritance of great wealth, a principle so early and so long cherished by Tawney, the New Liberals, and the old Labour party.[16] The second and third Thatcher governments adopted a policy of 'popular capitalism' through wider ownership of equity shares. From the point of view of Tawney's socialism this meant spreading the evils of avarice, or property without function, into an extended context of speculative gains. Bulls and bears were added to dogs and horses in the gambling menagerie.[17] A sense of grievance was manifest that some people had the resources to benefit from share ownership while others did not; but the echoes of Tawney's view that it was wrong in principle to do so had grown faint. Casino capitalism pushed back the hope of a society united by the service of its members to the common weal. Shortly before the end of a fifteen-year period of booming share prices the 1986 salaries of some employees in their early twenties in 'the City' were reported to be in excess of

[13] T. H. Marshall, *Social Policy in the Twentieth Century* (1965), 2nd edn. (London, 1967), 181.
[14] F. Zweig, *The Worker in an Affluent Society* (London, 1961), 212.
[15] C. A. R. Crosland, *Social Democracy in Europe* (London, 1975).
[16] *The Times*, 22 Mar. 1986.
[17] 'Boost to People's Capitalism', *The Times*, 19 Mar. 1986.

£100,000[18]—far indeed from Tawney's central concern with the corrupting influence of a false standard of values. Idolatry of possessions and of success in terms of money attained new triumphs. Few could remember Tawney's warning that it was this enemy with which socialists had to grapple, not least within themselves.[19]

Correspondingly, Tawney's notion of satisfaction with an adequate minimum came under severe scrutiny. The 're-discovery of poverty' during a period of rapidly rising standards of material living occupied a conspicuous place in the social history of the 1960s. Absolute definitions of poverty, among which Tawney's was a generous if ill-defined type, fell into academic disuetude. On the political right an adequate standard for the poor was reformulated along utilitarian lines as that level of income which was sufficient to prevent serious civil unrest. On the left the tendency was to assimilate the problem of poverty to that of inequality. Improvements in the absolute level of social security payments were thus deprived of their capacity to eliminate poverty in what were now perceived as Tawney's naïve and complacent terms. For each improved level was itself the basis of a new definition.

Thus Atkinson was able to show in 1969 that five million people in Britain were in poverty because they were living at or below the standard which the government itself felt to be the national minimum.[20] The theme once introduced was then available to be elaborated in various ways. By combining the concepts of relative poverty and relative deprivation with that of a poverty line defined by the current minimum scale of state benefit, Townsend was able to demonstrate that although material standards had risen through-out the population, poverty as he defined it had not diminished.[21] By 1987 a frequently quoted figure for those in poverty in Britain was eight million, but respectable academic commentators could say ten or even twelve million and not be challenged.

Those among the poorest who felt relative deprivation most

[18] *The Spectator*, Mar. 1986.
[19] R. H. Tawney, *The Radical Tradition: Twelve Essays on Politics, Education and Literature*, ed. R. Hinden (London, 1964), 180.
[20] A. B. Atkinson, *Poverty in Britain and the Reform of Social Security* (Cambridge, 1969).
[21] P. Townsend, *Poverty in the United Kingdom: A Survey of Household Resources and Standards of Living* (Harmondsworth, 1979).

keenly, i.e. who were least successful in matching their expectations and management of income to their resources, were accorded an increasingly sympathetic hearing. Those who adapted themselves most successfully to the national minimum tended to be overlooked if not despised by the metropolitan intelligentsia. Tawney saw greed more as a problem for the rich than as a danger to the welfare of the poor. But he in no way justified the feckless handling of such resources as were available. On the issue of the material standard of living, therefore, Tawney's comment on Harrington came partly to apply to himself: his Utopia became a fading mirage; he slipped from his pedestal and passed from the ranks of the prophets to those of the eccentrics.[22]

Tawney did not live to see the reconstruction of secondary education along comprehensive lines, the Robbinsian expansion of universities, the rise of the 'public sector' of higher education, or the development of the Open University, though he would have applauded the direction while deprecating the timidity of these measures of governmental patronage of a more democratic access to the nation's cultural heritage. At the same time he would surely have been disappointed by some other features of cultural development. Certainly the 'high culture' he took from Balliol was transmuted in ways he never anticipated. A later Balliol graduate, Simon Frith, writing in the *New Statesman* as a music critic, used the phrase 'hedonistic greed' not to condemn the 1960s but to rescue the period from what he called its 'bad press'.[23]

Away from the privileged world of commentators and media entrepreneurs a significant strand in popular culture also departed from the pattern Tawney had envisaged. Some of the working-class institutions that had sought to inculcate a taste for serious activities or to promote comradeship and sportsmanship through games came to depend upon commercial interests and relaxed their voluntary effort. The Scottish Football League for a time took the name of, for example, a grocery supermarket chain and the English Football League the name of, for example, a Japanese firm of photocopying machine manufacturers. The membership card of a working-men's club might still carry in its motto the words 'Study and Recreation'; the decorative scrolls might still depict debates, essays, and lectures on science and art. Legally, profits from

[22] Tawney, *History and Society*, 66.
[23] S. Frith, 'Confessions of a Rock Critic', *New Statesman*, 23 Aug. 1985.

refreshments might still be applied to the establishment of classes, examinations, and scholarships, or in maintaining circulating and reference libraries. But in practice little remained except the refreshments and the successors to bagatelle. Men like Aneurin Bevan, who had spent his time away from work 'reading everything he could lay his hands on' from Tredegar Workmen's Library,[24] did not live to see the great working-class libraries of Wales sold to Americans in job lots to make room in the clubs for snooker tables and one-arm bandits.

Tawney's assumptions about family, gender, and the domestic division of labour now seem remote and outmoded. He ignored domestic life. He took for granted a particular set of fallible arrangements for the personal, material, and emotional security of adults and children—the ordinary family with its binding statuses of spouse and legitimate child, capable of being cancelled only under strict conditions of failure. At the end of Tawney's days there were statistical reasons for believing that the family in its nuclear form of husband, wife, and dependent children was stabilizing and perhaps even recovering its institutional position. It seemed to be increasingly recognized and used as the one remaining possible, though by no means guaranteed, source of securely dutiful relationships in an otherwise egotistical and impersonal world.[25] Subsequently the efficacy and the personal and social costs of family life became the subject of renewed and intensified doubt and attack. Proposals to diminish further the legal and informal requirements that a biological father should take steady responsibility over a period of many years for the welfare of the biological mother and their children became acceptable not only to men but also to many women.[26]

[24] A. Bevan, *In Place of Fear* (New York, 1952), 19; M. Foot, *Aneurin Bevan: A Biography* (1962) (St Albans, 1975); J. Campbell, *Nye Bevan and the Mirage of British Socialism* (London, 1987).

[25] N. Dennis, 'Secondary Group Relationships and the Pre-eminence of the Family', *International Journal of Comparative Sociology*, Sept. 1962.

[26] By the 1980s arguments which a few years before had been seen as too silly to be seriously discussed had easy access too intellectual journals—e.g. the view that the family is 'the last sacred cow' or 'a capitalist prison'. The observation, true or false, that 'human beings are the only species who attempt to keep their families together for any length of time', which once would have been taken as evidence in favour of marriage and duty-bound parenthood, now appeared as an argument against it. For the family is an institution designed by males for males. 'Family interests still mean men's interests. . . . A man may be pushed around in the marketplace all day, but as long as he can bash his wife and rape his daughter he still

More generally, in the 1960s and 1970s, Tawney's moralizing style was discarded by influential non-Marxists in the Labour party (as it had, of course, been undervalued by them in his lifetime). Harold Wilson's opportunism stood in striking contrast to Tawney's combination of principle and pragmatism. In three major works, *The Labour Government 1964–70, Final Term*, and *The Governance of Britain* Wilson offered little discussion of Tawney's or any other type of socialist ideal.[27] Tawney's moralism also came under renewed and confident attack from academic Marxists. 'Kant's ethics tell me that the world should be corrected and reformed', a Marxist mockingly wrote in 1972. 'Socialism is the result of good wishes. Change the minds of men! Abandon scientific socialism for utopian socialism. Reality is not important. Facts are of no account.' Such ideas were simply 'contemporary Bernsteinism' and 'petit-bourgeois anarchism'. Only in a post-revolutionary society would values become effective in controlling human conduct.[28]

Meanwhile post-war consensus government gradually turned into a politics of frustrated intentions. The 'serviceable drudge' of the parliamentary state became for the political right an overweening government and for the old or sick or unemployed the faceless bureaucracy of 'Them'. Nationalization in its standard form disappointed ethical socialists and affronted economic liberals. The Labour governments of 1964–70 and 1974–9 lacked lustre either in edifying nobility of aims or in effective socialist performance. The Labour party lost support from mid-century—a loss partly disguised by declining support also for the Conservative party in an increasingly volatile electorate. Still more ominous, the party programme seemed increasingly out of line with the wishes of Labour supporters.

Tawney's confidence in the institutions of a parliamentary democracy thus became increasingly questioned. His constant

feels like a man.' Because, for girls, promiscuity and academic achievements are still wrongly portrayed as bad, unsatisfying things—the exponent of this point of view continues—girls who on this view ought to be 'sleeping around and studying for their A-levels' regrettably get married and have babies instead. (J. Burchill, 'The Last Sacred Cow', *New Society*, 20–7 Dec. 1985, 518.)

[27] H. Wilson, *The Labour Government 1964–70* (London, 1971); *The Governance of Britain* (London, 1976); *Final Term: The Labour Government 1974–6* (London, 1979).

[28] L. Colletti, 'Marxism: Science or Revolution?', in R. Blackburn (ed.), *Ideology in Social Science: Readings in Critical Social Theory* (London, 1972), 374.

references to local government officials as the dutiful and efficient
servants of the public told against him when their actual activities—
as health officials, housing managers, planners, and lawyers—were
closely scrutinized in connection with, for example, town planning
and slum clearance.[29] The national Civil Service lost prestige—not
only among socialists—as dilettante and inexpert, ignorant of
modern conditions and politically over-powerful.[30] Weakening
confidence in the ability of the Labour party in Parliament to
inaugurate socialist measures showed itself in the rapid growth of
such national organizations as Shelter and the Child Poverty Action
Group and, locally, community groups of all kinds. Though their
raison d'être was to claim welfare benefits, they were all sceptical
about the efficacy of the welfare state. Could it after all establish a
civilized minimum and distribute the common wealth so that men
and women might live in Tawneyesque fellowship in a socialist
society?

The political organization of ethical socialism had fallen into
patent and painful disarray by the 1980s, falling far behind the
Conservatives in General Election votes. The shifting ideological
compound of economic liberalism, monetarism, and presidential
parliamentary government, 'Thatcherism', dominated politics in
Britain through successive governments, holding secure Westminster
power. The minority who voted for the Conservatives was
substantial—over 40 per cent of the vote, over 30 per cent of all
those entitled to vote—and it reflected the opinion that the best
society was one of prosperous and successful individuals and that,
given the existence of the welfare state, such a society was to be
attained by increasing individual responsibility and diminishing
government.

Electoral arithmetic, in other words, could not be interpreted
plausibly as the frustration of a majority of ethical socialists by the
exigencies of the British electoral system and party organization.
The electoral success of Thatcher and the electoral failure of
Labour were the political manifestation of popular experience and
opinion. In the jargon of psephologists, the 'natural level of
support' for the Labour party from the end of the 1970s into the
1980s was between 35 and 38 per cent. Nor could Labour lay

[29] J. G. Davies, *The Evangelistic Bureaucrat* (London, 1974); N. Dennis, *People
and Planning* (London, 1970) and *Public Participation and Planners' Blight*
(London, 1972); E. Gittus, *Families, Flats and the Under-Fives* (London, 1976).
[30] H. Thomas (ed.), *Crisis in the Civil Service* (London, 1968).

unchallenged claim to be the party of ethical socialism. Liberals, Social Democrats, and anglican bishops saw themselves at least in part as inheritors of this moral tradition. Mr Edward Heath attacked the Queen's Speech in 1987—and particularly the proposed poll tax to replace rates, as an offence to the principle of levying tax most heavily on those best able to pay. Even Mrs Thatcher spoke of a 'contrite heart' at the plight of the inner cities as she re-entered Downing Street in June 1987. The tradition exacted its salutations, if only in humbug.

The task of the alternative ethical-socialist politics was to persuade the majority of Tawney's view that true wealth is communal, that the ugly face of individualism is egoism, that civilized opportunity requires fairness to the disadvantaged, and that the strength of the successful individual has its highest expression in care for the weak.

These disparate elements of interest and ideology contended for the soul of the nation. None of them had a monopoly of any class or region or gender. The traditional Labour base in the industrial working class was never complete and became increasingly irrelevant in a country which, while once the most proletarianized in the world, had passed through a transformation involving the reduction of the urban industrial workers to a diverse minority which could not be recognized in any version of George Orwell's description of the respectable working man and his family. The reinstatement of ethical socialism was only possible through the education and persuasion of people in the south as well as north, in owner-occupied as well as council houses, in every kind of full-time and part-time employment, in the formal as well as the domestic economy, in health as well as sickness, on salary as well as supplementary benefit, the young as well as the old.

The general election of 1987 could reasonably be described as a television-staged national debate over whether the British government should base its policies on economic liberalism or ethical socialism—on the 'enterprise' or the 'caring' society. The stage was indeed a stage with all the illusions, manipulations, and management of the dramatic arts. But while the actors were indeed actors, they were seen by the electors as to be judged ultimately not so much by present dramatic performance as by future authenticity in government and relevance to the anticipated future life of the voter. And the play was confused, as any such drama must be, where many playwrights compete to define the plot. Nevertheless the point is that the ground was lost by the party that historically represented ethical socialism and won by the exponents of Thatcherism.

What sort of country then was Britain to become? In the aftermath of the 1987 election there were facile answers from the House of Commons. The massed supporters of the government believed that Thatcherism had already restored greatness and a third term would make Britain 'mightier yet'. From the opposite benches came discordant versions of a divided society destined to fragment further, north against south, white against black, man against woman, government against people, rich against poor, confident against demoralized. The discordance of these voices challenged ethical socialists to identify possible collective action in aid of an attainable society.

THE PROSPECT FOR ETHICAL SOCIALISM

Happy is the country whose experience improves on its fears and whose expectations exceed its hopes. International polls in the first half of the 1980s recorded Britain as such a happy country. Compared with other Europeans the British on the whole expressed rather more satisfaction with their jobs, their spouses, their governments, and their police. The majority and the average had experienced increasing material prosperity since the coronation of the second Elizabeth. During a quarter of a century they had become twice as well off in terms of real income per capita: and they were working for their plenitude shorter hours with longer holidays. By the mid-1980s more than one in four Britains thought of themselves as having moved into a higher social class and less than one in ten as having come down in the world compared with their parents. From the slump years of the 1930s the British had lived with better todays than yesterdays and the expectation of still better tomorrows. Even after the oil crisis of the mid-1970s and the tripling of unemployment under the first two Thatcher governments, the majority continued on this upward path.

Why then should we peer anxiously into an uncertain future? Prophesies of doom whether from Jehovah's Witnesses, or Marxists, or Peter Jay,[31] though one or other may turn out, of course, to be

---

[31] P. Jay and M. Stewart, *Apocalypse 2000* (London, 1987).

right after all, were difficult to reconcile with the record of performance by Britain as a productive organization. Indeed the main plank of the celebratory optimist's platform remained that, for all its peculiarities, Britain was an advanced industrial nation and it was the distinctive mark of such societies that they produced more and more with less and less effort. On past expectations and objective physiological needs neither the mountains nor the lakes of EEC food and drink were required to convince Britons that the future could be for them one of economic sufficiency. While it was true that many cities had lost their manufacturing base and lacked adequate sewers, schools, and hospitals, these problems were not intrinsic to productive power. They arose essentially out of the mismatch of power over nature compared with power over ourselves. They lay in other words in the realms of organization rather than technology, distribution rather than GDP, and reproduction rather than production.

As to production the tragic problem was that more return from less labour yielded the curse of idleness rather than toil. People were not needed. So the class structure of industrial societies, including Britain, developed an under-class of those who could not be placed in the stable work-force of the formally employed. Ralf Dahrendorf described them as 'a cancer which eats away at the texture of societies'. They suffered from a cumulation of social pathologies—educational failure, illiteracy, broken families, high crime rates, poor housing, and spatial concentration in the inner city. They were disproportionately recruited from the young and the ethnic minorities and they tended to adopt a 'ghetto' existence outside the normal social contract of citizenship, with little or no stake in official society.

They are the extreme social manifestation of a class structure tending towards in terms of money a richer rich and in terms of quality of life a poorer poor. It bears little or no resemblance to the marxist picture of the future (endlessly repeated from the 1840s) which was to culminate in revolution. On the contrary, majority affluence in privatized security is possibly stable, even though it does suffer from public squalor, unsafe streets, mounting crime, and spasmodic riot. The majority of the prosperous in a political democracy can control its alienated minority by the twin weapons of state welfare and efficient police. Class politics can take the form of the containment of poverty and the control of disorder. Such a society is the likely outcome where private sector economics dominate impoverished public services. Nor is the price adequately reckoned in spending on burglar alarms. The total burden of unrestrained individualism is the incalculable cost of endemic distrust of all our neighbours. It is a society from which the interests of the elementarily prudent would demand their withdrawal. It is a society to be contemplated in terms of the ideals of ethical socialism only with the bleakest distaste.

As to reproduction Britain again illustrates the unforeseen and unresolved problems that accompany the transition of advanced industrial societies to a population balance of low fertility and low mortality. Indeed a more compelling case can be made for a crisis of reproduction than of production in such societies. The EEC populations were not replacing themselves. Between the end of the Second World War and the mid-1980s the size of the UK population, though 16 per cent up in absolute terms, had declined from constituting one-fiftieth to only one-hundredth of the population of the world as a whole. Meanwhile there had been a multiplication of nearly four in the proportion of illegitimate to total births. Not only had reproduction made a significant shift out of the framework of the traditional family but the family itself was less stable in the sense that there was a more than fivefold increase in the divorce rate between 1961 and 1985; in 1985 remarriages accounted for over one-third of all marriages. And one-person households which amounted to less than one-tenth of all households before the war added up, in an ageing population, to a quarter of them.

The new demographic regime brought a marked worsening of the ratio between tax-payers and pensioners. In 1931 the ratio was 9 : 1 between those aged 15 to 64 and those who were over 65. In 1981 it was 4.3 : 1. In the twenty-first century, when those born in the post-war baby boom start to age, the number of pensioners will increase and have to be supported by a reduced working population. The calculations are that the ratio of persons of working age to pensioners will fall below 3 : 1. A society, however rich in productive capacity, is unlikely to survive as a civilization if it leaves such problems to the mercies of the market.

Moreover in any realistic appraisal of expectations we must note with alarm that the built-in benefits of the long post-war boom with respect to opportunities may be withdrawn from us. The twentieth century has seen the gradual diminution of the industrial working class, as people have moved upwards in an increasingly middle-class occupational structure. Nor did Thatcherite policy destroy opportunities of upward mobility for working-class and lower-middle-class children. Indeed the Oxford Mobility studies comparing 1983 with 1972 samples produced evidence of still rising rates of absolute upward mobility. In 1983 nearly a quarter of middle-class professionals and an additional quarter of lower-middle-class clerical and other white-collar workers had been born into working-class homes. But meanwhile unemployment rates had risen into double figures and well over a million had been out of work for at least a year. The unemployed were a depressed class denied the opportunities of both the market and citizenship. The dispossessed, young and old, depended on a welfare state which was deliberately minimized by the policy intentions of Thatcherite governments.

By the second half of the 1980s a new politics of the public interest had become urgent. It became a commonplace of political discussion that a truer reflection of public preference in Parliament depended upon organized renewal of the political left. In that context the fate of Tawney's socialism turned first on the struggle within the Labour party so to reform itself as to re-emerge as a successful contender for office.

It was to mobilize the non-marxist elements in the Labour party against Trotsky's world-view as propagated by the Militant Tendency that Neil Kinnock, as Leader of the Labour party, turned to Tawney in the mid-1980s. He argued that although 'patriotism' was now little heard in the Labour movement, it was one of the values on which it had been founded and from which it had drawn its vitality.[32] It had been built on the particular experience, altruism, and commonsense of the people of Britain.[33]

A principal belief of British socialists, he said, was that political economy was not ultimately a question of historical inevitability but of moral choice. Its principal feeling was moral revulsion against the injustices of contemporary society. Its task was to create a strong body of moral opinion which (Kinnock quotes Tawney) 'knows what it fights for and loves what it knows'.[34] In his peroration Kinnock again referred directly to Tawney: the way

---

[32] N. Kinnock, *The Future of Socialism* (London, 1986), 3.
[33] Ibid. 12.   [34] Ibid. 1, 3.

forward for democratic socialism was to 'put the nation on its mettle'.[35] He, like Tawney, put 'the elevation of all individuals' as one of the foremost aspirations of democratic socialism. A socialist society was one in which there was a flowering of all talents, where all citizens could 'grow to their full stature, develop to their upmost limits the ranging capacities with which nature had endowed them'.[36]

The ideal behind the institutions of a democratic socialist society was, Kinnock said, a viable balance of liberty, equality, and democracy. It is the recognition of their interdependence which differentiates democratic socialism from ideologies which believe in the overriding importance of one or other of them—in the practicability of having a free society with little fraternity or equality, a fraternal society with little freedom or equality, or an equal society with little fraternity and personal liberty.[37]

Roy Hattersley argued in similar vein in his 1987 book on the future of democratic socialism, using *Choose Freedom* as the title.[38] Both he and Kinnock conceded that the Labour party itself had allowed it to appear that liberty was not for it a prime value. They wanted to restore the position represented by Tawney that democratic socialism was the friend of liberty. It was not impossible under socialism, as anti-socialists believed. Nor was it a bourgeois fad to be gladly discarded in favour of a higher concept of emancipation, as some sectarian socialists believed. Liberties are fictions unless men and women have the practical means for enjoying them. The Labour party's mission was to provide them collectively. The democratic state was available to be used by the community as an 'enabling power'—the Tawney doctrine.[39]

Kinnock's concept of an equality which is consistent with liberty and fellowship also coincides with Tawney's. Equality does not mean either that everyone naturally is or can be made uniform with everyone else in ability or external circumstances. Such beliefs are variously 'romantic', 'socially repulsive', 'biologically preposterous', and 'economically impracticable'.[40] It does mean that removing all barriers to practicable equality is an essential prerequisite to the

[35] Ibid. 12.   [36] Ibid. 7, 11.   [37] Ibid. 4, 12.
[38] R. Hattersley, *Choose Freedom: The Future of Democratic Socialism* (London, 1987).
[39] Kinnock, *Future of Socialism*, 2, 4–5, 11–12.   [40] Ibid. 7.

common good. Equality signifies that means must be provided to equalize the rights of individuals to realize their own particular capabilities[41] and that persons must be accorded the dignity of citizenship whatever their social position. Within this framework of factual and moral belief, inequality is seen as basically unjustifiable unless there is some clear mutual benefit to the worse off.[42] In a democratic-socialist society in which a dominant egalitarian spirit prevails, all inequalities are questioned and forced to justify themselves as means of contributing to the common good.[43]

Kinnock gives Tawney pride of place as the exponent of the value that stands out above all in British democratic socialism—fellowship. The society to which the British Labour party ought to be committed is: 'a community of responsible men and women, working without fear in comradeship for common ends'.[44]

To reach such a society, Kinnock writes, there is no surer course than through parliamentary democracy at local and national level. 'Democratic socialism in Britain is built upon parliamentary democracy . . .We can agree, again, with Tawney . . . "For socialists to give the impression that they, too, have reservations would be to give the enemies of socialism a present of what should be one of socialism's chief assets".'[45] In discussions of the 'Party Objects' of Labour—Clause 4 of the Constitution—it is sometimes overlooked that the very first object of the party in general is to organize and maintain a Labour party *in Parliament.*

As we have already remarked, the 'nationalization' objective does not mention nationalization at all. The actual wording forms the constitutional basis for pragmatism of the Tawney type. For the 'common ownership of the means of production, distribution and exchange, and the best obtainable system of popular administration and control of each industry and service' can embrace self-help groups, tenants' associations, housing co-operatives, and decentralized municipal administration. It can exclude unaccountable state bureaucracies. Democratic socialism 'recognizes that the re-examination of the strategies, attitudes and style of socialist politics is a continual imperative'.[46] Freedom, justice, and equality are meaningless as abstractions, and they can only be translated into

---

[41] Ibid.   [42] J. Rawls, *A Theory of Justice* (London, 1973), 78–9, 511.
[43] B. Crick, *Socialist Values and Time* (London, 1984), 17.
[44] Kinnock, *Future of Socialism*, 12.
[45] Ibid. 1, 6–7.   [46] Ibid. 2.

reality by men and women working with men and women as they actually are in the everyday world.[47]

With the experience of totalitarian democracy in France under Robespierre, Germany under Hitler, and the USSR under Stalin to consider, J. L. Talmon concluded that the distinction between an absolutist and empirical attitude to politics was fundamental. 'It is a harsh, but none the less necessary task to drive home the truth that human society and human life can never reach a state of repose . . . that life is a perpetual and never resolved crisis.'[48]

Tawney agreed with that, and had perhaps an even more sombre respect for the politician who works in the full light of the difficulties of creating and perhaps even more of maintaining a society of democratic socialists. He wrote once of the time when as Sergeant Tawney he led his men out into the Battle of the Somme. People and societies walk between precipices, he said, and they do not know the rottenness in them until they crack. On that day he recalled some lines from *The Pilgrim's Progress* which had always struck him, he said, as one of the most awful things imagined by man: 'Then I saw that there was a way to Hell, even from the Gates of Heaven, as well as from the City of Destruction'. To have gone so far and to have failed at last![49] Whether that was to be the fate of British ethical socialism lay beyond Tawney's horizon, as it still lies beyond ours.

[47] Ibid. 12.
[48] J. L. Talmon, *The Origins of Totalitarian Democracy* (London, 1961).
[49] R. H. Tawney, *The Attack and Other Papers* (1953) (Nottingham, 1981), 14–15.

INDEX